Ego Psychology

Ego Psychology

Theory and Practice

SECOND EDITION

▼

Gertrude and Rubin Blanck

Columbia University Press
New York

Columbia University Press
New York   Chichester, West Sussex
Copyright © 1994 Gertrude and Rubin Blanck
All rights reserved

Library of Congress Cataloging-in-Publication Data

Blanck, Gertrude
Ego psychology : theory and practice / Gertrude and Rubin Blanck.
-- 2nd ed.
p.   cm.
Includes bibliographical references and index.
ISBN 0–231–08292–4
1. Ego (Psychology)   2. Psychotherapy.   3. Psychoanalysis.
I. Blanck, Rubin.   II. Title
BF175.5.E35B53   1993
616.8'917—dc20   93–15638
CIP
∞

Casebound editions of Columbia University Press books
are printed on permanent and durable acid-free paper.

Printed in the United States of America
c 10 9 8 7 6 5 4 3 2 1

Contents

Introduction to the Second Edition

In 1974 we noted that for theory construction to advance it must rest on a solid base. New theory cannot but be influenced by Freud's discoveries. This applies even to those innovations that claim to be non-Freudian or even anti-Freudian. Freud's work has entered twentieth-century thought so thoroughly that its influence extends to the arts, especially literature, as well as to psychology. And within psychoanalytic circles, despite some claims to the contrary, modern theory construction is also influenced by the contributions of the ego psychologists who carried Freud's work forward. Rangell (1989) advocates theory construction "by accretion rather than by repetitive new and partial theories" (194), and he adds:

> The march of new theories and explanatory systems, which have been alternative rather than additive to existing theory, have typically had a rapid rise accompanied by excitement and huge followings, followed by a quiet decline and disappearance. During the years of their ascendancy however, cumulative theory has been excluded or set back, usually for decades at a time. Advances by accretion . . . are typically not furthered by contagious enthusiasm fueled by group pressures . . . What may be

absorbed from the new approaches, which in each case is a partial advance, could have been contributed without an eclipse, stagnation or even regression of the total accumulated body of theory.

The new theory currently on the "march" to which Rangell alludes is self psychology. Created by Kohut (1971), it claims to have bypassed ego psychology. Since Kohut was a contemporary of the major ego psychologists, he could not have avoided their influence unless he neglected to read the literature, which is hardly likely.

The International Psycho-Analytical Association has become considerably more ecumenical than in the days when Rank, Adler, Horney, Sullivan, Alexander, and others were forced to leave. On the current scene, self psychology, along with Kleinian theory and some of the French deviations, remains within the fold of the International. But this will not be a survey of all the points of view within and outside the International. Nor is it designed to be eclectic in its approach. In order to retain the focus of ego psychology and the developmental object relations theory contained within it, we eschew all those theories that are not consistent with it.

Although we contend that theory does not arise anew in each generation, but rather that each theorist stands on the shoulders of those who went before, we do not imply that everything is to be retained. Psychoanalytic theory has undergone extensive revision almost from the beginning—by Freud himself and later by his successors. Nevertheless, there is much that is basic and remains as the foundation of further theory construction. Although much revised over the years, there remain the concepts of transference, resistance, the unconscious, conflict theory, drive theory (including infantile sexuality), structural theory, and dream theory. In the area of technique, also much revised, especially by Kris (see chapter 5), there remains the goal of making the unconscious conscious to a certain extent.

Among Freud's own revisions are his drive theory, his theory of anxiety, and his addition of the structural theory to the topographic. There are also aspects of Freud's work that have had to be discarded in part or in toto. His death instinct is not accepted by many analysts, although some still adhere to it. Totally discarded are his notions about female sexuality. Freud was egregiously mistaken on this matter, and his error, unfortunately echoed by his early female disciples, has been corrected by modern psychoanalytic theorists. Those corrections are not known in some circles, and so the dead horse of Freud's outmoded notions about female psychology is still being beaten. We attribute this to poor scholarship.

While continuing to stand on fundamental psychoanalytic theory that was developed for the neuroses, our principal thrust is to understand more clearly the understructured personalities—the so-called narcissistic and borderline conditions—because these pathologies are not as well understood as the neuroses. Also influencing our decision to devote less attention to the neuroses here is that there is so much in the literature about their structure and about the techniques for treating them that to repeat it would be redundant.

Developmental theory explains the quantitative and qualitative differences between the borderline or narcissistic personalities and the neurotic by the level of structuralization that has been reached. Because of their developmental lags, understructured personalities have not reached psychological birth. Therefore the self representation is merged with the object representations to a greater degree than in the normal neurotic, who has reached psychological birth and can thus regard others as separate, whole persons. Several other differences between the neuroses and the borderline and narcissistic conditions will be elaborated further in our text.

Immersion in developmental theory furthers continuous elaboration of theory. This has kept us on the move, so that our thinking has advanced considerably since 1974. When we began our work we regarded our role as that of integrators of the contributions of the several ego psychologists. Inevitably, that role has changed somewhat. In the course of many years of working with theory in teaching, supervision, thinking, and clinical practice, ideas have evolved. We have presented some of these in *Ego Psychology II: Psychoanalytic Developmental Psychology* (1979) and in *Beyond Ego Psychology: Developmental Object Relations Theory* (1986), as well as in the *International Journal of Psycho-Analysis* (1977), and the Journal of the American Psychoanalytic Association (1988). Some of our newer ideas, particularly in the area of object relations, are unpublished and will be presented for the first time here.

With those few innovations, we remain integrators. Therefore we shall once again present a unified theory, incorporating the works of the two Freuds, Hartmann, together with the latter's two collaborators Kris and Loewenstein, Spitz, Mahler, Jacobson and the contemporary child observationalists, particularly Emde. We shall also cover the contributions of

Kernberg, who has played a prominent role in exploring the nature of the borderline and narcissistic conditions.

An integration must have as its objective something more than the obvious one of pulling things together. It must also be selective, for true integration can be only of elements that fit together by virtue of internal consistency. Therefore, as in the past, we make no apology for omitting some theories. To be suitable for integration, theory must meet a requirement beyond merely being on the current scene. It has to be consistent with the mainstream in order to fit comfortably with the flow. Therefore we shall not survey all current theories, such as the British object relations school. Were this book designed as a comparative study of schools of object relations, it would have been included. That would make an interesting study, but that is not our objective here. We intend to explicate developmental theory as it exists today. Thus the several theories that lie outside the developmental psychology that has evolved from ego psychology, while worth studying, are beyond the scope of this project. Some, such as Kohut's self psychology, are stand-alone theories that Kohut himself stated do not fit into the framework of ego psychology.

This also holds true for certain current techniques. Some arise from a theoretical position outside ego psychology, some as fads of the moment. We have yet to see a technique that does not originate in some facet of psychoanalytic technique. Some, such as hypnosis, were discarded by Freud, yet they crop up over and over again with mutations that make them appear to be new. Others take a small part of psychoanalysis and develop it as though it is a total psychology.

The overall organizing theme of this revision of our earlier work is built on the emergence (from recent infant observation) of the concept that drive and ego organization evolve from birth on within the medium of a relationship with an object, the mothering person. In a sense this is but an extension of Hartmann's concept of adaptation (1939) and of the ego as organizing process (Blanck and Blanck 1979). Adaptation ensures survival and to that end has at its disposal mechanisms that serve that purpose. With each deployment of such a mechanism, the individual is thrust into an ever-expanding environment in which the impact of stimuli from within and without impinge in ever-greater quantities. In the face of this barrage of stimuli, survival is ensured, not by the simple deployment of survival techniques but because each added stimulus becomes organized into a new and larger whole, within the context of the dyadic experience.

While the synthetic function of the ego is of course operative here, more than simple synthesis is necessary if the individual is to endure the barrage of stimuli. A central steering organizer, or superordinate ego, is essential to provide cohesion to synthesis. That added factor is necessary because synthesis alone is not selective. In certain pathologies such as psychosis, where the synthetic function operates without selectivity, everything that is experienced is brought together without sorting out that which fits together and discarding that which does not fit. As we shall elaborate, Hartmann regarded fitting together as even more important than adaptation precisely because synthesis without fitting together is not adaptive.

The concepts of synthesis and fitting together, intended as contributions to ego psychology, are remarkably pertinent to the organization of a book such as this. To carry out our organizing theme, we shall summarize the works of the several theorists whose contributions fit together, and we shall combine these internally consistent parts into an integrated whole. We have given this integrated theory several designations over the years. All remain valid. The theory may be termed *ego psychology* or *psychoanalytic developmental psychology* or *psychoanalytic developmental object relations theory*. We use the term ego psychology in our title because the theory is most widely known by that term.

Part 1 presents a brief survey of the evolution of psychoanalytic theory from its historical roots to its modern form. Because of a tendency to divide rather than integrate, a false dichotomy between drive theory and ego psychology has arisen. Therefore we discuss drive theory to show its compatibility with ego psychology. In summarizing the contributions of the several ego psychologists, we go beyond our earlier edition by adding detail and explication derived from the greater understanding we have arrived at over the years. We show how ego psychology has become an object relations theory, and we explain the nature of structure in object relations terms.

In part 2 we explore once again the differences between psychoanalysis and psychotherapy. We improve upon our continuous search for a diagnostic scheme to describe the whole person rather than the symptomatology. This has led us to a greater understanding of the severe pathologies that this theory continues to illuminate. And we deal in detail with the technical implications of the theory as they have developed since 1974.

Ego Psychology

Part One

Theory

1

▼

Historical Roots of Ego Psychology

E go psychology is a continuation of the basic psychoanalytic theory
Sigmund Freud began to evolve at the end of the nineteenth century. Freud was a neurologist who became interested in the grand
hysterias so prevalent at that time. He went to Paris to study with Charcot,
the famous French neurologist who was investigating functional losses—
paralyses of arms and legs, blindness, loss of voice, loss of memory—for
which no physical bases could be found.

The treatment Freud learned at Charcot's clinic was hypnosis. In some
cases this procedure helped patients retrieve memories of forgotten events.
That they were forgotten was responsible for the paralysis. With the recovery of those disturbing memories, usually sexual in nature, function was
restored. It seemed too magical, and it was.

On his return to Vienna, Freud began to study those hysterias that
either did not yield to hypnosis or that recurred after hypnotic treatment.
After trying various intermediate methods, such as exerting pressure on the
forehead to encourage memory, Freud invented free association. By
instructing his patients to allow their thoughts to wander freely without
exercising censorship, clues were provided that led to the "uncovering" of

the repressed memories that Freud thought were the source of the difficulties.

As the nineteenth century ended and he became increasingly interested in the psychology of the hidden recesses of the mind, Freud moved away from neurology. He found that a part of the mind is outside of awareness and exerts powerful, albeit hidden, influences. This he called the *unconscious*. There reside the darkest wishes of which mankind is capable and there the repressed memories are stored.

Not content with investigating the unconscious of his patients, Freud analyzed himself, including his dreams. Out of this self-analysis came his major opus, *The Interpretation of Dreams* (1900). In it he set down why we dream, how dreams are created, and how to unravel the hidden meanings of dreams. He found a force that censors unacceptable wishes, causing the "dream work" to disguise them. In 1923 Freud designated the censoring force the *ego*. Here lies the beginning of ego psychology.

Had Freud done no more than discover the meaning of dreams he would be famous for that alone. But he did not restrict himself to dreams. He became interested in the unconscious part of the psyche that is operative in waking life as well as in sleep. By analyzing his own neurosis, he discovered his unconscious conflict—his childhood love for his mother and rivalry with his father, which resembled the plot of Sophocles's play *Oedipus Rex*. Recognizing that the Greek myth dramatizes a universal truth, Freud termed this first love of childhood the *Oedipus Complex*. He found that it existed in all his patients and that it constitutes the core conflict of neurosis.

By 1905 Freud had discovered that infantile sexuality is broader than oedipal wishes alone and even precedes the Oedipus Complex. Infant sexuality is first focused on the earlier erogenous zones—mouth and anus—progressing to the genitals. Freud referred to this diffuse sexuality as *polymorphous perverse*. It contributes to the pleasure of foreplay if it develops normally by yielding to the primacy of genitality. However, it can contribute to formation of perversions if the forepleasure becomes end pleasure (chapter 12). The medical community denounced Freud for suggesting that young children are endowed with sexual interest.

From the publication of *The Interpretation of Dreams* (in 1900) until the early 1920s Freud thought of the ego as synonymous with consciousness, while the id was thought to be the repository of all that was unconscious. But Freud's clinical experience did not bear this out. That led him to propose in 1923 that a part of the ego is also unconscious. Ego psychology proper has its inception here. It came to be known as the *structural* or *tripartite theory*. Before then Freud worked only with the topographic theory, the layers of the mind—conscious, preconscious, and unconscious. Arlow and Brenner (1964) believed that the *topographic theory* is superseded by the structural theory. Most analysts find it useful to work with both theories.

The tripartite theory proposes that the psyche consists of the id, the ego, and the superego. The id is unconscious, while the ego and the superego are partly conscious. The ego has many functions—including perception, cognition, memory, motility, intentionality, anticipation, judgment, decision, and many others. A comprehensive list is not possible. Many of these functions are at the same time partly conscious and partly unconscious.

After proposing the structural theory, Freud realized that anxiety is not, as he first believed, the consequence of accumulation of toxic substances that were blocked from discharge and became "dammed up." By 1926 he was forced to think of anxiety as the consequence of conflict. This is known as his *second theory of anxiety*. The role of the ego attains even greater prominence here, for it is the structure that experiences anxiety and tries to deal with it in some way. How it does so is a factor of the competence of the ego. The most competent ego can experience anxiety unconsciously as a signal for the employment of defense.

Confusion about the strength of the drives remained, however. Freud believed that the id can overpower the ego. Several theories attempt to explain how the drives are "tamed." They may be fused, in which instance aggression is subsumed under the dominance of libido; or the ego may be strong enough to overpower aggression. Hartmann (1939) tried to resolve the puzzle of drive taming by proposing the concept of *neutralization* whereby drive energy is transferred to the ego for its use and thereby no longer needs to be "tamed." This, too, did not turn out to be a convincing solution to the issue. Our own proposal is that the drives are necessary to the developmental process, eliminating the need for taming. (For a complete discussion of this issue, see chapter 2).

Inspired and given direction by the structural theory, others were active in theory construction at approximately the same time, the late 1930s. Harry Stack Sullivan proposed a theory of interpersonal relations. Paul Federn extended the theory of the ego in psychosis. Heinz Hartmann introduced the idea of an adaptive function of the ego. Anna Freud detailed the operation of the defensive function, thereby inserting a major alteration in the technique of psychoanalysis. Before then, psychoanalysis was concerned solely with uncovering memories and fantasies hidden in the id. With her father's discovery that part of the ego is also unconscious, she was able to point out that the functioning of the ego in the analytic process—specifically the manner in which the defensive function of the ego operates—requires as much analytic attention as does the id.

Because Freud himself was one of his first patients, he evolved a theory and technique for psychoanalysis for the relatively benign pathologies—the neuroses. He was not unaware of the more severe pathologies, the so-called borderline, narcissistic, and psychotic conditions, but he did not regard them as analyzable precisely because the egos of such patients were not strong enough to endure the method. The psychoanalytic patient needs to have a "strong" ego, first to have been able to elaborate a neurotic compromise, and second to be able to withstand the treatment. This includes lying on the couch in order to regress; to allow one's thoughts to flow freely; to endure the analyst's refusal to gratify wishes that persist from the past; and to tolerate interpretation of unconscious defenses and the wishes that lie behind them.

Modern-day issues differ from those that intrigued Freud and the early-twentieth-century psychoanalysts. Thanks to the contributions of the ego psychologists in the latter part of the twentieth century we came to understand the more severe pathologies, the borderline and narcissistic conditions that Freud had regarded as unanalyzable. The long delay in arriving at a theoretical and technical understanding of these severe pathologies may be attributed to the fact that Freud's work was essentially restricted to patients whom he thought were neurotic. He was not optimistic about the prognoses for the understructured personalities because they were not amenable to the psychoanalytic method. It was left to his successors to discover that the roots of the more severe pathologies lie in the vicissitudes of preoedipal life and to elaborate methods for their treatment.

The question arises: would we have become cognizant of the etiology and treatment of the more severe pathologies sooner had Freud devoted more attention to them? We think not. The intense knowledge of the workings of the human psyche that Freud provided was needed before one could examine why the ego in the borderline and narcissistic conditions is not equal to the psychoanalytic method. The ego, in those pathologies, is less able to endure anxiety and conflict and can employ only primitive defenses against them. It was not until the mid-twentieth century, after the neuroses were fairly well understood, that theoretical examination of how the ego develops could begin to enlighten us about these more severe pathologies.

Meanwhile, in the first part of the twentieth century, the psychoanalytic method was being applied in the treatment and study of neurosis. Thereby it became increasingly refined as a treatment tool. In some instances it was used with limited success in the treatment of the borderline conditions. This usually came about because analysts were not yet skilled in making a diagnostic distinction between the understructured and the structured personalities and sometimes undertook treatment of a borderline case unknowingly. Remarkably, some such treatment succeeded. We attribute this to the likelihood that the analysts of such cases were attuned to the special needs of such patients and engaged in ego supportive measures. Because such deviations from standard psychoanalytic practice were not generally accepted by the psychoanalytic community, these pragmatic measures were given some word of mouth acknowledgment but little of it found its way into the literature. Where accurate diagnosis was made, psychoanalysts followed Freud in declaring such patients unanalyzable. Orthodoxy exacts a price.

Another reason for the delay in coming to an understanding of the understructured personalities was rooted in world politics. The major ego psychologists—Hartmann, Kris, Loewenstein, Jacobson, Spitz, and Mahler—were all refugees from the Holocaust in Europe. It was not until the late 1930s that they could resettle and resume their lives and their work. To the benefit of psychoanalytic theory construction, they found opportunity in the United States; they were accorded the freedom (and in some instances the funding) that enabled their work to flourish as it might not have had they remained in Europe.

The Modern Era of Ego Psychology

With Hartmann's thoughts about the adaptive function, the modern era of ego psychology begins. Because of world events and the difficulty of translating Hartmann's original (1939) contribution from the German, it was not until 1958 that his revolutionary proposals regarding adaptation became available for study in English. This became the basis for the modern ego psychology that flowed from the structural theory. That theory has also become known as *psychoanalytic developmental psychology*, and as *developmental object relations theory*. We retain the term *ego psychology* because it is best known.

Just as Freud's introduction of the structural theory was seminal in the sense that it paved the way for further theory construction, Hartmann's introduction of the adaptive function of the ego opened the way for psychoanalytic theory to become, not only a study of psychopathology, but of a normal developmental psychology as well. It set the direction for investigation to proceed toward discovery of how the ego develops from birth onward.

Hartmann alone elaborates on the adaptive function of the ego and, with his collaborators Kris and Loewenstein (1945, 1946, 1949, 1962, 1964), presents theories of ego and superego formation. Spitz (1945, 1946, 1957, 1959, 1965) describes how the developing ego becomes organized. Jacobson (1964, 1971) explores the representational world, depression, superego formation in girls, among much else. Mahler et al. (1975) studies the process whereby the individual proceeds from physical birth to psychological birth. We shall summarize these works in detail.

Why are the names of these theorists of ego psychology not household words? They reported their discoveries in the psychoanalytic journals and in their own books, but are not widely read by the general public. They are known within the narrow confines of the psychoanalytic community, and even there one finds controversy and "competing" theories. Some, such as Kohut (1971, 1977), would discard all investigation that came after Freud. Others complain that Hartmann's writings are difficult to read. This is true, partly because of his labored literary style, partly because the subject matter is not simple. The complexity of the theory reflects the complexity of the human psyche. Rangell (1989) attributes the popularity of anti-Hartmann movements to anti-intellectualism.

There are currently four major points of view regarding the borderline and narcissistic conditions:

1. The psychiatric position follows the general medical tendency to diagnose by symptoms. The *Diagnostic and Statistical Manual of Mental Disorders* lists the symptoms of borderline pathology. This maintains the atheoretical stance of its design so that it may be universally applied. The narcissistic conditions are diagnosed according to whether there is a preponderance of narcissistic symptomatology, such as apparent absence of interest in persons other than oneself, a pervasive grandiosity, and hypersensitivity to the evaluations of others.

2. Kernberg modifies the psychiatric approach by integrating it with psychoanalytic considerations. He regards the borderline state as stable and therefore terms it *borderline personality organization* to connote that it is a distinct and stable entity. Although he takes the symptomatology into account, Kernberg goes further by adding concepts derived from psychoanalytic conflict theory. He also takes a more dynamic stance than the psychiatric one, elaborating a theory of causation and techniques for treatment. (Chapter 9)

3. The self psychology position is presented by Kohut and promoted by his followers. Kohut's point of view deviates markedly from the traditional psychoanalytic position and from the ego psychological developmental point of view. His is a developmental theory that attributes narcissistic pathology to an arrest in development at a point where a cohesive, grandiose self and a cohesive idealized object come into existence. Because of the cohesion, a stable narcissistic transference is possible. (Chapter 10)

4. The ego psychological point of view defines the borderline condition as arising from failure to have completed the separation-individuation process. Mahler's research shows that psychological birth is attained approximately three years after physical birth. Before psychological birth, the developing individual is marching toward, but has not yet attained, an identity separate from the unity created by the self images merged with the images of the mothering person. Thus the borderline patient is arrested somewhere along the developmental continuum, whereas the normal or neurotic person has acquired the separate identity that is the hallmark of psychological birth.

Narcissistic pathology, in the developmental scheme, is also viewed differently from both the psychiatric and the self psychology positions. Since merged self and object representations are the order of the day in the separation individuation process that culminates in psychological birth, this merged state provides narcissistic pleasure and is normal during the developmental months and years. In that state, narcissistic pleasure is dependent on gratifying merger with the esteemed object. With psychological birth, normal narcissism results in evenly distributed positive cathexis between the now (relatively) separate self and object representations.

Pathological narcissism as well as the borderline conditions, reflect inadequate development at some level of still-merged self and object representations. Thus the borderline and narcissistic conditions do not differ greatly in quality. They differ in terms of attempted solutions that can be regarded as failed attempts at adaptation. The borderline patient remains more accessible to transaction or negotiation with another person. In the treatment situation the borderline patient seeks the therapist for alleviation of the painful condition. The narcissistic personality, on the other hand, has an unconsciously arranged solution (Blanck and Blanck 1979) that renders him or her less available for therapeutic intervention. That is because, in pathological narcissism, there has been created a fantasy object that gratifies, rendering the patient less interested in dealing with the therapist. Yet, a permeability brings the patient to seek treatment and challenges the therapist to seek entry into the otherwise closed narcissistic system.

The work of the contemporary child observationalists, Emde (1988a, 1988b) in particular, demonstrates that the patterns of relatedness between self and other, evolved early in life, are enduring. While Spitz wrote of this in 1965, it was not until recent years that instrumentation has made it possible to confirm his work by more precise observation of infants.

We shall not detail the works of the many child observationalists who have come upon the scene since the groundbreaking work of Spitz and Mahler. Of the more current investigators, Emde (1988 a and b) follows in the tradition of the ego psychologists. Others, particularly Stern (1985), proceed in an entirely different and even opposite direction; therefore, his work does not fit the theoretical thrust of ego psychology. To engage in detailed comparison of these two diametrically opposite positions would take us so far afield that it would detract from our main purpose, which is to present the theoretical position of ego psychology as it has evolved to the present.

Even before publication of *The Ego and the Id*, in which he proposed the structural theory, Freud wrote in 1921 about a *gesamt Ich*, translated literally as a gathered-together ego or an ego as a whole. Freud did not develop that theme, however, and it lay dormant for many years. Yet, the idea of an ego that is more than one of the three agencies of the psyche runs through much subsequent psychoanalytic thought. It has especially influenced the work of Spitz, who writes about a central steering mechanism, and that of Rangell (1986), who ascribes an executive function to the ego; it led us to propose in 1986 that a superordinate ego supervises, controls, and maintains the stability of the entire organism.

We integrate the contributions of the ego psychologists in a single, all-encompassing theory and extrapolate from it techniques for the treatment of the borderline and narcissistic patients (1974, 1979, 1986). We also propose that this integrated theory expands the treatment of neurosis. In that more benign pathology, the first three years of life are presumed to have been experienced in a more rather than less adequate manner, thereby enabling the individual to attain identity and to approach the oedipal conflict less encumbered than is the case in the more severe pathologies. Nevertheless, the vicissitudes of experiences in early life, even where neurosis will ensue, also exert their influence on the nature of the Oedipus Complex (G. Blanck 1984). In the psychoanalysis of neurosis, therefore, early life determines the individual variations in each person's oedipal conflict.

Ego psychology illuminates that, while neurosis is the consequence of having foundered on the Oedipus Complex, borderline and narcissistic pathology is the result of having foundered on the developmental tasks preceding the oedipal crisis. This enables us to arrive at a new understanding of the less than neurotic pathologies. Believed correctly by Freud to be unanalyzable, they are nevertheless treatable by psychoanalytically oriented psychotherapy rather than by psychoanalysis proper. We shall describe how these pathologies develop and how techniques derive logically from the theory.

2

▼

Conflict Theory, Drive Theory, and Ego Psychological Object Relations Theory

F reud was a conflict theorist, a drive theorist, an ego psychologist, an object relations theorist. To him psychoanalytic theory is indivisible; the parts constitute a whole. There is an unfortunate tendency today to separate these out, so that one hears of drive theory *versus* ego psychology; or conflict theory *versus* object relations theory. Not only did Freud not regard these as separate, he did not regard one in conflict with the other, nor did he value one over the other. Psychoanalysis is a unified theory that must be discussed in its various facets separately for heuristic purposes. To regard each part as a separate theory is artificial and simplistic.

Conflict Theory

Freud's first conflict theory was presented in *The Interpretation of Dreams* (1900). The force that powers unconscious wishes is in conflict with a censor that exercises a counterforce. Freud was to spend the next twenty-six years refining these ideas, including his thoughts about the drives, about psychic structure, and about conflict. In that time span, he also investigated infantile sexuality (1905) and narcissism (1914), and presented his case histories (1909–14). He made recommendations on technique (1912–13), wrote papers on metapsychology (1914–16) and a major essay on depression (1917), and gave his *Introductory Lectures* (1915–17). He also presented his dual drive theory (1920) and some newer thoughts about the ego (1921). By 1923 he was able to present conflict theory as more complex than force versus counterforce, to define *ego* as a coherent organization of mental processes, and to show that ego is but one of three agencies of psychic structure. He describes the ego as a "rind" on the id, therefore never entirely separate from it. Nor is the third structure, the superego, anything other than a differentiated grade within the ego.

By 1926 Freud's thinking on these interrelated matters necessitated that he revise his first theory of anxiety which held that anxiety is the consequence of dammed-up libido. His new drive theory and his new conflict theory called for a more complex theory of anxiety, to which we have alluded as his second theory of anxiety.

Subsequent elaboration of the structural theory, especially as the various functions of the ego have been explored and identified over the years, sometimes results in unfortunate reification. We need to keep reminding ourselves that we are dealing with constructs that enable us to organize our thinking about psychic structure, that reification of constructs serves to obstruct that purpose.

That it is Freud's intent to present a holistic theory of psychic structure is illustrated in his diagrams (1923:24, 1933b:79). He sets no boundaries, draws no lines of demarcation between the several agencies of structure. He writes of the ego and superego melding into the id. Later he is even more emphatic in describing psychic structure as unified:

> In thinking of this division of the personality into an ego, a super-ego and an id, you will not, of course, have pictured sharp frontiers like the artificial ones drawn in political geography. We cannot do justice to the characteristics of the mind by linear outlines like those in a drawing or in primitive painting, but rather by areas of colour melting into one another as they are presented by modern artists. After making the separation we must allow what we have separated to merge together once more.   (1933b:79)

Thus it is the whole psyche rather than the parts that is the subject of psychoanalytic interest. We examine each part separately for the purpose of reaching ever greater understanding of the whole.

Drive Theory

Psychoanalytic drive theory began as a libido theory. Not until 1920 did Freud propose that there are two drives, libido and aggression, or Eros and Thanatos—a life instinct and a death instinct. The concept of the aggressive drive remains vexatious in the minds of many theorists. There are now five major positions on the aggressive drive.

One position retains drive theory in unmodified form since 1920. To those who hold that view, such as the followers of Melanie Klein, the life and death instincts are taken rather literally and are important components of Kleinian theory and technique.

In a second position the concept of a death instinct is eliminated or played down; substituted for it is a theory of an aggressive drive that is not involved with the compulsion to return to the inorganic state. That view, represented by Jacobson (1964), considers that a death instinct is not necessary to theory construction.

A third point of view arises out of the necessity to account for assertiveness. In the interest of separating that from destructive activity, terms such as *aggressivity* (Erikson, personal communication) were introduced, but have not taken hold.

A fourth attempt to account for behavior that is active but not destructive posits that the aggressive drive may be thought of along a spectrum, with destructive aggression at one end, ranging through more moderate forms, to nonhostile aggression at the other end (McDevitt 1983; Parens 1979). This was prompted by Mahler's discovery that aggression powers the thrust into the separation-individuation process. Deployment of aggressive energy for that purpose is not destructive but is life-enhancing in the sense that it propels the individual forward developmentally.

We present a fifth position because it appears awkward and even paradoxical to us to view drives as affective phenomena. Drives serve development independent of accompanying affect. In Freud's 1940 (posthumously published) restatement of his drive theory he defines *libido* as the force that seeks connection, and *aggression* as the force that seeks to sever connection and thus destroy. There he no longer writes of a death instinct, although he retains the destructive connotation of the aggressive drive in this, his last statement on the drives. Can it be that he was moving toward regarding aggression as the disconnecting (separating) force that powers development? It was left to Hartmann to propose the concept of differentiation and integration, thereby providing the basis for regarding differentiation as nondestructive.

Beginning with the thrust down the birth canal and the severing of the umbilical connection, physical and psychic life require processes of disconnection. But those differentiations are always followed by integration— that is, consolidation at a next higher level of organization. There is a rhythm of differentiation, then integration, followed once again by a new round of differentiation in ever-widening sweeps that encompass more and more experience. In this manner are connections severed only to be resumed again, maintaining connections on higher levels in the very process of severing them on lower levels of organization.

We continue our theorizing from Hartmann's concept of the *undifferentiated matrix*. He proposes ([1939] 1958) that ego and id are at first undifferentiated; they separate out after birth. Jacobson (1964) expands on this idea to propose that the two drives are also undifferentiated at first, to separate out into libido and aggression under the auspices of adequate mothering. We (Blanck and Blanck 1979) expand further, proposing an affect theory which suggests that affects, too, are not drive-borne but arise out of the undifferentiated matrix. Love does not arise out of libido, and hatred does not arise out of aggression; the two sets of affects follow their separate developmental pathways.

Additional theoretical problems arise in relation to the aggressive drive. The very manner of its introduction to theory contains an inherent difficulty. Drive theory remained a libido theory for more than twenty years until Freud added the aggressive drive. Can it be that Freud was loathe to alter all the theory construction that was so laboriously elaborated before 1920? The fact remains that the concept of an aggressive drive was merely tacked on to libido theory, leaving us to assume that aggression goes through the same vicissitudes as does libido in the psychosexual progression that constitutes early psychoanalytic developmental theory.

Anna Freud, at the Twenty-Seventh Congress of the International Psycho-Analytical Association (1971), pointed out some of the shortcomings of a "tacked on" theory. Principally, she thought, it is not reasonable to believe that the aggressive drive follows precisely the same course as the libidinal drive through the psychosexual phases. She posed that theoretical puzzle without offering a solution.

It is noteworthy that, although psychoanalytic theorists have difficulty with the theory of the aggressive drive, they are quite comfortable with the idea of a libidinal drive. Perhaps connection is valued over disconnection, that libido is regarded as "good" and aggression as "bad." Is the lingering connotation of destruction that Freud failed to reconcile with the life force hampering further understanding of the workings of the aggressive drive? Loss of objectivity is especially dangerous in the clinical situation where countertransference may impose values, often against the analyst's better judgment.

Our theory of derivation of affect separate from drive is designed to offer a solution to the problem of usage arising from Freud's dual drive theory—the tendency to confuse *drive* with *affect* and to use the concept of aggression as though that drive is palpable. What has been overlooked is that one cannot see or feel the drives, but only their derivatives. Value judgment has crept into the very designations that are ascribed to affect—positive and negative. It is this that leads one to regard not only expression of anger, but also the important matter of seeking disconnection in the service of development, as negative, undesirable, or even "bad."

The problem transcends semantics. Drive and affect are all too commonly spoken of as though they are synonymous, yet they cannot be the same. It may be argued that affect derives from drive, but that is a matter having to do with the origin of affect about which there are also differing theories. The dominant theory about the origin of affects is that they do derive from the drives. We believe, rather, that our proposal that affect originates in another part of the undifferentiated matrix obviates much error in the way analysts think about and use both drive and affect technically. Support for our position may be found in the observation that the very young child has the developmental task, among so many others, of differentiation of affect. At first the child experiences and expresses affect in global terms—"all good" or "all bad." That suggests that the process of affect differentiation is a factor of development. As development proceeds, shadings of affect begin to appear. And as affect differentiation proceeds beyond "all good" and "all bad," on the one side will be elation, joy, happiness, contentment, and the like; on the other side will be depression, sadness, despair, unhappiness, discontent, and the like.

That drive and affect are not the same is highlighted by Freud's realization, late in his life, that the aggressive drive serves to sever connections. It remained for the ego psychologists to note that severing connections is not necessarily destructive, that indeed life would be destroyed if connections were retained. This applies even in the realm of physical connections. The umbilical connection must be severed at term if child and mother are to survive. The story of ego psychology is that psychological connections must also be severed in order for the individual to attain an identity.

This distinction was not so important to early theorists of psychoanalytic technique because, in dealing with the structured (neurotic) personality, one was dealing with a person who had completed the first round of the separation-individuation process reasonably satisfactorily. Now that we have the means with which to work with the understructured (borderline) personality as well, we have to consider that such patients have not succeeded in using the aggressive drive in the service of separation in the first round of development; therefore these patients will need to employ that thrust within the therapeutic process in order to attain the identity that the structured personality already possesses.

As we shall show in chapter 18, this has enormous consequences for dealing with resistance in the treatment of the understructured personality. There we shall urge that the therapist distinguish between transference behavior that reflects hostility and that which reflects the thrust toward a separate identity. Often this means that the very treatment of the understructured personality calls for support of the separating thrust. If the therapist confuses drive with affect in the clinical situation, there is the danger of making an erroneous interpretation. The suggestion that there is nonhostile aggression puts this matter aright somewhat; yet it remains awkward to retain that link between drive and affect because it serves to perpetuate the tendency to regard the aggressive drive as having undesirable aims as well.

It serves theory construction and clinical accuracy better, we believe, to think of drive and affect as two separate lines of development, deriving from different parts of the undifferentiated matrix, as we have described. Then one can be clear that anger, rage, hostility, dislike, and similar affects, although often accompaniments of the separating thrust, are not the same as movement toward differentiation.

Object Relations Theory

Even as Freud was developing his drive theory, allusions to object relations inform us that he had that matter in mind from the beginning. We are unable to account for the lack of emphasis. Yet as early as 1905 he says: "In view of the importance of a child's relations to his parents in determining his later choice of a sexual object, it can easily be understood that any disturbance of those relations will produce the gravest effects upon his adult sexual life" (228).

In 1914 Freud writes: "Here we may even venture to touch on the question of what makes it necessary at all for our mental life to pass beyond the limits of narcissism and to attach the libido to objects" (1914c, 85). He adds: "We must begin to love if we are not to fall ill, and we are bound to fall ill if, in consequence of frustration, we are unable to love" (85).

As though anticipating contemporary ego psychological object relations theory, he writes of the anaclitic form of love as distinguished from the narcissistic form. Of anaclitic love he says that a person may love the woman who feeds him, the man who protects him, and the succession of substitutes who take their place (90).

In 1917 Freud devotes an entire essay to the effect of object loss on depression. And by 1921 he is even clearer about object relations, commenting on the mutual relationship between the object and the ego (105–10).

The next step in Freud's developing theory of object relations is taken in his 1923 work where he writes as though he takes it for granted that an object relations theory is an integral part of his total psychoanalytic theory. There he refers to object relations in counterpoint, as it were, even as he pursues his main theme, description of psychic structure. He says: "We cannot avoid giving our attention for a moment longer to the ego's object identifications . . . There remains the question of conflicts between the various identifications into which the ego comes apart, conflicts which cannot after all be described as entirely pathological" (30–31).

With the theoretical tools of ego psychology available today, we are in a position to see that the conflict theory that Freud clarified in 1923 is more complex than intersystemic conflict alone. There can also be intrasystemic conflict, between the self representation and the object representations, for ego psychological object relations theory is a theory of the relationship between those two sets of representations. It is not a simple theory of action of one individual on another but a complex theory of intrasystemic interaction.

In chapter 11 we discuss more fully our position on object relations theory.

3

▼

The Contributions of Heinz Hartmann

As Freud is indisputably the father of psychoanalysis, Hartmann is known as the father of ego psychology. Hartmann expands psychoanalysis from a psychopathology only into a normal developmental psychology.

Some believe, erroneously, that ego psychology is a psychology of conscious processes. That fallacy derives from the fact that Freud did, in his early writings circa 1900, think of the precursor of ego—the censoring force—as synonymous with consciousness. The influence of Freud's early thinking persists in the tendency to retain the idea that ego psychology is concerned solely with such functions as perception, cognition, judgment, and the like. These do indeed lie within its realm. But that is far from all.

Hartmann carries far forward Freud's later recognition that the ego is in part unconscious. Not only does he clarify how the ego functions, he also identifies the very composition of ego and some of its component elements. It is by combining defense, adaptation, and fitting together that Hartmann brings psychoanalysis to the status of a normal developmental psychology. This is of inestimable importance to psychology in the broader sense because there are many psychologies of normality and pathology, some of which attempt to understand human behavior from its conscious manifestations alone. Hartmann shows that a depth psychology can explain normality, as well as its pathological deviations, more profoundly than a psychology that omits the essential dimension of the unconscious.

Hartmann affirms that conflict is part of the human condition: "The development of the ego may be described by tracing those conflicts which it must solve in its struggle with the id and the superego, and if we include the conflicts with the external world also, then we see it in terms of the war it wages on three fronts" ([1939] 1958:11).

The seminal quality of Hartmann's work is noteworthy because his ideas constitute the foundation on which the later ego psychologists were to build. Thus the relationship of Hartmann's work to basic psychoanalytic theory is that of offspring of Freud's fundamental theory and progenitor of the theories that were to follow.

At the time he writes (1939), Hartmann finds it necessary to defend his innovations. He says: "The resistance to a new discovery is clearly not a measure of its scientific significance" (6). We might add, because of the many fads that come and go, that the popularity of a new discovery is also not a measure of its scientific significance.

The value of building theory in progressive steps is demonstrated later in an essay by Hartmann, Kris, and Loewenstein (1949). Rangell deplores the fact that Hartmann is not well enough known to the new generation of psychoanalysts because of "an anti-intellectual bent, or a reaction against science, which asserts itself periodically in favor of humanism" (1989:135). Mainstream psychoanalytic theory, as it has evolved, proceeds from basic psychoanalytic theory to ego psychology to developmental object relations theory.

Anna Freud, in referring to the structural theory, comments on intellectual inertia, the reluctance to accept new ideas. It is that inertia that has also retarded full acceptance of ego psychology. She refers to the difficulty of analysts of her era to apply the structural theory because they were so bound up in id psychology. She says: "Any piece of ego analysis is much less satisfactory than analysis of the id" (1936:14). Therefore one can appreciate that, when psychoanalysis was so new, the first generation of analysts were fascinated with the id.

Hartmann (1964) comments, not only on the rejection of new ideas, but also on the difficulty in absorbing complex innovations. This is especially applicable today because there are so many competing theories that some would wish to integrate to make matters simpler. Hartmann believes this is not yet possible. He says: "But, as for the present, the concepts of developmental phase, conflict, trauma have become much more complex for us, and, I think, they will become ever more complex before we again reach that beautiful, peaceful state of affairs where both simple and general formulations become possible" (1964:209).

Hartmann is not deterred by complexity. He plunges into exploration of the extraordinarily intricate features of the ego in extension of the structural theory. By focusing on the major ego functions, adaptation and fitting together, he leads ego psychology toward the complex object relations theory into which it has evolved.

His lecture to the Vienna Psychoanalytic Society on "Ego Psychology and the Problem of Adaptation" was presented in 1937 and published in German in 1939. It did not appear in book form in English until 1958, although Rapaport, his translator, referred to it extensively as early as 1951. Difficult to comprehend because it exposes hitherto unidentified aspects of human psychological development, it is nevertheless the major contribution to psychoanalytic theory since Freud. It is both innovative in its own right and seminal in the sense that all the developments in ego psychology that have taken place from 1937 to the present, and foreseeably beyond, may be traced to Hartmann's extensions of Freud's basic work. His major extension is an integration of defense with adaptation. The concept of adaptation cannot stand alone without theories of drive, conflict, and defense.

Below we summarize Hartmann's major theoretical concepts.

Adaptation

The ego has an adaptive function. *Adaptation* is defined as a reciprocal relationship between the organism and its environment. It is guaranteed by the possession of primary (inborn) equipment, by the maturation of these apparatuses, and by ego-regulated actions that improve the individual's relationship to the environment. Noteworthy is that Hartmann here posits a modification of Freud's structural theory. He offers the thought that the ego is inborn, that it does not arise as the result of the experience of the id with reality, as Freud thought. Here we see the forerunner of Mahler's work in which she is to discover the importance of the inborn endowment to the ability of the neonate to enter into and interact within (adapt to) the mother-child dyad.

Adaptation is brought about by activity that directly changes either the environment or the individual. Alloplastic alterations change the environment; autoplastic action adjusts the individual to the environment. A higher ego function decides whether alloplastic or autoplastic action is appropriate in a given situation. No value judgment applies to either action. In some circumstances alloplastic behavior serves adaptation; in others autoplastic behavior is more adaptive.

Development employs regressive as well as progressive means; therefore there can be regressive as well as progressive adaptations. Regression can be to an earlier stage of fitting together, to a feeling of being at one with the object. Here again Hartmann illuminates the complexities of human behavior as he postulates that retreat need not be seen as defeat, and may at times be even more appropriate than continuing to press on. Regressive adaptation is related to detour through fantasy (A. Freud 1936). Kris (1952) was later to elaborate on this in his concept of regression in the service of the ego.

Adaptive abilities are not guarantees of successful reality relationships and mastery of environment, nor does a single instinctual drive guarantee adaptation. But the whole ensemble of instinctual drives, ego functions, ego apparatuses, and the principles of regulation, as they meet the environment, do have survival value. Hartmann avoids simplistic reductionism of his ideas by maintaining here that only continuous functioning of the entire apparatus provides the capacity for ongoing adaptive moves.

A state of adaptedness in the broad sense (phylogenetic) provides a relationship to the external world from the beginning. The neonate is not wholly a creature of drives. Here is another definitive statement designed to move theory away from exclusive preoccupation with the drives. There are inborn apparatuses that perform protective and perceptual functions that mature in the course of development. Mahler et al. (1975) were to observe many years later that the neonate is at the height of its adaptive capacities. After differentiation of ego and id we attribute these functions to the ego.

The Undifferentiated Matrix

There is a matrix out of which structures differentiate and inborn apparatuses (capacities) develop. This is a theory of inborn equipment. Hartmann proposes that both ego and id are products of differentiation out of the matrix.

The later ego psychologists use this concept of an undifferentiated matrix as a feature that accounts for many capacities not created in inter-action with the environment but, being inborn, serve development—enable the individual to use the environment for developmental purposes.

Jacobson (1964), in her expansion of Hartmann's work, was to use the concept of an undifferentiated matrix to show that not only ego and id, but the two drives as well, differentiate after birth. We (Blanck and Blanck 1979) are to use the concept of the matrix to argue that affects arise from still another part of the matrix, and that they too differentiate. Mahler et al. (1975) were to propose that the capacity to extract from the environ-ment derives from the undifferentiated matrix. Emde (1988), in his research on neonatal life, was to find a host of capacities that had hereto-fore been believed to develop out of experience, to be innate.

The concept of an undifferentiated matrix led to the concept of differ-entiation that, together with integration, became fundamental elements of developmental theory. Differentiation, the specialization of a function, leads to integration on a higher level of structuralization, which in turn leads to new differentiations emerging out of that more complex level, and is once again followed by new integrations. This process goes on through-out life.

The Conflict-Free Sphere

Although the wording appears to connote a locus, Hartmann clarifies that, in proposing that there is a conflict-free sphere, he is not speaking of a province of the mind where there is no conflict, but of processes that have an intrinsic potential for development without requiring a conflictual expe-rience. He lists them: in the mental realm—perception, intention, object comprehension, thinking, language, recall phenomena, productivity; in the motor realm—grasping, crawling, walking, and other maturational and learning processes. This is not to say that these may not, under some cir-cumstances, become involved in conflict.

To illustrate how certain functions develop outside of conflict, Hart-mann describes thinking and learning as operating alongside the instinc-tual drives and the defenses, while at the same time being partly indepen-dent of both. Intellectualization is an adaptation of instinctual life to external reality. The interaction of the conflict-free sphere with other ego functions is to be taken into account in order to make a valid assessment of ego strength. The conflict-free ego functions contribute to the kinds and consequences of defense and resistance.

Drive Theory

Hartmann integrates drive theory with ego psychology, defense with adaptation. Conflicts are part of the human condition. The concept of adaptation cannot stand alone without the theories of drive, conflict, and defense. Defense may simultaneously serve both control of instinctual drive and adaptation to the external world, thus literally combining drive and ego function of defense. The development of the ego itself takes place within the milieu of interaction with the drives (and the external world and the superego).

Detour Through Fantasy

This expands Freud's idea that delay is achieved by the use of thought as trial action, and Anna Freud's description of denial through fantasy. In Hartmann's thought, a relation to reality can be achieved by way of detour through fantasy, involving an initial turning away from reality as a preparation for mastery of it. By such detour, fantasy connects needs and goals provisionally with possible ways of realizing them. Optimal functioning, in the intellectual realm in particular, is not attained in a straight line, but via a detour that travels through instinctual, irrational, unconscious life. Knowledge of reality, taken alone, is not synonymous with adaptation to reality. Affect, far from being an impediment to rational action, lends itself to mastery of reality because it can organize and facilitate many ego functions.

Change of Function

A behavior form that originated in a certain realm of life may, in the course of development, appear in an entirely different realm. For example, an attitude that arose originally in the service of defense against an instinctual drive may become automatized. Thereafter the instinctual drive triggers the automatized apparatus. As an independent structure it may come to serve other functions and may turn from a means to a goal in its own right.

We use the example of reaction-formation. It is initiated at the anal phase as a defense against the wish to soil. Normally, it changes function to become an adaptive, automatized mechanism that enables us to maintain order and hygiene in both our environment and our thought processes.

Automatisms

Hartmann's concept of automatisms has important consequences for understanding structure formation and transference phenomena. He finds that "not only behavior but perceptions and thinking, too, show automatization" (88). In the motor sphere, constant repetition integrates somatic systems so that the action becomes automatic. In this way a more efficient use of energy is achieved, since thought is no longer required to initiate the action.

In the mental sphere as well, repetition automatizes methods of problem solving. By this Hartmann means something much more than habit formation; the latter overlooks that human actions are regulated by an ego. Automatisms exemplify one of the characteristics of relatively stable forms of adaptiveness. Both flexibility and automatisms are necessary characteristics of the ego.

Automatisms can become "musts" for the ego, not as compulsions, but as important forms of adaptation. Hartmann gives as an example Luther's "Here I stand. I cannot do otherwise," as the opposite of pathology. The concept of a totally flexible ego is an illusion and must not become a goal of psychoanalysis. Automatisms applied only to somatic and preconscious ego apparatuses produce purposive achievements and have an important role in adaptive processes.

Structuralization

Structure formation serves adaptation The superego is an outcome of adaptation, the result of continuing ego development, including processes of identification. In turn, the identifications reflect the nature of the process of adaptation with parental figures. Within the superego as well as the ego we live, so to speak, in past generations as well as in our own. Although the ego has a share in building tradition, the superego is the agency that becomes the chief vehicle of that tradition and of all the age-long values that are transmitted from generation to generation.

Structure becomes increasingly complex as the processes of internalization create identifications that become component elements of the psyche. An "inner world" is thereby brought into being, functioning between receptors and effectors. This world enables the individual to adapt in two steps, by withdrawing from the external world and returning to it with improved mastery. It renders the human being less dependent on the environment, and profoundly influences thought and action. It distinguishes the human from other animal species that are dominated by instinct.

Object Relations

The social relations of the child are crucial for maintaining biological and psychological equilibrium. The adaptation one has to make is to the social structure and one's collaboration in building it. For the neonate, the social structure consists of the mothering person.

We should not assume that because the neonate and the environment interact from the outset that the child is psychologically directed toward the object as an object. The neonate, as Mahler was to confirm, cannot distinguish between self-images and object images. In fact, the entire developmental process can be described in abbreviated form as consisting of the gradual acquisition of representations of the self and of the object. Object relations, we know with hindsight, is to take on more and more importance as the works of the ego psychologists who follow Hartmann begin to accrue and culminate in the developmental object relations theory that we enunciate (Blanck and Blanck 1986).

Fitting Together

Fitting together has its origin in the synthetic function of the ego (Nunberg 1931), and in the regressive need to be at one with the world. In either event it serves adaptation.

The importance of fitting together, allied with the concept of an average expectable environment, has been confirmed by the many observers of infant development. That development takes place within the medium of a dyadic object relationship is based on the supremacy of the need to fit together. Fitting together "must be supraordinate to the regulation by the external world"

(55), and "knowledge of reality must be subordinated to adaptation to reality, just as we subordinated adaptation to fitting together" (66).

Modern neonatal research confirms that the early period of fitting together for neonate and mother has lasting impact on psychological structure formation.

Equilibrium

The equilibrium of the individual is constantly disrupted. Hence constant restoration of equilibrium takes place. Equilibrium must exist (1) between individuals and their environment; (2) between the instinctual drives; (3) among the mental institutions; and (4) between the synthetic function and the rest of the ego (the intrapsychic aspects).

The Two Principles of Mental Functioning

Pleasure must be considered in relation to stability of the total organism. The pleasure potentialities at the various levels of development of the ego and its functions and apparatuses are of great significance for the stability of ego organization and its functioning. Sexualization of ego functions may lead to their inhibition. The intactness of functions is, up to a point, a guarantee against the interference of libidinal with utilitarian functions.

The pleasure principle disturbs adaptation. When needs can no longer be satisfied by fantasy, we search the external world for pleasure possibilities that may not be adaptive.

Certain modes of behavior have greater pleasure potential than others. Using the example of the ego function, anticipation, Hartmann shows that the reality principle is a continuation of the pleasure principle, although its means are different. The primary function of anticipation is to delay pleasure. But anticipation can become secondarily pleasurable in its own right.

Adherence to the reality principle involves a certain level of ego development. This has to be understood in both the broad and narrow senses. The broad sense refers to the phylogenetic nature of adaptation to reality, while the narrow sense refers to its ontogenetic nature. A state of adaptedness in the broad sense provides a relationship to the external world from the beginning, as in the neonate's adaptive readiness to fit together with the mothering person. As the neonate becomes a child, however, adaptation in the narrow sense is also sought, which involves pursuit of individual and more autonomous goals within that same relationship. It is well exemplified by Mahler's later assertion that the individual person must be fully in this world (phylogenetic adaptation), yet fully separate from it (ontogenetic adaptation).

Differentiation

Differentiation and integration go hand in hand. As differentiations are made, integration of the newly differentiated functions takes place at a higher, more complex level. The development of reality testing, judgment, extension of the world of perception and action all involve differentiation, as does the ego function of thinking. Perception must be distinguished from imagery, cognition from affect.

Ego development is a differentiation by means of which primitive regulating factors are increasingly replaced or supplemented by more effective ego regulations. What was originally anchored in instincts may subsequently be performed by the ego.

Differentiation progresses not only by the creation of new apparatuses to master new demands and new tasks, but also and mainly by new apparatuses taking over on a higher level functions that were originally performed by more primitive means. The infant's quest for safety feeling resides in the infant's visual perception of the object; as the function of memory is differentiated and attains greater importance, a purely psychic and more efficient apparatus replaces visual perception as the source of safety feeling.

Ego Strength

Ego strength cannot be assessed solely by the relation of the ego to the id and the superego. The interaction of the conflict-free sphere with other ego functions is to be taken into account in order to make a valid assessment.

Although ego strength is usually defined in terms of tolerance for tension produced by the instinctual drives, Hartmann proposes that stability and effectiveness are influenced by intelligence, which coordinates and orders functions in terms of adaptation.

Intelligence

Regulation by intelligence takes first place among the ego's regulatory factors. It serves differentiation and integration, as well as adaptation. It is but one function among others and is not to be overvalued as militating toward rational behavior. Rational behavior has to be considered in terms of the effectiveness of that behavior.

Rationality

Rationality includes regard for irrational as well as rational elements. The completely rational man is not a paragon of mental health. Such a person would be a man without qualities. An action based *solely* on an understanding of reality would not necessarily be adaptive. What must be taken into account are the social consequences of that action.

Thinking

Man conquers his environment better than other animals despite inferior physical equipment because of intelligence, which liberates the individual from having to react to immediate stimuli. Here Hartmann does not mean intelligence in the narrow sense of a person's ability to think, but in the broad sense of detour through fantasy. The intellect decides whether to accept the event as it is, or to change it by means of alloplastic adaptation.

Psychoanalysis

Psychoanalysis is the highest development of thinking. It is directed toward the inner life. It regulates adaptation and fitting together. Hartmann's definition of thinking illuminates the theory of interpretation in the following way: defenses keep thoughts, images, and drives out of consciousness, thereby preventing assimilation. Insight depends on assimilation of unconscious tendencies. Making the unconscious conscious is not enough nor is the mere production of memories because the ways in which children make connections do not satisfy the mature ego. That is why memories are not elicited for the sole purpose of releasing them from repression, but in order for the mature ego to establish new causal connections.

Hartmann's later writings are concerned with normalcy, health, rational and irrational action, ego and its development, reality, schizophrenia, the drives, among other subjects. A major theme, recurring again and again, is his thought that all behavior—normal, neurotic, borderline, or psychotic— is overdetermined. Behavior reflects influences of the drives, of the super- ego, of all psychic systems. Human goals reflect relationships to the object world, to the instinctual drives, to moral values, to ego interests.

Hartmann defines the ego by its functions. This enables him to broad- en the concept of the synthetic function into an organizing function, thus bringing into prominence the concept of an overall organizing process. All psychic systems are subject to organization. This enables us to study the psychic systems and the processes of conflict, adaptation, and defense by observing the manner in which organizing processes succeed or are for some reason prevented from succeeding. An example is Hartmann's thoughts about the metapsychology of schizophrenia. Freud (1911) believes that Schreber's psychosis was brought on by an upsurge of drive energy. Hartmann asks why the defenses proved inadequate, thereby open- ing a new line of inquiry into psychotic and borderline phenomena.

Studying the organizing process brings Hartmann to consider that the psychic systems are not always in conflict with one another. The ego and id are not always in opposition; they also collaborate. Gaining and restor- ing equilibrium proceeds in everyday life by resolution of conflicts, not only by defense or stalemate. Hartmann also alters Freud's definition of narcis- sism, thereby opening the way to study the very composition of the orga- nizing process—that is, the composition of the ego. Instead of seeing nar- cissism as a cathexis of the ego (or of the self), Hartmann proposes that narcissism consists of hypercathexis of the self representation. This paves the way for more precise knowledge of the component elements of ego, principal among which are the self and object representations.

This logically leads Hartmann to add a new concept—intrasystemic operations and conflicts—to the already well-known concept of intersys- temic operations. Hartmann says: "If we let our curiosity tempt us to look into the future, we may say that technical progress might depend on a more systematic study of the various functional units within the ego" (1964:145).

This dictates important technical alterations in our use of resistance and interpretation. We must address not only the dynamic and economic aspects of resistance, but the structural components as well. The systems that are functionally employed in defensive operations derive from intrasystemic as well as intersystemic processes and are consequently far more complex than was believed until now. Study of a patient's resistances must address that patient's perception of his or her own reality, regardless of the analyst's differing "objective" perceptions.

Hartmann strongly supports the search for psychoanalytic data that may be derived from direct infant observation, a matter disputed by those who maintain that the only valid data are derived from the psychoanalytic treatment of adults.

Hartmann refers to Kris's "new environmentalism" as the "theoretical core for the turning to a closer scrutiny of the impact of object relations on development, and of the ego aspect of object relation" (1964:292).

Finally, we are left to deal with a concept that, in retrospect, is to be regarded as transitional and may now be discarded—namely, the concept of neutralization. It was needed in Hartmann's attempt to deal with the problem of drive energy. Neutralization, he argues, converts that energy to more adaptive purposes by transferring it to the ego. With our proposal regarding drive theory—that libido serves to create unity, while aggression serves separation that is not destructive—a concept such as neutralization of drive energy is no longer needed. The organizing function (ego) serves both drives, without requiring transfer of energy.

4

▼

The Contributions of Hartmann with His Collaborators

The Genetic Approach in Psychoanalysis (1945)

In this paper Hartmann collaborates with Kris to add a fifth consideration to the factors of metapsychology. To the topographic, structural, dynamic, and economic factors they add the genetic. They point out that psychoanalysis is threefold—a therapy, an observational method, and a body of hypotheses. This paper is on the hypothetical level.

Psychoanalysis, in its hypothetical stance, began as a libido theory. Freud presented the sequence of psychosexual maturation as he discovered it through his clinical observations. His genetic investigation then proceeded from the study of libidinal development alone to include inhibiting forces. Hartmann and Kris say:

> In summarizing what is explicitly and implicitly contained in Freud's concept as far as genetic propositions are concerned, we suggest the following formulation. In the life of each individual crucial situations occur. They may be due predominantly to external events or they may be due predominantly to predispositions in the individual which then may invest insignificant situations with high significance. In order to assess

the predispositions of an individual that meet those crucial situations, the data in every case would have to refer to his total past.   (24)

For a considerable time reference to the instinctual demands dominated the discussions of these predispositions, and the functions of the ego were either incompletely described or the description was limited to that of mechanisms of defense at its disposal. This created an imbalance in theory construction. Freud's emphasis was on the instinctual demands, while consideration of the ego's functions was limited to the defensive function. Thus one set of hypotheses was elaborated in greater detail than others. One consequence is that more was known about the development of the superego than of the ego. This leaves a gap in knowledge about genetic considerations.

Dynamic considerations are concerned with the interaction and conflict of forces within the individual and his or her reaction to the external world. An example would be the use of defense in situations involving conflict. Genetic propositions state how such reactions came into being and how they are used in the course of an individual's life. They have grown out of the individual's past and extend throughout the individual's life span. They refer not to a history of events, but to how a pattern is formed, a constellation of experiences that become part of structure. And they explain why a particular solution was adopted and what causal relation exists between that solution and later developments.

Genetic considerations explain why outdated conditions still exercise influence. They make it possible to establish typical sequences in development and to trace individual behavior to its origins. Thus one may now characterize psychological phenomena according to their position in the developmental process. Genetic considerations also permit careful distinction between behaviors that appear similar by examining their origins. For example, pacifism may in one case represent a reaction formation to the wish to attack; in another instance it may be the expression of a fear of being attacked. Did Hartmann and Kris overlook that it may also be conflict-free?

Hartmann and Kris use the classical example of castration anxiety for further illustration. Fears at the phallic phase involve the mistake of regarding girls as castrated, thus reinforcing the idea that castration is indeed a reality. This combines with fear of a similar fate because of erotic sensations directed toward incestuous objects and dread of retaliation. That dread revives memories of similar anxieties when desires for earlier gratifications were predominant, when the fear was not of castration but of not being loved. Their comment is noteworthy: "In other words: pregenital experience is one of the factors determining the reaction in the phallic phase" (22).

Hartmann's proposal that the ego as a psychic system controls perception and motility, achieves solutions, and directs actions—in other words, operates outside the sphere of conflict—also informs that these functions are of specific importance because they exercise a considerable influence as independent factors. On this Hartmann and Kris say: "The importance of an actual experience through which a child lives, and the direction this experience may give to his life largely depend on the specific phase of the child's development. This is the reason why a superficial collection of anamnestic data concerning an individual's childhood is frequently misleading" (25).

The paper also points out that psychoanalysis does not claim to explain behavior solely as the result of drives and fantasies. Psychoanalysis is applied social science in the sense that one must view experience in relation to the child's biological growth, as well as in relation to the world around it. Typical phases of conflict occur in the life of an individual, brought about by maturation or by the demands of the environment. Crucial phases of maturation and development coincide and are dependent on cultural factors.

Our own vantage point, so many years later, enables us to point out here that Spitz (1965) is to develop the importance of the coincidence of maturation and development in the life of the young child. He termed these points of convergence *critical periods* (chapter 7). Hindsight also enables us to point out that Kris was to present a paper on the patterning of childhood memories, the roots of which may be found here (chapter 5).

With apparent recognition that their contribution is not finite Hartmann and Kris advocate longitudinal research. They suggest that this be carried out by interaction of two methods—psychoanalysis and longitudinal study of life histories. They point to two areas in child development that require more attention—achievements of the ego that are independent of conflict, and experiences of preverbal life. Subsequent investigation has indeed followed this direction in the works of Jacobson, Spitz (1965), Mahler et al., and Blanck and Blanck (1979–1986).

Implicit in this paper, but not yet developed, is that some organizing or guiding force is needed that maintains an equilibrium among the many factors that contribute toward maturation and development in the life of the child, the adolescent, and the adult. Again we find roots of our 1986 proposal that a superordinate ego maintains the integrity of the psychic system as a constant force during the turmoil of constant change.

Comments on the Formation of Psychic Structure (1946)

In this essay Hartmann, Kris, and Loewenstein do not overlook drive theory in their focus on ego psychology. Here they weave together certain aspects of ego development that operate in concert with the drives. But their focus is on the concepts of differentiation and integration, as well as on maturation and development. They say: "Differentiation indicates the specialization of a function; integration, the emergence of a new function out of previously not coherent uses of functions and reactions. . . . Maturation indicates the processes of growth that occur relatively independent of environmental influences; development indicates the processes of growth in which environment and maturation interact more closely" (18).

They begin with the assumption that the essential elements in the structure of personality exist at age five or six and that developmental processes after that age are modifications, enrichments or, in pathology, restriction of existing structure.

They find certain disadvantages in Freud's assumption that the ego differentiates gradually out of the id. Freud's formulation suggests that the equipment that exists at birth is part of the id. To them it appears more useful to consider that there is an undifferentiated phase out of which both id and ego differentiate. Apparatuses that exist in the undifferentiated matrix mature and will later come under the control of the ego to serve motility, perception, and certain thought processes.

By means of differentiation the ego becomes a specialized organ of adaptation separated to some degree from the id. It is this that accounts for the difference between the instinctual drives in humans and the instincts in animals. Animals must rely on their instincts to mediate adjustment to reality; humans rely on an organization independent of the id—the ego.

The first step in ego formation involves the infant in beginning to distinguish between the self and the outside world. To make this distinction, the infant must experience a tolerable amount of frustration because, with total satisfaction, the infant would tend to experience the source of satisfaction as part of the self. While the object is still experienced as part of the self, the entire unit is cathected with value. A cathectic shift takes place as differentiation begins. The *primary narcissistic cathexis* that exists at birth becomes partly transformed into *object cathexis*.

Casting this in terms of object relations theory it may be said that, as differentiation proceeds, the infant establishes object relatedness with the mothering person. This suggests that borderline and narcissistic pathologies may be described as pathologies of object relations.

During the undifferentiated state the child's connection with the mothering person is profound. It is then that the child's earliest learning begins. The ability to anticipate future events and to delay gratification has its inception in the second part of the first year of life and operates in conjunction with maturational changes that give the child greater control over his or her body. This facilitates transfer from the pleasure principle to the reality principle. Learning to exchange immediate for future gratification is essential to the child's formation of the internal world.

Degree of need rests on degree of structuralization. The infant and child are in a state of intense object need that changes with development. With structuralization, accompanied by physical maturation, need diminishes as autonomy gains ground. By the end of the first year anxiety has begun to invade the child's life. He or she has developed to the point where fear of the loss of the object is superseded by fear of the loss of the object's love.

Distinction between id and ego becomes ever sharper as the child learns to control the drives. When the child has learned to anticipate the future, anxiety undergoes a change in function. It can now operate as a signal.

Mechanisms that have their roots in the reflex equipment of the newborn can serve the purpose of adjustment (adaptation) in infancy. Later they begin to function as mechanisms of defense and thus produce changes in the child's personality. Here the authors are contending that defense is at first adaptive.

Identification is seen as a normal developmental phenomenon and only secondarily might it also be a defense. As development progresses, identification is with the attitude of the parents from whom the child has learned that certain instinctual demands are undesirable. With those demands under control, the ego becomes free to be used in organizing the child's intellectual world. Thinking becomes gratifying in its own right. Thought interacts with fantasy.

The process of superego formation is independent of maturation because there is no bodily component. The authors retain the concept of the role of castration threat in superego formation, but their emphasis is on identification and idealization. In prephallic stages, the child's identifications were with aggrandized parents for the purpose of magically partaking in their protection and power. At the end of the phallic phase idealization is more concerned with moral behavior. The child identifies not with the parents as they really are, but with their superegos.

The process of identification in superego formation is different from the earlier understanding of identification as a defense. A change in distribution of psychic energy takes place. The identifications become part of the cathexis previously attached to the object. The superego is now an organization relatively independent of the objects and the ego. Libidinal energy becomes desexualized; aggressive attitudes toward the former rival are internalized to become the force that serves the superego in enforcing its demands.

As a consequence of this development, a new anxiety situation is introduced. It first manifests as a fear of loss of the now-perceived object; with development, it alters to become a fear of loss of love of the object; at the phallic phase, it becomes fear of castration; finally, the fear transforms to superego anxiety. Then the individual becomes morally independent of the environment. "Man has acquired an inner voice" (34).

Notes on the Theory of Aggression (1949)

In this paper Hartmann, Kris, and Loewenstein attend to the fact that, in presenting the dual drive theory, Freud (1920) sought a biological base for the drives; hence the death instinct, a matter these authors find irrelevant to psychoanalytic theory construction. Their own concept of the operation of the drives is based on the assumption that libido has a biological avenue of discharge in orgasm, but they are unable to find an analogous avenue for the discharge of aggression. This puzzles them because, although they find no merit in a death instinct, they are not liberated from the idea that aggression seeks to destroy.

This then leads them to consider the individual's concern about danger of destruction of the object. They have to search for theories of how aggression is modified so that the object is preserved. They speculate that aggression can be modified by: (1) displacement; (2) restricting the aim; (3)sublimation; and (4) fusion with libido in which libido dominates.

They further clarify the difference between instinct in animals and drives in humans. In animals, instinct serves preservation of the individual; in humans, not instinct, but the ego function of self-preservation is operative.

This essay approaches our theory that the aggressive drive serves growth rather than destruction, but does not go quite that far. The precursor of that developmental use of aggression may be found in their thought that aggression is manifest in control of the body, control of reality, and in the formation of psychic structure.

The Function of Theory in Psychoanalysis (1953)

In this work Hartmann, Kris, and Loewenstein wish to counteract the tendency to extract parts of the whole of psychoanalytic theory and to present that part as an entirely new theory. They also oppose the tendency to restrict interest to the clinical aspect only, at the expense of overlooking theory altogether. They believe that theory directs the clinician toward intelligent questioning. They say:

> Not even the simplest clinical observation in psychoanalysis would be meaningful without assuming the existence of dynamically active unconscious processes, of processes which cannot be observed but merely inferred. Thus the everyday tools of all analysts, whatever their insight into or evaluation of theory, include the necessity not only of "descriptive" but also "explanatory" concepts. Every psychoanalytic case report, however "factual," is replete with inference based upon theoretical assumptions. (15)

They give as an example the theory of dreams, which have an immediate bearing on the psychoanalysts' attitudes to theory in general. The interpretations offered patients are thereby based on theoretical assumptions that might otherwise be speculative. A more modern example is that of child observation, which has produced a considerable number of hypotheses about stages of early personality development.

To illustrate their position they review Freud's major theoretical discoveries over time. They make the often overlooked observation that Freud did not usually undertake to integrate his new findings with those that went before, a fact that probably lends itself to fragmentation of theory. Nevertheless, one finding logically does follow the preceding one in the accretion of proposals that has become the whole of psychoanalytic theory.

Fragmentation stresses one proposition at the expense of another, such as emphasis on ego psychology at the expense of id psychology, or the other way around. Simplification of theory always diminishes its usefulness.

With considerable prescience, since they write so long before the advent of self psychology, they assert that a given author's work may result in a highly personalized theory. Anticipating Rangell, who stresses that theory is cumulative, they conclude: "Progress in psychoanalytic theory has led to a better integration, an ever clearer connection of its various parts" (35).

Notes on the Superego (1962)

In this essay Hartmann and Loewenstein discuss superego formation, anticipating Kohut by ten years. Particularly clarifying is the distinction they draw between superego as a discrete structure, and superego forerunners. In separating genetic roots from functional entity, they explain that the beginning internalizations are variously described in the literature as primitive, archaic forms of superego, or as precursors. They prefer to reserve *superego* as a term and concept for that structure that crystallizes out of the oedipal conflict. In that struggle, the disparate aspects become integrated and merged into a new structure which is the superego. In an oversimplified analogy, it would be incorrect to describe flour, eggs, shortening, and other ingredients as forerunners or archaic forms of cake. The cake becomes an entirely new structure. To refer to the ingredients of what are to become combined to form the superego as archaic forms of that structure as an entity is to deny the essence of the ego's capacity, namely its organizing function. To the authors, the superego is "a dynamically, partly independent center of mental functioning with aims of its own" (65). Its development does not proceed in the direction of increased detachment from the ego, but is bound up with it. The ego ideal is regarded as one of the functions of the superego, as are conscience and moral values.

In summary, then, superego development depends on ego development, according to Hartmann and Loewenstein, and "once the superego as a system is set up, its normal functioning is constantly bound to certain activities of the ego; and the further evolution of the superego does not diminish the developing ego's influence, but tends to increase it" (64).

Jacobson was to develop further this interesting spiral effect of ego development enhancing superego development, and she discusses how both are mutually reinforcing.

Some Thoughts on Interpretation in the Theory and Practice of Psychoanalysis (1957)

Loewenstein, in this paper, builds on Kris's work on the patterning of memory (chapter 5) and adds comments on the timing of interpretation, on genetic interpretations, on the relevance of verbal communication to interpretation, and on theory as a guide to interpretation. He shows how ego psychology sharpens and refines our knowledge about what Freud had already discussed concerning the timing of interpretation.

Loewenstein defines genetic interpretation: "Genetic interpretations essentially are re-constructions of psychological events considered to be the prototypes or the causes of later psychological manifestations whose significance or determinants are thus being explained" (143).

On the role of speech in interpretation Loewenstein says that speech is the vehicle that lifts psychological processes out of the unconscious into the preconscious and finally into consciousness.

And, last, Lowenstein cautions that in every psychoanalysis, theory is never to be taken for granted because that would bar the way to new discoveries.

5

▼

The Contributions of Ernst Kris

While it is commonly acknowledged that Hartmann is the father of ego psychology, less well known is that Ernst Kris is ego psychology's theorist of technique. Kris proposes some major alterations in technique in the very process of working with Hartmann and Loewenstein on their groundbreaking contributions to theory. Usually, technique lags behind theory. In this instance, however, technical considerations are introduced side by side with theory.

It is unfortunate that Kris died at a relatively young age. Had he lived longer to continue his work, the technique of psychoanalysis might now be more advanced. As it is, few texts on the technique of psychoanalysis have appeared in the modern era. The last text to have been influenced by ego psychology was begun by Greenson (1967). He, too, died before he could finish the second of a projected two-volume work. We are left, therefore, with the standard texts—Freud (1912), Fenichel (1941), Glover (1955), Sharpe (1950), Menninger (1958), and the one volume by Greenson. With the exceptions of Hartmann, Greenson, and G. Blanck (1966), ego psychological considerations have not been made explicit in the literature; they are implicit throughout, however, beginning with Freud. All analysts employ ego psychological considerations without necessarily having conceptual knowledge of them. Moreover, a number of unpublished papers and panel discussions add an ego psychological note to contemporary practice. Kris points out that, despite the paucity of recording, technical questions concerning the functioning of the ego continue to increase in importance.

Ego Psychology and Interpretation in Psychoanalytic Therapy (1951)

In this paper, Kris notes that the principles of ego psychology were anticipated in Freud's papers on technique. Ego psychology, Kris says, enlarges the scope of psychoanalysis. He is not alluding to the treatment of the borderline structures when he introduces the relevance of the mother-child relationship, a matter we would now place under the aegis of object relations. He would apply this knowledge about preoedipal life in the psychoanalysis of neurosis proper.

Kris also rediscusses resistance. Analysts used to regard resistance as an obstacle to treatment in the days when the analytic objective was to arrive at id content as expeditiously as possible. Kris found it necessary to remind analysts of what Anna Freud had already said, that resistance is the use of defense in the analytic situation and thereby provides an opportunity to observe how the ego functions. (We elaborate on the subject of resistance in chapter 18.) Kris also describes evenly suspended attention here. He defines it as oscillation among empathy, self-observation, and judgment.

Of special importance is his thought about the technique of interpretation. Interpretation, he says, is to be designed to convey the broadest possible meaning rather than the narrow one of id content alone. We elaborate on this in chapter 21 by describing how interpretation is made from the narrow (immediate) material, with the broader interpretation in mind.

Psychoanalytic Explorations in Art (1952)

Here Kris deals with the creative process. Among the organizational functions of the ego are capacity for self-regulation of regression and for control over the primary process. As is well known, the ego in psychosis does not have control but is overwhelmed by the primary process. The artist, on the other hand, is subject to an ego regression during inspiration, but it is partial, temporary, and controlled by the ego, which retains the function of establishing contact with the audience. That regression is purposive, temporary, and pleasurable while remaining in the service of the ego. The ego of the artist may use the primary process without being overwhelmed by it. The ego of creative persons employs the integrative function, including self-regulation, which permits daring intellectual activity.

The Personal Myth (1956)

In this work Kris describes two cases in which the patients maintained unconscious fantasied biographies as though they were real, without losing their real life histories. This paper adds emphasis to the importance of exploring unconscious fantasy.

On Some Vicissitudes of Insight in Psychoanalysis (1956)

Kris's best-known paper has a nickname, "The Good Hour." He makes the important point, new at the time, that psychoanalysis heretofore had been concerned with intersystemic conflict; now intrasystemic functions are of equal importance. Focus on defense and resistance is supplemented by considerations concerning the integrative function because that function includes intrasystemic as well as intersystemic factors.

The "Good Hour" begins unpropitiously, with a mild negative tinge. That it is to be a good hour only becomes apparent after ten or fifteen minutes. Then there might be a dream to which the patient associates spontaneously. In good circumstances, there might also be recovery of a memory. New elements appear that fit into the context of that which had gone before as though they had always been familiar. If the analyst interprets, it need only be in question form because the patient's autonomous functioning is in tune with the material. Because of that, the patient may even arrive at the interpretation without the analyst's help.

This process cannot be explained simply by stating that the repressed has reached consciousness; the integrative function must be at work. The Good Hour appears as though it had been prepared, for indeed it has been, but outside of awareness. The Good Hour can only arrive as the result of work that has gone before. It depends on the crumbling of a resistant structure, not on interpretation of a single resistance. Kris's thoughts about the manner in which material arrives in consciousness in the Good Hour, is that it is analogous to the activity of artistic creation. Thus he does not restrict creativity to the artist. All significant intellectual achievement is the product of preconscious mentation.

He accounts for the mild negative tinge at the beginning of the Good Hour by using Hartmann's concept of *neutralization* of drive energy. Although we have already explained why we no longer subscribe to the concept of neutralization, at that time Kris was working with Hartmann. Therefore he supposed with Hartmann that aggressive energy has to be neutralized in order to be transferred to the integrative function of the ego. Now we have Mahler's studies (chapter 8) to explain the negative tinge at the outset of the Good Hour as the use of the aggressive thrust, resembling the thrust of the separating toddler who uses that thrust in the service of attainment of autonomy.

Kris contrasts the Good Hour with the "Pseudo-Good Hour." There is an element of compliance in the Pseudo-Good Hour. The work is not pursued autonomously, but in order to please or defy the analyst. It serves to gain praise, love, or even merger, which may provoke defense against merger. It overshadows the opportunity to gain insight. It hypercathects the relationship with the analyst at the expense of autonomous functioning.

Another form of the Pseudo-Good Hour, according to Kris, might be an attempt to gain independence prematurely, resulting in self-analysis that is competitive and tinged with hostility. Yet a third form, more common in borderline phenomena, is misuse of the integrative function to attribute all factors in the patient's life to a single experience in infancy. Here the synthetic, but not the integrative, function is at work. That allows unrelated matters to be synthesized. Finally, Kris makes the point that control over acting out is one of the requirements for attainment of insight.

Recovery of Childhood Memories in Psychoanalysis (1956)

Here, Kris shows that analysts are not to be misled by memory of distinct events, for memory is dynamic and telescopic. Behavior, as well as memory, is influenced by derivatives of archaic material. Analysis deals with patterns rather than with real events. To be taken into account is the result of the interaction of childhood experiences, preverbal unconscious fantasy, and later events—an interrelation between past and present. The present selects, colors, and modifies the past. Memories are revived in analysis when the influence of instinctual forces and unconscious fantasies on current conflicts are analyzed. Spontaneous recall of childhood material might then ensue.

Dynamic interpretation of conflicts concerned with the current situation is combined with genetic interpretation. Kris notes that Freud might have had this kind of integrative interpretation in mind when he said that all interpretation is construction or reconstruction. It is the historical context into which such interpretation fits that constitutes a biographical picture of a special kind, not one that would meet the requirements of a biographer who strives for accurate replication of precise experience, but one that interweaves the present with the past in a way that includes unconscious fantasy as well as real experience. Kris says: "We are no longer satisfied to view the development of the child in terms of his psychosexual maturation only; we find that the development of ego functions and object relations . . . are of equal and intrinsic importance" (67).

Kris gives as an example a child whose mother was absent because of illness and hospitalization. While the mother was away, the child became ill and had to be hospitalized on the mother's return. In the past, the child's reaction to the mother's absence might have been analyzed by emphasis on libidinal and aggressive drives—that is, by making an id interpretation such as "You became ill because you were angry." Kris warns against interpretations that provide the patient with an "empty id vernacular" that serves only to reinforce repression. Now that we know about the effect of separation on children, the correct interpretation reflects the effect on the child's development of an untimely physical separation from the mother.

The content of this review of Kris's major contributions to technique appears familiar, as though we always knew it. That fact resembles the "good" interpretation that, Kris notes, feels to the patient as though it was known all along. That we now use so much of what he has added to the theory of technique speaks for the enormity of his impact. His observations on technique have so permeated modern procedure that we scarcely remember that psychoanalysis used to be restricted to id content alone.

6

▼

The Contributions of Edith Jacobson

Edith Jacobson was a prominent psychoanalyst in Berlin before World War II. She was imprisoned by the Nazis because she refused to disclose information about a patient, a government official whose secrets they wished to know. She was incarcerated in a women's prison for political, not criminal, offenders. There she observed the behavior of normal women who, in order to cope with the cruelty of interrogation, used depersonalization, until then believed to be a psychotic defense. It was out of that experience that she later (1959) writes about *depersonalization* to describe how normal people under stress may use depersonalization.

In her major work, *The Self and the Object World* (1964), Jacobson struggles to master two languages—English and the vocabulary of ego psychology. These are difficult for someone who had been trained in Germany, not only in classical psychoanalytic theory, but in the literary style of German philosophy. She is hampered by having to express her innovative ego psychological concepts in the more familiar but limited terminology of drive theory. One has to "translate" some of her thoughts into the newer terms that have by now become familiar to us.

Jacobson carries forward some of Hartmann's ideas and introduces new concepts that expand ego psychology. Her contributions are far ranging. They span such subjects as acquisition of identity, including gender identity; the processes of internalization; the representational world; superego formation in girls; depression; and the psychoses and borderline states.

She clarifies the distinctions among *ego*, *self*, and *self representation*. *Ego* is one of the parts of the tripartite structure, used to provide analysts with a construct for the purpose of organizing clinical data. *Self* is the totality of the bodily and psychic person as it develops after birth. Before birth psyche, soma, drives—in potential form in the undifferentiated matrix—are undistinguished from one another. Differentiation begins at birth and, with it, the sense of self begins to be acquired gradually, altering continuously with experience. *Self representation* is the unconscious, preconscious, and conscious endopsychic representation of the bodily and mental self in the system ego. This locates the representational world within the ego.

Deficient identity formation is the major ego deficit in psychosis. That discovery led Jacobson to study the manner in which identity is formed. She was dissatisfied with the then current conceptions of identity because they were either broadly sociological or, as in Erikson's (1959) work, rested on ambiguous terms like *ego identity*. Identity, she found, is essential to the state of intactness and cohesion. As she put it: "I would prefer to understand by identity formation a process that builds up the ability to preserve the whole psychic organization—despite its growing structuralization, differentiation and complexity—as a highly individualized but coherent entity which has direction and continuity at any stage of human development" (1954:27).

Thus she addresses the whole structure, as well as its component elements, and shows that while massive development (differentiation, integration, and structuralization) is proceeding, identity in the very process of formation provides stability in the midst of change. She explains how identity is formed out of "those essential identifications on which the experience of personal identity is founded" (viii).

She carries forward Hartmann's concept of a representational world, a cornerstone of ego psychological object relations theory. Self representation and object representations arise out of experiences of the self in interaction with the object. These experiences register in that part of the ego where the representations "reside." Mahler et al. (chapter 8) were later to clarify that interaction between neonate and mothering person is at first interpersonal. As the representational world comes into being, interaction shifts to the internal world to take place between the self representation and the object representations as well. Object relations then have become intrapsychic, intersystemic, and interpersonal.

Jacobson describes the establishment, development, and cathexes of the self and object images and representations and their interaction. She highlights the importance of maternal care, its contribution to structural differentiation and to the development of specific functions, thereby heralding the emphasis that later ego psychologists will place on the importance of the dyadic experience.

This forces a review of the psychosexual phases with a new emphasis, to view them more broadly than impelled by the drives only. Drive theory appears to limit psychosexual progression to the zonal feature—oral, anal, phallic. Taking into account all that impinges on the life of the infant and child at each psychosexual phase broadens the picture considerably. We may use the experiences of the oral phase as an example. There is more to the life of the infant than feeding alone. As Spitz (chapter 7) is to investigate, feeding alone, with a propped bottle and minimal human contact, does not even assure survival. Jacobson describes the behavior of an adequate mother performing the routine tasks of child care, such as feeding, bathing, and diapering. These tasks involve her, simultaneously, in interaction—in playing with the baby, talking, cooing, stimulating, responding to the infant's responses in an "action-reaction-action" cycle (Spitz). These interactions "start up" the child's latent ego functions. Some, such as motility, will mature according to a biological timetable. Others, such as perception, thinking, memory, judgment, and the less tangible functions such as latent talents, are enhanced by the interaction. These observations about the broader experience in each psychosexual phase show that the individual develops within the context of self and object interaction rather than by drive maturation alone.

Jacobson introduces the concept of "selective identification," an unconscious process by means of which the child identifies, not with the entirety of the other person, but selectively and more autonomously, with admired aspects. At this level of development, the ego has become capable of thinking less globally than in infancy. In order to select admired aspects of the object, the child must become able to partialize, while at the same time becoming able to realize that the object is more than the parts. By means of selective identification, the child combines his or her own qualities with selected features of the object to create a new and unique personality. Especially because popular psychology fixes simplistically on "role models," we find it necessary to emphasize that the matter is not as simple as copying another person.

Selective identification is a compromise between symbiotic yearning, on the one hand, and striving for autonomy, on the other. Both the *transitional object* (Winnicott 1953) and *selective identification* exemplify how differentiation and integration interrelate. At the developmental level where the transitional object is created, the infant differentiates from the mothering person by extracting aspects of the mother to form a new creation. This act consists of differentiation on one level only to integrate on a higher level. The transitional object—diaper, teddy bear, blanket—becomes the concrete symbol of the state of transition between merger and differentiation. Selective identification may be thought of as a device at a somewhat higher level with a similar developmental purpose. At the level of selective identification the child no longer requires a concrete article because self representation and object representations have formed; the newly created structure now exists in the representational world. Differentiation followed by integration have formed a new *internal* structure. In that way, selective identification creates profound modification of the ego—a new self representation that includes likeness to an object without loss of identity.

Jacobson's study of the mechanisms of drive discharge led her to revise Freud's ideas about primary narcissism and primary masochism. Freud presented his thoughts about those matters before he altered theory radically in 1923. Because he preferred to march forward in his theory construction without returning to revise earlier formulation, analysts are left with some of his early thoughts that remain unreconciled with later ones. This explains why, in reading Freud, one is baffled by the fact that he writes about primary narcissism and primary masochism in terms of drive discharge on an "ego" that he had not yet defined. He considers narcissism to be the consequence of libidinal cathexis of the ego. That left theory with a most imprecise understanding of narcissism, which Hartmann amended by redefining narcissism as libidinal cathexis, not of the *ego* but of the *self representation*. That emendation eliminated the vagueness about the site of cathectic discharge and also made room for consideration of normal as well as pathological forms of narcissism. Today we may think of normal narcissism as consisting of appropriate valuation of the self representation, whereas in pathological narcissism the self representation is either cathected with too little value, or is overvalued in relation to the object representations.

Even when corrected by the concept of cathexis of the *self representation* in place of *ego*, however, the concept of primary narcissism remained hazy. Jacobson attempts to clarify this concept. She shows that discharge on the not-yet-existent self representation is not possible. A similar theoretical problem exists with regard to primary masochism. Freud (1920) equated it with the death instinct. Jacobson is among the many theorists who do not find the concept of a death instinct useful. She says:

> A glance at the psychoanalytic literature discloses that most analysts, although they accept the existence of two inherently different kinds of drives, refuse to work with the death instinct theory. The main reason for this rejection may be that Freud's proposition, of life and death instincts is founded on rather speculative assumptions foreign to his earlier conceptions and definitions of the drives. In any event, valid arguments can be raised in objection to the death instinct theory.
>
> (1971:30)

Much confusion remains about the psychological state of the neonate. The infant is said to be in a state of primary narcissism and primary masochism (Freud), undifferentiation (Hartmann), nondifferentiation (Spitz), in a dozing and splanchnic state (Mahler), or, in opposition to the ego psychologists, in possession of a cohesive self (Kohut; Stern). Confusion will probably continue to exist until instruments are devised that can "ask" the baby. Jacobson deals with these issues in terms of the infant's relatively undifferentiated state. "What precisely is the meaning," she asks, "of narcissism and masochism in the primitive psychic organization prior to the child's discovery of his own self and the object world?" (7). At the beginning of life neither masochism nor narcissism can be said to obtain because there is not yet a self representation to be cathected. Jacobson advances drive theory in three ways:

1. Elaborating on Hartmann's postulate that ego and id differentiate after birth out of an undifferentiated matrix, she proposes that the drives also exist only as potential and differentiate out into libido and aggression after birth under the auspices of adequate mothering.

2. Departing from earlier concepts of discharge processes, she proposes that the ego exercises control over discharge. Thus she is able to offer a comprehensive summary of infant development in which drive maturation proceeds hand in hand with structural development.

3. She finds that there are positive uses of the aggressive drive, disputing the idea that this drive serves destructive purposes only. She notes that certain behaviors that appear to be manifestations of the aggressive drive contribute to growth and development. Here she agrees with Freud's 1940 view that aggression is the force that severs connection, but she does not go far enough to dispute his thought that it destroys. Yet she notes that ambitious strivings, using aggressive energy, can promote growth and development where the life circumstances offer gratification in equal balance with tolerable frustration. That the aggressive drive serves growth is one of the most revolutionary ideas presented by the ego psychologists. If one were to distinguish between drive and affect—between the aggressive drive as an energy source, on the one hand, and as a hostile affect, on the other—matters would be even clearer. Immersed in drive theory and its terminology, Jacobson was not yet able to make that distinction.

Object relations (interaction between the self representation and the object representations) develop out of mental registration of affectively charged experiences that become established in the ongoing process of organization. Whereas Melanie Klein (1948) deals literally with the reality of the object, Jacobson points out that there is a difference between *representations* of the self and object in the psychic structure, and between the self and object as they really are. In early life our view of the world is distorted by inadequate perception. It is probably not possible ever to form absolutely realistic self and object representations because there is always an element of subjective, affectively colored distortion. But capacities for introspection, realistic perception, discrimination, and evaluation do improve with development and experience. We shall show in chapter 11 that this makes for a complex theory of object relations because some patterns are laid down when distortion is still very great and these tend to become more or less rigidly fixed for life.

Jacobson presents a major revision of superego theory. She alters Freud's view that the threat of castration is the incentive that forces the boy to abandon his oedipal strivings and to acquire a strong superego instead. This formulation led Freud into one of his most egregious errors, for he could not then account for superego formation in the girl. Reasoning that girls have no such incentive, he was led to the logical (but not clinical) conclusion that superego development in girls and women must be incomplete. Jacobson regards the superego as a most complex organizational outcome of development, agreeing with Freud that superego formation accompanies oedipal resolution. She does not altogether refute the role of castration wish and castration threat in superego formation. But she regards this as a projection of the boy's ambitious and rivalrous relationship with the oedipal father. This establishes the castration threat, not as real, but as a projection of the boy's fantasy.

To amend Freud's theory of superego formation, especially in girls, Jacobson takes a step backward to look at an earlier stage of development. Boys and girls acquire knowledge of anatomical difference not at the oedipal period, but within the second year of life. Both boys and girls then experience a castration "shock." This is borne out later by child observation (Mahler; Galenson and Roiphe 1976). The boy recovers more readily because he has the assurance of the continuing presence of his phallus. The girl, lacking such assurance, compensates for the absence of that body part by displacement on her entire body. She displays it and adorns it. In addition, she seizes on the value system that has been presented to her in the process of her toilet training, which coincides in time with discovery of anatomical difference. She becomes a neat, clean, obedient little girl. Superego formation is thereby achieved earlier in girls.

Jacobson adds the important dimension of object relations to the puzzle of how the Oedipus Complex is resolved. This emphasizes the effect on the child of positive parental affect—tenderness, warmth, love—which promotes positive identification. In this way, she extends her ideas about identification to the theory of oedipal resolution and superego formation. Love for and identification with the parent of the same sex overcome rivalry. The superego is the repository of identification with moral and ethical values, with prohibitions, and includes also identification with the loving aspects of the parents.

In her revision of the theory of superego formation, she adds emphasis to the well-known superego function of regulations enforced by ethics, morals, and conscience. She suggests that the superego governs moods and regulates the entire ego state; she adds the important idea that the superego oversees the development of a coherent, consistent defense organization. In essence, she suggests a kind of superordinate superego.

A major revision of psychoanalytic thought about the perversions also arises out of Jacobson's work. She proposes: "The child's experience of sexual identity does not by any means rest exclusively on genital comparisons" (1964:72). Sexual identity, she suggests, rests on identification with general physical and mental characteristics, and comes about long before castration problems arise. She adds: "Identity formation and the feelings of personal identity are not quite as dependent upon the heterosexual position as one might imagine; they are largely influenced by the extent to which consistent and enduring identifications leading to secondary autonomy and independence of the ego can be established, even if they lead to sexual pathology" (1964:73).

Jacobson makes a major contribution to the psychology of the affective disorders, pathologies closely involved with identity formation, and with superego development. She regards depression as a complex syndrome that cannot be viewed from the standpoint of ego psychology alone. She says: "An ego-psychological approach to the problem of depression would . . . not be psychoanalytic if it neglected drive theory" (1971:183). She believes that depression involves an underlying conflict in which aggression is turned against the self-images. (Having stressed that aggression is not hostile but growth promoting, here she reverts to her roots in drive theory by confusing the aggressive drive with hostility.)

Depression is an ego state that may be embedded in a variety of pathological structures. Diagnosis is complex. There are neurotic depression, borderline depression, and psychotic depression. And in psychosis, it matters greatly whether one is dealing with manic-depressive depression or schizophrenic depression. Jacobson concludes:

> A sound psychoanalytic theory of depression presupposes a "multiple-factor" genetic approach. It must take into account the nature and intensity of the drives involved in the conflict, the instinctual constitution; the quality of the drives in terms of deneutralization and defusion; the special drive fixations and regressions, the nature of cathectic conditions, the drive discharge processes, and the changes in the cathexes of the self and object representations, since all these have a bearing on the level of ego functioning.   (1971:183)

This exemplifies the orientation in drive theory that leaves Jacobson appearing to have one foot on either side of the fence. She is forced to express her thought in the language of drive theory and then to tack on that ego functioning and developmental factors must also be considered. Today we would think of one integrated theory that includes both drive and ego considerations.

Jacobson discusses the origin of the defense mechanisms, projection and introjection. In infancy perceptual capacity is not yet mature enough to distinguish internal from external. Therefore the infant cannot identify the source of stimulation. There are constant cathectic shifts; libido and aggression turn continuously from object to self with, as yet, weak boundaries between them. Affective expression by the mother induces affect in the infant who attempts to maintain symbiotic merger by making imitative movements. This is an empathic exchange that results in the establishment of primitive affective identifications.

Introjection and projection originate in early, infantile incorporation and ejection fantasies. Jacobson adds: "Hence in adult patients, we must not confuse transference processes based on displacement from one object image to another, such as from the mother onto the analyst, with projections" (1964:47).

Thus both defense and transference phenomena have to be reconsidered in order that they not to be confused with the phenomena that exist before there is a distinct boundary between self and other. Where the boundary remains unclear, projection is to be regarded, not as a normal mechanism of defense, but as the consequence of deficient distinction between self and other. This also bears on the development of the capacity for empathy which, we believe, has its roots in the state of merged self and object images. An infant whose emotional needs have been well attended will probably develop a good capacity for empathy.

Despite the fact that Jacobson's ideas, as well as her literary style, are complex, much of her work has become so thoroughly incorporated into the totality of theory and technique that we use her contributions in our daily clinical work without always knowing its source. Internalization, identification, gender identity, superego formation, object relations, the value of defense and the formation of defense mechanisms, the positive use of the aggressive drive, the representational world, all have become part of our theoretical and clinical repertory. In addition to providing such rich addenda to psychoanalytic theory, Jacobson paves the way for future theorists to advance theory construction.

7

▼

The Contributions of René A. Spitz

Freud, Hartmann and his collaborators, Jacobson, and Mahler are aware that psychoanalytic theory is an object relations theory. But it fell to Spitz to explore the very beginnings of object relations and to leave no doubt of its centrality in human psychology. At the core of Spitz's discoveries is that development takes place in interaction with the mothering person. The result of this interaction is more than the sum of the contributions from each partner in that dyad. This was to be developed even further by Mahler (chapter 8).

Spitz was both a psychoanalyst and an infant observer. That combination enabled him to bring psychoanalytic insight to his observational studies. As he put it (1965), he was a lonely figure at a time when a large segment of the psychoanalytic community believed that the only valid source of psychoanalytic information is provided by the adult psychoanalytic patient on the couch. At present, there are a few who still believe that interpretation of child observational data is subject to adultomorphic speculation. Overlooked there is that psychoanalytic discipline guards against such error.

Spitz's work constitutes an indispensable addition to psychoanalytic theory and, as is true of the works of those ego psychologists who precede him, he builds another bridge to further theory construction. Leaning on the shoulders of Freud and Hartmann, he advances theory in several directions. He explores the whole person and, simultaneously, the minutiae of component elements of the person, the sources of those elements and their pathways of development. He asserts that there are "three developmental currents, namely the crystallization of affective responses, the integration of the ego and the consolidation of object relations [which] are interdependent although different aspects of the total personality" (151).

Spitz's aim was to create an overall understanding of development in which "the ontogenesis of the ego, the unfolding of object relations, the foundation and the establishment of personality structure, and the ultimate achievement of social relations" may all be described in a psychoanalytic frame of reference (1957:ix). He viewed miles of film to study the behavior of infants with and without the presence of the mothering person. He concludes that growth and development in the psychological sector are essentially dependent on the establishment and progressive unfolding of ever more meaningful object relations, that is, social relations (1965:4).

Spitz's observation of development in the first year of life demonstrates that "before our very eyes, a state of social unrelatedness, a purely biological bond is transformed step by step, into what is eventually to become the first social relationship of the individual" (11). It is to be noted that Spitz's studies include several ethnic groups—Native American, black, and Caucasian, rendering his conclusions universally applicable.

The essential nature of early object relations is now so taken for granted that one can too easily overlook Spitz's pioneering discovery of its vital importance to life itself. He says: "I realize that my attempt to define normal object relations is vague, groping and tentative. It is difficult, if not impossible, to find a formula to express the multiform, silent ebb and flow, the mute invisible tides, powerful and at the same time subtle, which pervade these relations" (205).

His studies brought him to the conclusion that, from the beginning of life, it is the mother who "mediates every perception, every action, every insight, every knowledge" (96). He adds:

> What makes these experiences so important for the child is the fact that they are interwoven, enriched and colored by the mother's affect; and to this affect the child responds affectively. That is essential in infancy, for

at this age affects are of vastly greater importance than at any time later in life. During his first few months affective perception and affects predominate in the infant's experience, practically to the exclusion of all other modes of perception . . . the mother's emotional attitude, her affects will serve to orient the infant's affects and confer the quality of life on the infant's experience. (99)

Following Hartmann and his collaborators, Spitz affirms that psychic structure develops; it does not exist at birth, and function exists only in potential form in the undifferentiated matrix. Development is quickened in the dyadic interaction as the result of myriad experiences of gratification and frustration, for each plays an important part. Gratification has to be the preponderant experience for development to be favorable, but Spitz insists that the role of frustration is essential to promoting growth toward autonomy.

One of Spitz's major studies was of infants whose mothers were prisoners. They had been permitted to nurse their babies for three months before the babies were taken from them. Then the babies were transferred to an institutional setting. Spitz was called to investigate because there was an extraordinarily high death rate among the infants despite "good" care. He reported this study in two papers on "Hospitalism" (1945–46). His discovery, new at the time, was that the infants were dying of psychological neglect in spite of adequate physical care. They were tended in assembly-line fashion, with propped bottles and minimal human contact. Having had mothering for the first three months before being so totally deprived, these infants developed what Spitz called *anaclitic depression* because of object loss. They could not tolerate life without a partner; they simply gave up and died of marasmus, infantile wasting away.

Spitz also studied the genesis and gradual development of the capacity to communicate. The most potent incentive for this, as well as for other forms of learning, are the emotions that develop within the framework of the first object relationship. Detailing this, Spitz notes that the newborn responds initially to inner stimuli only. At the beginning, the most reliable and specific reflex action is taken via the *primal cavity*, the mouth and snout area. Within a brief time external stimuli are noticed, although probably not yet perceived, as emanating from outside the self. After one week the head will turn toward the chest of the person who picks up and holds the neonate in a horizontal position. The rooting reflex causes the infant to turn its head seeking to close its mouth on a nipple. These movements are associated with gratification of need.

With experience of gratification during nursing, the infant begins to stare at the mother's face. In this state of profound gratification and relief from organismic distress, memory traces of the face begin to enable the infant to shift from the more primitive form of perception, tactile contact, to a more advanced form, distance perception utilizing the visual function. As the newborn's eyes begin to focus on the face, and even to follow movements, one notes an interest (cathexis), a psychological investment in the human face that is the precursor of the smiling response.

Although the neonate responds to stimuli from the start, this is not conscious or organized. Stimulus and response travel reflexively along inborn pathways. Despite the absence of conscious awareness, infants have a capacity to "sense," a primitive form of reception. "Sensing is extensive, primarily visceral, centered in the autonomic nervous system, and manifests itself in the form of emotion" (44). At this early period of life the newborn employs a primitive form of perception that Spitz terms *coenesthetic reception*. That will change at about the third month of life when *diacritic perception* (judgment) replaces coenesthetic reception to a large (but not total) extent.

Spitz believes that the role of coenesthetic reception has been vastly underrated. He places great emphasis on its persistence throughout life. He says:

> The coenesthetic organization continues to function throughout life, powerfully one might say, as the wellspring of life itself, even though our western civilization has fitted a silencer on its manifestations. In emergencies, under stress, the archaic forces sweep the silencer away and break through with terrifying violence, for they are not under rational control. Then we are confronted with the more or less random explosive discharge of primal emotions, with malignant psychosomatic disease, or with certain forms of psychotic outbreaks. (46)

Affect, to Spitz, is the "trail breaker" of development (84). At that early time of life, affect is global—all good or all bad. Life is experienced in a sequence of quiescence alternating with unpleasure, such as hunger. Thus the earliest affective experiences evolve in the rhythm of pleasure and unpleasure. Global affects can be intense, although often they tend to be overlooked or are thought to be trifling by the unskilled observer. They become observably significant, however, if they persist into later life, as may happen when there is no opportunity to internalize the modulating influence of experience with the partner in the dyad. In such unfortunate circumstance, the experience of an "all bad" object world remains dominant. This can result in paranoia or, somewhat less pathologically, in a negative attitude toward others.

Thus Spitz affirms from a new perspective the crucial importance of the relationship between mother and neonate. Some of his conclusions, if heeded, can influence society in general. The neonate, he found, arrives with enormous developmental potential that must be quickened in the relationship with the mothering person within the first few weeks and months of life. Failure in this early mother-child relationship can cause failure in development and lasting psychological damage. Spitz attributes much of the violence that is so prevalent in our large cities today to deficits in the "dyadic dialogue." It is in that dialogue that the infant learns how to learn. Spitz says:

> From the societal aspect, disturbed object relations in the first year of life, be they deviant, improper, or insufficient, have consequences which imperil the very foundation of society. Without a template, the victims of disturbed object relations subsequently will themselves lack the capacity to relate. They are not equipped for the more advanced, more complex forms of personal and social interchange without which we as a species would be unable to survive. They cannot adapt to society. They are emotional cripples . . . their capacity for normal human and social relations is deficient; they were never given the opportunity to experience libidinal relations and to achieve the anaclitic love object . . . The misery of these infants will be translated into the bleakness of the adolescent's social relations. Deprived of affective nourishment to which they were entitled, their only recourse is violence . . . Infants without love, they will end as adults full of hate.   (300)

He added that therapeutic or preventive intervention, if it is to avert damage, must be instituted early in the infant's life; programs such as Headstart, which generally begin when the child is four, are too late (personal communication, 1967).

The self is seen as a cognitive precipitate of experience, beginning at about fifteen months. This is a phenomenon that takes place approximately one year after the infant has become aware of the existence of a Non-I. According to Spitz: "Genetically, the self can be traced to the 'I,' while the 'I' originates from the infant's emotionally cathected physical relations with the 'Non-I' " (1957:120–21).

Perhaps the most widely known aspect of Spitz's work is the identification and description of the three organizers of the psyche. Mahler et al. (1975:45) refer to Spitz's "ingenious lucidity." We believe that it is nowhere better reflected than in his in-depth description of the process whereby the psyche is organized. Psychological development keeps uneven pace with physiological maturation. Although physical and psychological factors are inextricably intertwined, maturation (physical) and development (psychological) may take separate courses for brief periods of time. There are moments, however, when convergence of physical and psychological factors is essential for development to proceed more or less normally. Such moments of convergence are termed *critical periods*.

Spitz uses the analogy of three cones vertically attached to illustrate how one level of development and maturation is dependent on the one that preceded it. A ball can be dropped from the tip of one cone to fall to the bottom rim. Whether it falls to the proper place or deviantly, the next organizational task proceeds from there. If the fall has been deviant, the next drop will inevitably be deviant also, and will result in pathological development.

To augment Spitz's analogy of the cone and ball, we use that of the weaver who makes an error in the design but continues without ripping it out. The flaw is incorporated in the design (Blanck and Blanck 1979). These analogies help explain how it happens that, in the adult patient, the therapist does not find simple arrest at a given point in development, but has to deal with the totality of organization.

Spitz borrows from embryology where specialization of a function results from organization to describe psychological organization. He posits three *organizers of the psyche*, each of which connotes new integrations. Each of the three organizers has its own *indicator*, a behavioral manifestation that signals that a new level of organization of the psyche has been reached. Because psychic structure becomes increasingly complex as more and more newly achieved functions accumulate, reorganization to integrate the new with that which already exists from past organization must continue throughout life, although it is most accelerated in infancy and early childhood.

The first indicator of organization, the smiling response, was at first observed to occur at approximately three months. Spitz states however, that all his timings are approximate; the differences can be plus or minus two months. The earliest smile he records occurred at about twenty-six days. The smiling response is the indicator of the following bursts of development: The infant turns from passive reception of stimuli from inside, to active perception of stimuli from the outside. This means the infant now has the capacity to delay drive discharge. The reality principle has begun to function alongside the pleasure-unpleasure principle. Recognition of the human face is an unmistakable indicator that memory traces now exist. Topographical division—conscious, unconscious, and preconscious—has been made.

The smiling response also shows that the infant can now combine perception in the present with a memory trace from the past, a cathectic shift. Such a shift corresponds to Freud's definition of the thought process, which is now operative.

Finally, Spitz sees the smiling response as representing the inception of a rudimentary ego that can now take over the protective function of the stimulus barrier. It enables the infant to engage in directed activity, as opposed to the previous passivity and random activity. Of major importance, it marks the beginning of social relations. The infant has now inexorably turned toward that which is destined to become the object world. At this point that world consists of the symbiotic relationship with the partner, but ultimately it will enlarge to become the wider world.

The second organizer of the psyche is indicated by fear of strangers, which Spitz terms *eight month anxiety*. Now the infant no longer smiles at *any* human face, but reserves the smile for the mothering person and other very familiar faces. The child may exhibit reactions ranging from anxious curiosity to bitter crying when approached by an unfamiliar face. From this Spitz concludes: "A 'thing' has been established in the optic sector that has achieved cognitive constancy" (161). Going beyond behavioristic conclusions, however, Spitz finds that anxiety, an affect, plays the decisive role in this phenomenon. Once the "libidinal object" (mother or mothering person) has been discovered, a secure exclusiveness is established. "The child has found the partner with whom he can form object relations in the true sense of the term" (182). Diacritic functioning is now possible, aided on the physical side by neurological development that enables the musculature to be used to serve directed activity.

Directed discharge can lower affective tension intentionally, enriching the ego organization by augmenting its regulatory function. This is one of the areas of Spitz's work that complements Mahler's work remarkably, specifically her concept of the symbiotic tie between infant and mother.

The first indicator of organization, the *smiling response*, is the affective indicator of anticipated gratification. The second indicator, *eight month anxiety*, usually but not always marked by crying, is the result of acquisition of a level of organization that recognizes the "libidinal object proper." Crying is the result of mounting tension, fear of loss of the object when a stranger appears. As organization proceeds to higher levels, ego functions—perception, memory, anticipation—quicken.

Like Jacobson (chapter 6), Spitz stresses the importance of negative affect to development. Both affects, pleasure and unpleasure, have to be experienced before "the function of judgment can be crystallized" (146). Following Freud's thought that reality testing develops out of the experience of losing an object that once brought gratification, negative as well as positive affect must be experienced if development is to proceed normally. Frustration forces creation of adaptive coping mechanisms that further the organizing function. Spitz inveighs against the kind of "progressive" education that seeks to prevent frustration.

With attainment of the second organizer, development in the area of social relationships proceeds rapidly. Social gestures are understood and even used as a vehicle for reciprocal communication. The child's inanimate environment also expands; he or she can now begin to discriminate between animate and inanimate things. In the affective realm, subtle shadings begin to form.

All that goes before leads to the establishment of the third organizer of the psyche, the indicator of which is the acquisition of *semantic communication* and the capacity to say NO by using the defense mechanism, *identification with the aggressor*. Spitz refers to this third organizer as "perhaps the most important turning point in evolution, both of the individual and of the species. Here begins the humanization of the species. Here begins the *zoon politikon*; here begins society. For this is the inception of reciprocal exchange of messages, intentional, directed; with the advent of semantic symbols, it becomes the origin of verbal communication" (189).

Semantic communication is to be distinguished from the ability to speak. Except in rare and unusual circumstances, everyone learns to speak. The object relations theory that Spitz explores in such detail combines the human capacity to formulate words with awareness of the need to communicate with another person in the secondary process. The social life of the human begins in earnest when he or she realizes that communication can no longer be with the symbiotic object who understands nonverbally, or preverbally. Now and forever, one must communicate across that which

Spitz refers to as a "chasm," the vast distance between one differentiated individual and another. With acquisition of the third organizer, that chasm is only breached thereafter at moments of pleasure and union, of regression in the service of the ego (Kris; chapter 5).

The validity of Spitz's work has become more apparent with the passage of time; very little requires alteration to accommodate new findings, and much of it furthers new exploration. In his final work Spitz approaches the mind-body problem that has vexed philosophers through the ages. Here Spitz may have taken but one bold step toward a solution that may require the work of many more thinkers before it is solved, if indeed a solution is possible. In that last paper Spitz says: "Forgive me if in my attempt at orientation I stumble over my own mixed metaphors when I speak of the bond between affect and percept as a bridge, made of duration, anticipation, and meaning; a bridge to span the void across the chasm in front of the soma, a bridge reaching toward the shore of an as yet nonexistent psychic system" (1972:734).

8

▼

The Contributions of Margaret S. Mahler

B orn in Hungary, Margaret S. Mahler began her professional life as a pediatrician and was later trained in psychoanalysis in Vienna. She came to the United States in 1938 as a refugee from the Holocaust in Europe and began her work in this country training residents in child psychiatry at the New York State Psychiatric Institute.

One of her first research projects was to investigate childhood psychosis. The methodology, which remained as the pattern for later investigation of normalcy as well, was observation of psychotic children and their mothers by psychoanalytically trained observers. This methodology meets as closely as is possible, in working with human beings, the experimental psychologists' insistence on replicability. Without cruelty or damage to the infant, the experiments can be repeated. Now several "second generation" child observers are engaged in further study of mother-child and father-child pairs and of infant behavior, patterning their designs after Mahler's pioneering studies.

In her study of psychotic children Mahler found that an outstanding feature of their pathology was lack of separate-from-the-object identities. She was led to hypothesize (1958, 1963, 1965, 1968, 1971) that separation-individuation might be the key factor in the establishment of identity. In order to validate that hypothesis she set up a parallel study of normal mother-child pairs. The findings of that study (Mahler, Pine, and Bergman 1975) led her to the dramatic discovery that psychological birth normally takes place approximately three years after physical birth.

Mahler's contributions have become popular because they are less abstract than those of some other theorists and are readily applied to normal development as well as to understanding where and how pathology ensues. Perhaps for that reason one hears it referred to as separation-individuation *theory*. This is an error. Mahler has contributed not a holistic, stand-alone theory, but a *subtheory* that follows the direction pointed toward by Freud and Hartmann and that is complementary to the works of the other ego psychologists. This in no way diminishes the importance of Mahler's work.

As is true of the work of the other pioneer child observer, Spitz, Mahler's subjects have always been available for study; there have always been babies. But the "decoding" of infant behavior awaited these creative scientists who linked observation with psychoanalytic insight to elaborate theory.

Mahler describes how, from birth on, there begins a complex, multiform and circular developmental process. The first weeks of life are spent in a state of primitive hallucinatory disorientation in which the goal is homeostasis. Mahler designated those first few weeks as the *normal autistic* phase. She did not wish to give the impression that there is absolute imperviousness to the outside world, although that may be conveyed by the term *autism*. The term has led to misunderstanding of the concept behind it. She was trying to distinguish normal from pathological autism by pointing out that, in the normal condition, there is responsiveness to external stimuli. Later studies (Brazelton et al. 1975; Osofsky 1979; Stern 1985; Emde 1988a, 1988b) confirm and elaborate on this, although Stern would argue that his work refutes it.

Responsiveness increases to the point where, by the second month of life, the neonate is dimly aware of a need-satisfying object. That ushers in the *symbiotic* phase, which is at its peak for approximately six or seven months. Symbiosis wanes as the *separation-individuation* thrust begins. Mahler stresses that symbiotic need is never completely superseded, that residues of earlier phases overlap the next ones and continue to pervade later life. This coincides with Spitz's assertion that even the earliest forms of coenesthetic sensing, "the mute, invisible tides," remain with us for life. Residual symbiosis, in particular, persists as the reference point for regression in the service of the ego—for pleasure in the deepest forms of temporary, reversible union as in sexual and aesthetic experience.

Mahler's discoveries have come under severe criticism, particularly by Kohut and Stern. Kohut (1971) accuses Mahler of adultomorphic speculation, overlooking that hers were the observations of an experienced researcher and psychoanalyst. Stern argues that his neonatal observation does not bear out that the neonate is, as Mahler thought, in a dozing, splanchnic state. He asserts that his studies prove that the neonate is differentiated at birth, and he argues that there is neither an autistic phase, a symbiotic phase, nor a separation-individuation process. His assumptions are designed to support the self-psychologists' assertion that the goal of development is to seek connection rather than to separate and individuate. To us it appears a long and hazardous leap from the observation that the neonate has brief periods of alert activity to the conclusion that this proves the existence of a self. Kaplan (1987) finds a serious methodological flaw in Stern's work. She points out that states of arousal vary in the same infant at different times of the day, that the laboratory baby does not behave as the same baby would in the home environment. Stern's conclusions from his laboratory studies are based on observation during a segment of the infant's day when he or she is at the height of stimulation.

Nevertheless, the videotapes of the neonate staring at the mother's face are impressive. As an open-minded scientist, Mahler took the newer observations under consideration. She conceded that her choice of the term *autistic* was unfortunate because it was influenced by her observation of psychotic children. What she wished to convey is that this first phase of life is characterized by a search for the maternal niche. She had discovered that psychotic infants do not have the capacity to find this niche, that is, to enter *symbiosis*. Our own proposal (1986) is that this first phase, then, might more felicitously be termed *preparation for fitting together*. We remind ourselves here that Hartmann regarded fitting together as even more important than adaptation. Our suggestion that fitting together prepares for symbiosis, which is adaptive in the sense that it orients the child to the world of reality, also fits together Mahler's observation with Hartmann's theory. The concept is more important than the term that might be selected. Our term retains the concept, yet obviates the confusion between psychotic and "normal" autism, and might contribute toward elimination of unrewarding semantic argument.

How did a former pediatrician and psychoanalytic observer fall into such an apparent error? One conjecture is that the neonates she observed were less alert because they were delivered under anesthesia, which is no longer common obstetric practice. Also to be considered is that these later investigators have available more sophisticated instrumentation, such as video cameras, split screen projection (to show simultaneous interaction between neonate and other persons), electroencephalography, and the like. It is predictable that, in the not too distant future, even prenatal life will become available to investigation as ever more refined instrumentation is developed. Then we will discover more about the innate endowment. Emde has already begun research into endowment as it influences infant development.

Symbiosis *is* the maternal niche. In borrowing the term *symbiosis* from biology, Mahler clarifies that it does not carry precisely the same meaning in psychology. Biologists refer to two organisms that are mutually and equally interdependent. Mahler recognizes that the mother in the symbiotic unity is not at the same developmental level as the infant and, although she enters symbiosis with her infant, she has needs and requires gratifications outside that symbiotic orbit as well as within it. In the psychological sense, symbiosis is a state in which the infant experiences himself or herself as living within a common boundary. That there are two individuals who are physically separate is a reality unknown to the infant.

An adequate symbiotic phase is marked by experience of tactile contact of the total body. The essence of symbiosis is that the chaos of neonatal psychic life becomes organized in the milieu of the mother's holding behavior. An adequate symbiotic phase paves the way toward organizing mental processes that will ultimately lead to secondary process thought. The baby who does not experience adequate symbiosis either because of an innate inability to enter the dyad or because of absence of a symbiotic partner is doomed to chaos.

Toward the end of symbiosis the child "hatches." *Separation-individuation* is an intrapsychic process in which actual physical separation plays only a minor role. Mahler introduced the hyphenated term to indicate that there are two tracks, intertwined but not always proceeding at the same pace. The separation track involves distancing, boundary formation, disengagement from mother. The individuation track involves intrapsychic autonomy and quickening of ego functions such as perception, memory, cognition, reality testing. These open the way toward developing specific interests, directions that define the person's individuality.

The thrust into the separation-individuation process begins with the first subphase, *differentiation*. Expansion beyond the symbiotic orbit begins. The infant acquires a new look of alertness, persistence, and goal directedness, which Mahler takes as a sign that the infant has "hatched." The hatched, or differentiated, infant strains his or her body away from the mother in order to have a better look at her, to scan her and the environment, as contrasted with simply molding onto the mother's body as in the symbiotic phase. The differentiating infant scans the mother's face and body. Visual contact gradually replaces bodily contact, thereby establishing a form of mental imagery that retains the object image while differentiating.

Differentiation is overlapped by early *practicing* as the child becomes able to move away from the mother physically by crawling. With attainment of upright locomotion the practicing subphase proper begins, accompanied by an upsurge of exhilaration. Mahler et al. say: "The chief characteristic of this period is the child's narcissistic investment in his own functions, his own body, as well as in the objects and objectives of his expanding 'reality' " (1975:71).

Mahler regards elation as the "hallmark" of the practicing subphase. It derives from the joy of exercise of ego functions and of escape from the engulfment of symbiosis. Greenacre (1957) describes practicing as a "love affair with the world."

Toward the end of the practicing period, with increasing capacity for reality testing, the child begins to realize that he or she is a very small person in a very large world—as Mahler puts it, the world is not his oyster. The need for closeness to the mother, which appears to have been held in abeyance in the practicing subphase, reappears as the result of the rebuffs and disappointments of normal living in the wider world. The *rapprochement* subphase begins with reversal of direction *away* from the mother that had characterized the practicing subphase. Now the child moves *toward* her once again.

The developmental task of the rapprochement subphase is a tremendous one and requires the mother's optimal emotional availability. This is difficult for her because the child behaves in a confusing and contradictory fashion. There are normal misunderstandings as the child becomes more and more aware of his or her separateness and tries to undo it. Yet no matter how the child might wish it, mother and child can no longer function as a dual unity. Painfully, the delusion of grandeur and of participation in parental omnipotence must be given up. The child often engages in dramatic fights with the mother in what Mahler terms the *rapprochement crisis*.

There are structural gains. A higher level of object relations is reached in which fear of loss of the love of the object replaces fear of loss of the object qua object. Verbal communication becomes the order of the day. The affective range widens. The mother-child world is extended to include the father in a new way, no longer as an alternate need gratifier, but as a distinct person.

Gender identity begins to be established. In that regard, the development of boy and girl takes divergent courses. The boy in the upright position gains a new perspective of his penis. Awareness of his difference from females accelerates separation from the mother. Becoming a separate individual is more difficult for the girl. The authors say: "Girls, upon discovery of the sexual difference, tended to turn back to mother, to blame her, to demand from her, to be disappointed in her, and still to be ambivalently tied to her" (106).

As she had already begun to indicate in an earlier paper (1971), Mahler found that failure to consolidate a separate identity during the rapprochement experience may constitute the etiology of borderline phenomena. Where successful, the rapprochement subphase results in acquisition of a unified self representation demarcated from the object representation.

The fourth subphase, *on-the-way-to-object-constancy*, is not a subphase in the temporal sense as are the others because it is open-ended—that is, it will continue to develop for an indeterminate period, perhaps throughout life. It is characterized by individuality. Structuralization and internalization have proceeded apace, with gradual internalization of a constant, positively cathected mental representation of the mother and a stable sense of self. This subphase is reached where trust and confidence through predictable relief of need tension have begun to build from as early as the symbiotic phase. Gradually, in the subphases that follow symbiosis, relief is connected with the need-satisfying, differentiated object. With internalization, images of an object who brings relief are transferred to the specific mental representation of the mother. The former ambivalent love relationship that existed only as long as it was satisfying gives way to a more mutual give-and-take relationship. Those developments are marked by the dominance of verbal communication over earlier forms, by the beginning of fantasy play, by increasing interest in the real world, by a sense of time and spatial relations, and by increasing capacities to delay gratification and endure physical separation. Psychological birth takes place as identity is born.

In addition to informing about child development, which can be useful for primary prevention, knowledge of the vicissitudes of life before psychological birth informs a great deal about borderline phenomena and neurosis. It is at that early period of life that patterning for later pathology or normalcy is laid down. The very definition of the borderline problem is, according to this scheme, a developmental one—failure to have attained psychological birth.

Mahler's work is so alluring that, in the beginning, it was thought that one could simply extrapolate from it to the treatment of the adult patient. This, it turns out, is too simplistic. Taking into account that the adult, and even the latency and adolescent child, continues to develop and that organization is continuous, it is apparent that the therapist is dealing with a person who has incorporated whatever inadequacies existed in the first round of development in the sweep of organization. This makes the treatment far more complex than was heretofore believed.

It is not generally remembered that the search for techniques for treatment of borderline patients goes back no more than forty years. Many techniques have been elaborated and then discarded in favor of more sophisticated ones. Some theorists and technicians have thought that reparenting an adult patient, as though to encourage reliving the subphases in a better way, can be curative. We now know that the adult understructured (borderline) patient is one with skewed organization, and that matters are more complex than need for mothering. In addition to malformations in organization, the early developmental experiences shape character and determine the patterning of object relations. These factors resonate throughout life and challenge the technical creativity of the therapist who undertakes to treat such patients.

Periodically, in the history of psychoanalytic theory construction, new organizing principles appear that bring theory to a point of culmination and, simultaneously, provide a new point of departure for future theory construction. These organizing principles are analogous to the organizers of the psyche as described by Spitz—a period of extensive ego building culminates in a new level of organization that in turn leads to a greater degree of integration and to a next higher level of organization. It remained for

Mahler and her co-authors to provide yet another organizing principle, embodied in the statement: "A major organization of intrapsychic and behavioral life develops around issues of separation-individuation" (4). That organizing principle paves the way for further elaboration of theory, giving it new direction. It was the major stimulus for our 1979 book in which we show that ego psychology has become a psychoanalytic developmental psychology.

9

▼

The Contributions of Otto F. Kernberg

E xploration of the more severe pathologies was delayed by Freud's
belief that only the transference neuroses are analyzable. The
"narcissistic neuroses," as he called the pathologies that we now
designate as psychotic, borderline, or narcissistic, fell outside his investigation into the neuroses proper. Freud's legacy diverted theoretical and technical attention to the neuroses for many years. Much was gained thereby in
understanding the neuroses and in refining treatment techniques for them.
Perhaps an understanding of the more severe pathologies had to await its
turn in this historical sequence.

While refining their psychoanalytic techniques, some psychoanalysts
also treated the more severe pathologies that came their way. Most analysts
in the United States had been residents in psychiatric hospitals before their
analytic training, were familiar with the severe pathologies, and had some
pragmatic ways of dealing with them. Perhaps because psychoanalytic
training followed after psychiatric or other preliminary training, psychoanalysis was (and in some quarters still is) regarded as superior to psy-

We are indebted to Dr. Kernberg for reviewing this chapter and for making corrections
where needed in order to represent his work accurately.

chotherapy. This is strange logic. The superior form of treatment for any pathology is the one that is designed for it based on diagnosis. And, if we are to make a comparison, it is to be noted that psychotherapy is the more difficult form of treatment because (1) the pathology is more severe than the neuroses, making for management problems as well as problems intrinsic to the pathology per se, (2) the levels of pathology range more widely, and, consequently, (3) etiology, diagnosis, and treatment techniques are not easily systematized.

Study of the severe pathologies as an appropriate area of investigation entered the psychoanalytic arena slowly. Not until the 1950s were psychoanalysts willing to talk about them openly as a legitimate concern rather than as an inferior departure from psychoanalysis proper to be hidden in the psychoanalytic closet. Knight (1954) was one of the first to discuss the borderline conditions. In that same year Stone participated in a panel of the American Psychoanalytic Association on "The Widening Scope of Indications for Psychoanalysis." The theme was that some patients formerly considered to be unanalyzable, those suffering from the so-called narcissistic neuroses, could be treated. This began conceptualization of a treatment already prevalent in practice—namely, that the analytic method is not restricted to neurosis. It can take us to a more profound understanding of narcissistic and borderline pathology.

Kernberg is to be credited with being the first to study these more severe pathologies in depth. He is the principal systematizer of borderline and narcissistic pathology within mainstream psychoanalytic thought. He deals with the etiology, diagnosis, and treatment techniques for these conditions. Kernberg would "widen the scope" somewhat differently from Stone, reserving psychoanalysis proper as the treatment of choice for neurosis. For the more severe pathologies, the therapeutic approach calls for expressive psychotherapy where that mode of treatment is tolerable for the patient and his or her pathology, and he would employ supportive psychotherapy if the patient cannot endure and cannot be expected to benefit from growth-promoting measures.

Kernberg finds the etiology of the severe pathologies in abnormal development of internalized object relations, which impedes and disrupts ego integration. With this as his theoretical backdrop, he presents a conceptualization that integrates psychoanalytic dual drive theory with ego psychology. He suggests that drives are first expressed as affects—that is, inborn behavior patterns activated in interaction with the maternal object, leading to internalization of object relations and to affective memory linked with them. Kernberg proposes that aggression and libido are supra-ordinate organization of their component affect dispositions. That developmental process, if it proceeds well, organizes structuralization and promotes its progress in a normal direction. If it proceeds badly, it leads to pathology.

Earlier he delineated four stages of development. In accord with recent infant research, he now questions the earliest stage (autism) as one that precedes the establishment of the undifferentiated self-object, and believes that symbiotic development under peak affective conditions occurs in parallel with differentiated internalization at low affect conditions.

There is popular controversy about autism. Ego psychologists refer to it variously as undifferentiation (Hartmann), nondifferentiation (Spitz), autism (Mahler). Mahler in particular, is under attack, especially by Stern, who undertook to provide observational support for self psychology. For that theory to stand up, it needs the assertion that a self exists at birth. Stern believes that that is so.

For Kernberg the earliest affect-driven behavior patterns are soon replaced by internalization of object relations as mothering functions and interpersonal interaction organize structuralization and promote its progress. He proposes there are three stages of development along this line: the symbiotic, separation-individuation, and object constancy stages—following Mahler's developmental schema in this regard. As already mentioned, Kernberg believes that an autistic phase does not precede symbiosis normally, and that childhood autism is always a pathological development, most frequently caused by deficient cognitive development related to organic pathology.

At the earliest, normal symbiotic stage, consolidation of a libidinally invested, undifferentiated self-object representation takes place under the impact of gratifying interactions with the mother. In that event, an intrapsychic structure will develop, with memory traces carrying a positive affective charge. Out of painful psychophysiological experience, a separate structure with an "all-bad" self-object representation is built, the aggressively invested self-object representation. Thus there arises an "all good" self-object separate from the "all bad" self-object with no separation between self and nonself and only rudimentary ego boundaries. Fixation at or regression to this stage of development consists, in the main, of an imbalance on the side of the "all bad," aggressively cathected self-object representation and promotes defensive refusion of the primitive "all good" self and object representation as a protection against excessive frustration and rage. Such defensive refusion, if carried beyond the early infantile states, constitutes a psychotic identification. Reality testing is lost by blurring of the limits between self and object images resulting in loss of ego boundaries.

Here Kernberg is referring to psychosis proper and to the threat of ego dissolution. In schizophrenia this phenomenon is clinically observable in the defensive flight into a mystical, ecstatic, primitive, idealized self-object fusion. Secondarily, additional defensive operations are triggered, particularly the use of primitive projective mechanisms. These are designed to expel the "all bad" internalized object; this process leads to paranoid distortions.

Kernberg defines splitting as pathological dissociation of polar opposite ego states. Splitting is brought into play for the defensive purpose of preventing all-pervasive anxiety and fear of destruction. He believes that, prognostically, schizophrenic psychosis is treatable if the patient attains the capacity to establish object relations in the present. This accords with our view that the technical procedure in the treatment of the very severely disturbed patient involves the use of the therapist as a real object for the purpose of building object relations. Obviously, this is the opposite of psychoanalytic technique, which presupposes that object constancy and reality testing exist, rendering unnecessary and even contraindicating the use of reality to bring the patient into the object world.

At the second stage, from approximately six to eighteen months, borderline pathology will ensue if development ceases there. Primitive idealization of the mothering person as "all good" is employed in defense against contamination of this image by the "all bad" object image. Kernberg suggests that the stranger anxiety described by Spitz may be caused by projection onto the stranger of the "bad" self-object image dissociated from the "good" one.

Splitting is the defensive arrangement at this second stage of development. It dissociates "all good" from "all bad," which interferes with further integration of self and object representations. It keeps the good relationship with the mother intact in the face of frustration and protects the self against overwhelming contamination of love by hatred. If it persists beyond this level, however, the result is pathological splitting.

Thus Kernberg presents his principal theoretical contribution to the understanding of borderline pathology. He designates failure at this second stage of development of internalized object relations as the determining factor in borderline personality organization. Included within this category are several types of severe character pathology—addictions, narcissistic personalities, infantile personalities, antisocial personality structures, the "as if" personality, and other types of personality disorders.

In the borderline personality organization, a level of differentiation of self representation from object representation has been attained. Although incomplete, it is sufficient to permit the establishment of integrated ego boundaries and differentiation between self and others. However, primitive aggression prevents development to the third stage as domination of splitting prevents integration.

Distinguishing between the borderline states and psychosis, Kernberg asserts that, while in both pathologies active splitting is (unconsciously) employed and is reinforced by primitive idealizations and projective identification, the purpose of splitting in the borderline personality organization is to separate love from aggression, while in the psychoses the purpose is to prevent engulfment and annihilation. Although borderline patients preserve reality testing, they retain serious difficulties in interpersonal relations in their subjective experience of reality. This coincides with our view of fixed object relations patterns, established in early life and remaining inflexible despite the reality that the object in the present is not the same as the subjectively experienced object from the past.

Borderline patients also demonstrate contradictory character traits, chaotic coexistence of defenses against primitive impulses, lack of empathy, identity diffusion. Ego weakness is also present and manifests itself in lack of impulse control, lack of anxiety tolerance, and lack of capacity to sublimate. In addition, one finds pathological condensation of pregenital and genital aims, with pregenital aggressive strivings dominating.

Superego integration, too, is defective because of the absence of an integrated self-concept and of integrated object representations. This further interferes with overall ego integration. Absence of an adequately integrated superego deprives such persons of those superego functions that operate as internal guidance systems. This leads to overdependency on external sources of reassurance, praise, and punishment.

Also, there is contamination of sexual with aggressive drive derivatives resulting in premature sexualization of relationships with incestuous figures accompanied by aggressive contamination of the relationships as well of the later sexual life of borderline persons.

At the third stage, neurosis is the outcome of development. Neurotic patients have identity, a well-integrated ego, and stable self and object representations. Defensive mechanisms center around repression rather than splitting. In normality, which might be designated as a fourth stage, there is a benign superego and realistic superego demands. Ego ideals and ego goals make for harmony in dealing with the external world and with instinctual needs. Repression successfully bars residual instinctual demands. There is a large sector of conflict-free functioning in conjunction with capacity to repress and suppress ungratifiable needs without excess stress.

10

▼

The Contributions of Heinz Kohut

Heinz Kohut's earlier contributions to theory construction span almost twenty years, resulting in 1971 in *The Analysis of the Self.* His interest was narcissism as he defined it, "that is, of the cathexis of the self" (xiii). He credits Hartmann for the conceptual distinction between *self* and *ego*. Then he goes on to establish his own theory of a self, the crystallization of a separate psychobiological existence. This forms the basis for what was later to become known as self psychology.

Especially in the light of Kohut's later (1977) work, it is important to be precise about the exact content of Hartmann's contribution. In elaborating and amending Freud's reference to narcissism as a libidinal cathexis of the ego, Hartmann believes it would be "clarifying if we define narcissism as the libidinal cathexis not of the ego but of the self" (1964:127). Jacobson adds the suggestion that it is not the *self* but the *self representation* that is involved here. Hartmann and Jacobson are but two of the several theorists who precede Kohut; yet Kohut avers that they have not influenced his thinking, indeed that he has had to erase from his mind all work subsequent to Freud in order to be able to develop his own thinking in a straight line from Freud.

He says:

Finding myself floundering in a morass of conflicting, poorly based, and often vague theoretical speculation, I decided that there was only one way that would lead to progress; the way back to the direct observation of clinical phenomena and the construction of new formulations that would accommodate my observations. . . . Having thus shed the ballast of taking into consideration the various concepts and theories used by other researchers, I trust that my own basic viewpoint will emerge.

(1977:xx–xxi)

Whether Kohut succeeds in shedding the ballast of previous researchers is open to challenge. He was an active part of the mainstream psychoanalytic movement during the years when ego psychology was being presented and he held the position of President of the American Psychoanalytic Association for a term. Thus he was in close contact with the ego psychologists and knew their contributions. Although he expresses the wish to expel their influence from his mind, one finds their work reflected in some of his concepts and terminology. For example, he coins the term *transmuting internalizations*, which appears similar in terminology and meaning to Jacobson's *selective identification*. Jacobson has priority by some seven years. Also, his unhyphenated *selfobject* resembles Mahler's early-in-life *self* merged with *object*.

The cornerstone of Kohut's theoretical reasoning is the postulate that there are two lines of narcissistic development. Pathology consists of arrest at a point where a cohesive archaic grandiose self and a cohesive archaic idealized object have come into being. These are revived in the transferences of the narcissistic personalities. Two types of transference ensue—the idealizing transference and the mirror transference. In the former the therapist represents the idealized *selfobject*, and in the latter the grandiose self is revived. There can be horizontal or vertical splits in the ego that render the individual unable to maintain basic narcissistic homeostasis.

In his 1977 work, *The Restoration of the Self*, Kohut extends his theoretical and clinical approach to the larger patient population, contending now that all patients suffer from narcissistic pathology. This book announces the introduction of a new theory, *self psychology*, that posits the existence of a self at birth. This is directly antithetical to a theory of development that proposes that it takes approximately three years for identity to be acquired.

Self psychology deals with the same patient population that we designate as understructured. Or, to put it differently, the ego psychologists and the self psychologists are equally concerned with the early months and years of life to which Freud had not devoted much attention. Yet ego psychology and self psychology arrive at diametrically opposite conclusions. Kohut makes his assertion before having the benefit of observational support. Stern (1985) provides that support retroactively, claiming that the neonate is alert at birth and therefore there is a *self*.

The etiology of narcissistic pathology, in Kohut's view, lies in failure of parental empathy. Cure rests on ascertaining the exact place where absence of empathy caused the narcissistic injury. Once the narcissistic deviation is corrected, development will proceed normally. Neurotic conflict is not material for therapeutic intervention because such conflict will right itself automatically once the parental empathic failure is repaired. Kohut does not intend that "corrective" empathy be applied in a simplistic way; he maintains that empathy must be applied to the precise empathic failure that is the cause of the narcissistic problem. He adds: "And empathy, especially when it is surrounded by an attitude of wanting to cure *directly* through the giving of loving understanding, may indeed become basically overbearing and annoying: i.e., it may rest on the therapist's unresolved omnipotence fantasies" (1971:307).

Many practitioners wish for a cohesive theory that would integrate the many competing theories that are extant. We believe the time has not come. Eventually, integration may be possible, but it must await clinical testing to retain that which is valid. That which fails to prove itself will be discarded and, we must add rather sadly, such an objective goal is hardly possible in the competitive, sometimes passionate climate of partisanship that unfortunately exists today.

In summary, the two major theorists in the area of borderline and narcissistic pathologies see the diagnostic and therapeutic matters quite differently. Kernberg, in conformity with mainstream psychoanalytic thought, defines borderline and narcissistic pathology in developmental terms. Kohut has created a new theory, first presented more modestly as a contribution to the theory of narcissism, but now expanded into a total and "free-standing" new psychology.

11

▼

Object Relations Theory and Structure Formation

The propulsive power of the structural theory is such that we have yet to see the end of its enormous potential for theory construction. After almost fifty years, its thrust still extends far into the future.
—Gertrude Blanck and Rubin Blanck,
Toward a Psychoanalytic Developmental Psychology

Thus we begin an essay that marks the evolution of psychoanalytic theory into a developmental psychology. We would alter it only in terms of time. It is now seventy years since Freud proposed the structural theory. Its thrust still extends into the future. In this chapter we shall show where it has led theory construction today. And we shall explore how structuralization comes about in the context of an object relationship. Our objective is to conceptualize ego psychological object relations theory.

Freud's definition of ego consists of a new and decisive integration of earlier theoretical propositions. It brought no final solutions, but a new set of issues and questions. A most interesting oscillation in Freud's thought appears in the very writing of *The Ego and the Id*. He wavers between the ego as a reflection of reality and rational thinking, and the ego that is also partly unconscious and therefore not necessarily rational. His definition of ego includes coherence and organization, which implies rationality: "We have formed the idea that in each individual there is a coherent organization of mental processes, and we call this his ego" (*S.E.* 19:17). He goes on to describe the rational ego: "The ego seeks to bring the influence of the external world to bear upon the id and its tendencies, and endeavors to sub-stitute the reality principle for the pleasure principle which reigns unre-strictedly in the id. . . . The ego represents what may be called reason and common sense, in contrast to the id which contains the passions" (25).

Taken alone, these passages have misled many into the egregious error of regarding ego psychology as a psychology of the conscious and rational only. But taking the historical view, one notes that the very presentation of the structural theory was necessitated by the fact that Freud found, in his clinical work, that a part of the ego is unconscious, "and Heaven knows how large a part" (1923:18). The unconscious part of the ego is believed to join *the repressed*, that is, that part of the psyche that is close to the id and therefore influenced by it. There it is far from rational because it is removed from contact with reality.

This relates to Freud's idea of the origin of ego. He says that it arises from the id as a "rind" upon it, as that part of the id that is modified by contact with reality. It may be taken that he infers that part of the ego remains part of the id, that all of the ego does not necessarily emerge. This appears con-tradictory and paradoxical until one realizes that, at the time, Freud was still equating id and unconscious, i.e., straddling the topographic and structural theories. Thus there is an unconscious that never becomes conscious; an unconscious that consists of the repressed that once was conscious and has been relegated to the unconscious defensively; and the id that is altogether unconscious. The assumption is that whatever is unconscious is in contact with the id and therefore is not subject to rational thinking.

A better way of reconciling the apparent contradictions in these ideas is to go back in time to when Freud began thinking about the ego before he proposed the structural theory. Two years before *The Ego and the Id*, he mentions a *gesamt Ich*, an ego-as-a-whole (*S.E.* 18:130). We understand this to mean that the so-called tripartite structure does not consist of three disparate agencies but, rather, that the three constitute a unity; that part of the ego that is unconscious unites with the id. Shortly, we shall discuss the third agency of structure, the superego, and we shall show that the super-ego, too, is part of the ego. It is this unity that Freud termed the *gesamt Ich*. We extend it to connote not only the ego-as-a-whole, but structure-as-a-whole. Interrelating the rational with the irrational (unconscious) part of the ego, Freud adds: "If the ego were merely the part of the id modified by the influence of the perceptual system . . . we should have a simple state of things to deal with. But there is a further complication" (*S.E.* 19:28).

The complication is that the ego is altered by means of identifications that form a new part of structure—the ego ideal or superego (which were synonymous in Freud's thought). It was not possible for Freud to be clear about the process of superego formation because he did not have the theoretical tools available today. As we understand how self images and object images come about and enter the representational world, we are better able to discuss superego formation, although many questions remain. Freud did not regard the superego as separate from the ego, but rather as a differentiated grade within it. As we see it, the differentiated grade within the ego consists of the object representations, including their value systems, that have been incorporated into the ego-as-a-whole, or the structure-as-a-whole.

We highlight some of the uncertainties about the process of superego formation: What is the psychic institution called superego? Is it the severe, moralistic, punishing voice of conscience and the vehicle for retribution, or is it a system of regulation—of self and object cathexis—of preservation of equilibrium and of self-esteem as well as object esteem? Is the superego a depersonified, observing agency separated from the ego which, in extreme cases, provides hostile auditory and visual hallucination? Or is it a differentiated grade *within* the ego, which changes the lowest part of mental life into that which is highest in the human mind, and is heir to the Oedipus Complex? Is it the agency that has selected only the parent's strictness and severity to abuse the helpless ego that is at its mercy? Or does it incorporate other, more loving aspects of the parents and, if so, by what means? Or is the superego a structure that is formed only out of parental prohibitions?

Such issues are brought toward resolution when the self and object representations are included in our considerations and are defined as components of structure. Then it may be understood that identifications are the means by which those representations are formed and by means of which internalization takes place as parental values enter the structure. Affirmation and disapproval are experienced first as emanating from the external object and later from the internalized object representations. The difficulties in establishing which functions belong to the ego and which to the superego become irrelevant when we consider that the object representations do indeed constitute a differentiated grade *within* the ego wherein the value system "resides."

Rapaport and Gill (1959) define structure as configuration with a slow rate of change, and they add that structures are "configurations within which, between which and by means of which mental processes take place" (157). That definition refers to the relatively fixed nature of structure, its stability.

> Rapaport was not content with merely defining structure without inquiring into the process of structure formation. He says: "The study of the process of psychological structure formation seems to be the prime requisite for progress towards dimensional quantification. *We must establish how processes turn into structures*, how a structure once formed, changes, and how it gives rise to and influences processes"
>
> (1959:98–99; italics ours)

> Moore and Fine define *structure* as: "enduring patterns and configurations in the mind, (motivational, defensive and controlling) that may be abstracted from behavior and the analysis of intrapsychic content. They are derived from the interaction of maturing constitutional givens and environmental influences in the various phases of development. They take shape through identification in early relationships, through learning, and through the resolution of adaptive conflicts"   (1990:187)

Moore and Fine are clear that structuralization comes about through identifications in early relationships. They bear out, as we showed in chapter 2, that an object relations theory was implicit in psychoanalytic theory from the beginning. It became explicit gradually in the modern era as ego psychology came into being and led to infant and child observational studies. Then no doubt remained that development takes place in the context of the very earliest dyadic relationship.

We believed, at first, that object relations is one of the several ego functions. Beginning with the observations of Spitz and Mahler and the theoretical contributions of Jacobson, it became evident that object relations has a special and crucially important role in development. That object relations has its inception early in life is confirmed by Emde who establishes that it is the very matrix within which development takes place.

Other theories of object relations revolve around concepts such as attachment, acquired from studies in ethology that show that animals "attach" to others, not necessarily of the same species. Because human psychology is so much more complex than animal psychology, we find attachment theories simplistic as an explanation of human behavior. Attachment has led to the lay concept of "bonding" with the implication that one individual bonds to another as though by a mastic.

Even physical maturation of the neonate is activated by mothering.

Neuronal pathways are established through the repetition of experiences that are provided in the dyad; maturation of the nervous system and the musculature are enhanced; functions such as locomotion and speech, determined largely by a biological timetable, are quickened. That does not necessarily mean that they are hastened, although that may be the case, but principally they are accomplished more surely. Potential from the undifferentiated matrix unfolds more thoroughly within the dyadic experience because competent mothering assures that it will reach optimal levels.

The object relations theory that has grown out of ego psychology is not a simple theory of action of the mothering person on the infant and child, but a complex theory of interaction in which action and reaction continually recur in endless cycles. The experiences of these actions and interactions lay down affectively charged memory traces that make for internalization and structuralization.

At first the transactions between mother and child are interpersonal. Visual tracking begins early and is a forerunner of the smiling response (Spitz 1957, 1959, 1965), which signals that memory traces are organized and influence behavior. When the child is approximately eighteen months of age, the midpoint in development between physical and psychological birth, development begins to shift more sharply as the result of internalization; then transactions begin to reflect intrasystemic operations in addition to the interpersonal. From that point on, in that part of the ego where the self and object representations are beginning to build, transactions between the two sets of representations begin to exert their effect on interpersonal transactions, altering those by virtue of the existence of a representation of the object as well as of the object qua object. These transactions become ever more complex as they operate in tandem; affectively laden experiences provided by the object are internalized as an aspect of the object representations that influence the quality of the self representation as well as the interpersonal interaction. As structuralization accompanies internalization of experience, patterns of relatedness are laid down that endure for life.

To define *psychic structure* as consisting of only id, ego, and superego is too simple. Matters appear far more complex as we begin to ask how these agencies are formed, what their component elements are, how they operate in concert and in conflict, and what effect they have on the nature of the personality. Jacobson rounded out the definition by including Freud's observation that the ego is first and foremost a bodily ego, thereby including the physical self and the endopsychic representations of self and object.

Although lacking the data from infant observation that were later to illuminate the process of identification in more minute detail, Freud knew much about the part identification plays in structure formation. He says: "The effects of the first identifications made in earliest childhood will be general and lasting" (*S.E.* 19:31). He discusses the role of identification in structure formation in three ways: (1) as the earliest and original form of an emotional tie with an object; (2) regressively, as a substitute for a libidinal tie by means of introjection of the object into the ego; and (3) normally, as arising from any new perception of a common quality shared with some other person who is not an object of the sexual instinct (*S.E.* 18:107–8).

Identification, then, is the means by which an object image is formed. Freud's definitions of identification suggest that an affective experience is triggered by or connected with perception of an external object or a quality of that object. An internal structure that retains the perceived and desired essence of the object is thereby created. The findings of neonatal research and infant observation are consonant with all three of Freud's definitions.

The first definition may be regarded as referring to symbiosis, the neonate's emotional tie with the object experienced as part of the self.

The second definition refers to regression as a device for dealing with object loss. An imbalance between the two sets of representations results. In the service of retrieving the lost object, the object representations are overvalued, thereby depleting the self representation of positive value. In other words, cathexis is withdrawn from the self representation and invested in the object representations. Where the affective relationship between the two sets of representations is predominantly negative, hostility attaches to the self representation in the course of the regression. In childhood this form of regression in the face of real or fantasied object loss is a necessary adaptation because of the totality of physical and psychic dependency. In later life such regression may become a reaction to actual loss, as in mourning. Freud (*S.E.* 19:30) refers to yet another instance in which a "disruption of the ego" occurs when the "object identifications" become "too numerous, unduly powerful," thereby causing a pathological outcome. In the instance of multiple personality, the self representation is overbalanced by multiple object representations, which Freud also regards as identifications.

The third of Freud's definitions informs how structure is formed by identification, which is regarded today as a normal process but previously was thought to be only a defensive one—by internalization of that which was once experienced as external. The ego can separate from objects by means of establishing identifications that retain them representationally. Freud thought of these internalized structures as precipitates of abandoned object choices. Rephrasing that with the benefit of contemporary theory, one may say that, by means of selective identification, features of the real external object are internalized, to be retained in the form of object representations. How images and representations are registered in the structure depends on the level of development. Early in life they are part of an undifferentiated self-object; at the other extreme, concomitant with psychological birth, registration is of a self representation differentiated from object representations. This aspect of structuralization constitutes an important component element of the ego.

It is useful to point out here the distinction we make throughout our discussion between *images* and *representations*. As the thrust toward individuation continues, and as experience affirms the reality of separate identities, the images are no longer fleeting; they approach some level of constancy. Here we follow Lichtenberg's suggestion (1975) that as images achieve constancy and stability they should be termed *representations* to connote that they have become a stable part of structure.

The propulsive power of the structural theory continues to fuel some current neonatal research. Findings of that research round out Freud's thoughts about structuralization by means of identifications. Maurer and Maurer (1986) find that the neonate, after approximately one week of extrauterine life, recognizes the mother's voice and prefers it to the voice of all others. Recognition and preference suggest there is mental registry, in this instance of the voice. This conforms with Freud's first definition of identification as an emotional tie before object cathexis. He says also: "At the very beginning, in the individual's primitive oral phase, object cathexis and identification are no doubt indistinguishable from each other" (*S.E.* 19:29).

The recent discovery that the fetus hears explains why the newborn recognizes the mother's voice so soon after birth. By the time the infant is born, the mother's voice is already familiar as the infant hears it again, probably now with a less filtered quality. Infants also possess an acute olfactory sense. Odor, voice, and bodily "feel" combine as the first, primitive means by which the infant begins to distinguish one person from another.

Considerable development is needed to achieve the advanced capacity for object recognition that is the indicator of the second organizer of the psyche (Spitz).

The complex process of organization begins immediately after birth. Mental registry is being established and will become an enduring configuration in the mind as neuronal pathways are laid down. A primitive form of structure thus begins to form that might be regarded as a precursor of structure, one of the myriad components that will eventually lead to relatively full structuralization.

With mothering, the neonatal cry—which has been described as an objectless wail—begins to change in quality (and sometimes in volume). This alteration comes about because of the repeated experience, in good enough circumstances, that the cry initiates a series of events. First, it brings the sound of footsteps, then a face appears above the crib, next there is tactile and bodily contact as the baby is picked up, and finally relief from hunger. This sequence of events, initiated by the cry which then changes from objectless wail to summons, brings into play several ego functions—anticipation, organization, and the capacity to delay because of the experience that relief is on the way. The cry may then cease, become less urgent, or become strident with excitement. Organization combines internal processing of events with experience not yet recognized as external. Out of this combination, a new configuration is formed, another primitive organization, another component that becomes a precursor of structure. As the infant begins to realize that it is he or she who produces and controls the cry that summons relief from distress, the cry is endowed with magical qualities that tend to persist throughout life. Shakespeare alludes to this enduring belief in the magic of the summons in *Henry the Fourth, Part I.* Glendower, retaining infantile belief in his magical powers, boasts that he can call spirits from the "vasty" deep. Hotspur, more reality oriented, replies, "Why, so can I, or so can any man; But will they come when you do call for them?" (3.1.56–57).

Identification, at first indistinguishable from object cathexis, produces a merged (symbiotic) image of self and object. This shapes structure in the direction of connection, first with the specific symbiotic object and, much later in the developmental process, with objects in general, thereby creating connection with the object world. The dim recognition that an external object provides relief comes about slowly. Countless daily repetition of experience is needed for the infant to become able to cognize and recognize the most important fact of early life—that *the object* restores equilibrium by relieving distress. Viewed by an objective observer, these experiences clearly take place between an infant and an external object. It is not clear to the infant at first; it will take a long time for the infant to become able, gradually, to distinguish inside from outside, self from object—to know that relief comes from outside.

Object need is part of the innate endowment of the human infant, an adaptive device to insure survival, both physical and psychological. That the infant requires physical care is obvious. Psychologically, the world of the newborn becomes organized around interactions with the caregiver. The mothering person plays a critical role in formulating the "rules" to live by.

Although one would like to believe that reality testing is based on objective perception, that is not so. In early life perception of reality remains the function of the caregiver who interprets reality to the child. Whether accurate or false, that becomes the view of reality that the child adopts. With smooth separation, the child begins to make his or her own interpretations of reality, even where they differ from the caregiver's perceptions. This forces the child to find ways of coping with difference and even with disillusionment.

Two sets of representations, of the self and of the object, begin to be formed and shaped in the process of gradual differentiation from the at-first merged self-object image. Characteristics of each set of representations will in some fashion complement or reflect the characteristics of the other set. At first these exist in the merged self and object images; later, as part of the process of differentiation, they accompany the now differentiated object representations. The object representations are always needed to restore and maintain equilibrium. Maintenance of equilibrium shapes subsequent structure formation. After symbiosis, self and object are continuously being sorted out, impelled by repeated experiences with reality that self and object are not the same. There is a self-object unity alongside a growing awareness that there is also an outside "something." As soon as the child develops this dim awareness of an outside object, interpersonal transactions take place. But at the same time the internal world is gradually being built. A theoretical paradox thus presents itself. The child deals with the object as part of the self-image and, with internalization and structuralization, intrasystemic transactions begin as well. When these become predominant, at approximately eighteen months of age, a turning point occurs that we regard as the *fulcrum of development*, a point where development takes a qualitative and quantitative leap.

In light of the most recent infant research, we have to alter our former position that object relations is merely one of the several functions of the ego, but instead, constitutes the very matrix within which structure is built.

Spitz shows that affective experiences that take place so early in life that self and object images are barely differentiated remain embedded in the structure. He describes the affective interaction between mother and infant as having the most powerful influence on development. This is because affects are predominant in the first months of life, so much so that in the infant's daily experiences affect practically excludes all other forms of perception. Thus the mother's affective responses, her emotional attitude, serve to orient the infant's own affects to a great extent, and confer the "quality of life" to the infant's experiences.

Emde extends Spitz's research. Especially affirmed is the enduring quality of experience with an object. Emde says: "What may be formative about infant experience is *not* that *infant* behavioral patterns get set in an enduring way, but rather that *infant-caregiver* patterns get set in an enduring way" (28).

The capacities for adaptation that derive from the innate endowment interact continuously with the more or the less facilitating environment, producing the unique resultant of these interacting forces which we have described as the *template of object relations* (Blanck and Blanck 1986). Emde supports this idea: "A great deal of evidence has accumulated to support the idea that the human infant is born with developmental agendas" (29). He also finds that the first basic motive of the infant is activity, which takes place within the medium of the relationship with the caregiver.

R. Blanck (1986) suggests that, in normal development, functions of the object representations become transferred to the self representation in the course of development. Freud quotes a similar idea from Goethe: "What thou hast inherited from thy fathers, acquire it to make it thine" (*S.E.* 12:158). Transfer of function from object representations to the self representation takes place *intrasystemically* (within the ego, where these two sets of representations "reside"). Autonomous functioning increases as the self representation becomes able, by means of transfer of function, to perform functions that were formerly performed by the object representations. With transfer, the functions become part of the self representation as a permanent part of structure. Because the socialization of the infant involves prohibitions, restraints, and the like, transfer of function also installs the function of drive mastery into the self representation. It may be recognized that we are describing an aspect of superego formation.

The level or degree of differentiation of the self representation from the object representation is of great significance. How well the differentiation process has proceeded will be reflected in the degree to which the always relative autonomy of the self representation from the object representations has been achieved. To take what has been inherited (internalized) and to make it "thine" represents a high level of identity formation in which characteristics, first internalized in the object representations, have been rendered more autonomous by being transferred to the self representation. Where they remain as characteristics of the object representations, they can reflect an entire spectrum of possibilities, from "normal" superego directives to excessively compliant responses from a highly dependent self representation. Where even minimal structuralization has not been attained, psychotic formation may result.

In good enough circumstances the many precursors of structure will progress toward coalescence into relatively full structuralization. Affective life accelerates with recognition of the external world. The smiling response indicates that the organization that precedes it has reached a new level. Now the sequence—cry, footsteps, bodily contact, relief from hunger—taken alone no longer restores equilibrium. The configuration of the human face is recognized as the equilibrium restoring object. That is because, with differentiation, the self representation becomes more independent of the object representations; testing of reality on one's own begins.

Perception of separate identity is promoted by

1. The normal separating thrust powered by the aggressive drive.
2. The maternal "nudge" from the symbiotic orbit.
3. The child's burgeoning interest in the wider world, usually represented by the father and encouraged both by his behavior toward the child and the child's own beginning capacity to form triadic object relations.
4. Tolerable doses of frustration, alternating with gratifying experiences that affirm the self-images, thereby contributing to differentiation, to diminution of magical thinking and of narcissistic omnipotence. Frustration is essential to differentiation. Moderate frustration forces the infant to realize that the object is not part of him- or herself because, try as he or she might, the spirits in the "vasty" deep do not respond to the

infant's summons. In optimal circumstances the overall affective balance is gratifying enough to enable the child to process frustration more or less comfortably. In addition, mastery of new functions produces intensely gratifying states that propel the infant toward individuation and the "love affair with the world" (Greenacre 1972). With total gratification the child is unable to come to the realization that the object is not part of the self because the overgratifying caregiver *does* respond to summons. Where frustration is excessive, however, without the leavening of gratification, it may become so intolerable that it would defeat differentiation and stall development. To compensate, the child might create a fantasy of a merged self and object representation that always gratifies. That results in a form of pathological narcissism (Blanck and Blanck 1979).

5. More general experiences in interpersonal transactions that become internalized to form patterns of affectively charged interaction, registered and contained within the internal world.

Assumptions about the self in relation to the object world that are established in the dyad tend to persist throughout life. Many such assumptions become *automatisms* (Hartmann)—automatic responses to stimuli. Hartmann describes these as serving the ego by rendering it unnecessary to repeat the steps in a thought process. Some such assumptions can also be pathological where they are perceived as though they are the same as the original experience with the primary object. The response, then, is likely to be more appropriate to the past. The automatic nature of the response overshadows reality testing and judgment that would, if operative, inform the individual of the differences from the past. We sometimes use the term *programs*, borrowed from computer language, because it aptly fits the concept of automatisms that run off automatically when certain "buttons" are pushed. These automatisms reflect the nature of the self representation, of the object representations, and of the state of affective negotiations between them. It is out of this aspect of structuralization that transference potentiality lies latent (see chapter 17).

Whether these assumptions are rigidly fixed or flexibly adaptive depends on whether a degree of autonomous functioning has been attained that permits testing of reality even if the independently perceived reality might contradict both the caregiver's interpretation of reality and the assumptions established early in life. Then new situations can be more accurately assessed in terms of differences from past experience with primary objects.

As the self representation continues to differentiate from the object representations, the affective relationship between the two sets of representations is also established. Inevitably, positive cathexis results from gratifying experiences and negative cathexis from essential frustration along with whatever inadequacies are suffered. These form a pattern of affective relationship between the self representation and the object representations. In excellent circumstances, an evenly distributed positive cathexis is achieved between the two sets of representations (Jacobson) which may be described as a healthy narcissistic balance; both the self representation and the object representations are valued. Narcissistic imbalance can result; the self representation can be overvalued at the expense of undervaluing the object representations. The opposite can occur—the object representations can be overvalued, thereby impoverishing cathexis of the self representation.

The innate striving toward mastery leads the child to investigate the wider world. Now fitting together is no longer restricted to accommodation to the caregiver; the differentiating child is led to seek fitting together with a larger world. This creates inevitable conflict between the perception of reality by the self representation and the perception by the object representations. Where development is proceeding favorably, such conflict is well enough tolerated to foster ever-greater autonomy. In poor circumstances it can lead to abandonment of one's own perception in favor of object retention.

The long separation-individuation process, a period of accelerated psychological development, leads to ever-greater autonomy. It is nevertheless fraught with growth-retarding hazards, although these are less threatening to life than in the case of very young babies, such as the hospitalized babies Spitz studied. Let us look briefly at the vicissitudes of the practicing subphase as an example. The crawler who shortly becomes a toddler needs to exercise and enjoy these newfound skills, to explore his or her expanding world. But if capacity to tolerate dawning awareness of separateness has not kept pace with physical maturation, tolerance for moving away from the object is strained. Excessive separation anxiety results; the toddler's own feet become his or her enemy.

Another kind of failure in the practicing subphase can be that the child's initiative and exercise of function meets with disapproval. Disapproval by the object representations of such important activity can pervade the self representation for the individual's entire life. For some it prevents venture into the wider world. Where individuation (a developmental track more autonomous than the separation track) proceeds, the individual ventures despite disapproval. Such persons may succeed in life without the joy of approving object representations.

Need for and connection with an object is retained throughout life by means of identification with the need gratifier. It is to be found in religion, in love, in friendship, in the need for a sexual partner, in feelings of community, among many other areas of life.

Continuing study and refinement of the structural theory leads to more specific knowledge, not only about the theory but in extrapolation to treatment techniques. Knowledge of the way in which component elements of structure develop and contribute to the overall functioning of the ego enables the therapist to understand the "nutritional" developmental requirements of some of the *critical periods* of development (Spitz). It provides a firmer grasp of how an ego deficit might have come about and what remnants of that deficit persist in the organization that has taken place since that usually unrememberable event. We are not implying that it is the therapist's function to provide "nutrition." That would be analogous to feeding a starving person a rich meal that the stomach is unable to digest. Knowledge of development, however, provides cues that enhance the therapist's attunement. Development at early levels cannot be reconstructed or relived in treatment in every case. Yet the therapist is better equipped to understand the effect on structuralization, and especially on the quality of the self representation, of failures in differentiation, absence of autonomy, separation anxiety, and fixed patterns of object relations.

We illustrate the role of maintenance of equilibrium:

A forty-year-old man fears his justifiable anger when he is offended in his real, current life. He is afraid he will go too far in his rage. He knows from an older sibling, but cannot remember except affectively, that their parents quarreled violently during his first and second years before they divorced. Using Mahler's discovery that affective storms occur normally in the rapprochement subphase (commonly known as the tantrums of the terrible twos), the therapist speculated that the child had had to restrain his tantrums while the parents were having theirs. Why could he not have joined them? Because the object has the function of maintaining equilibrium. A child can only have affective storms where there is assurance that the object will act as a "container" for them. The child who knows the tantrum will be contained feels assured that the object will help the ego regain control before identity is lost regressively. In this case, since the parents could not control themselves, the child had no assurance that they would control him. Therefore his affective storms can only rage within, turned against the self representation. At best, this results in lowered self-esteem with overvaluation of the needed objects. Structuralization is inevitably impaired.

For the structured (neurotic) personality, it used to be believed that knowledge of preoedipal and preverbal experience is not necessary to psychoanalytic treatment. Now we find, however, that the vicissitudes of early life exert powerful influences on even the well-structured personality. We can put this very simply indeed: it is not possible for the first three years of life to be entirely smooth. A good enough first round of development will foster structuralization and neurotic formation, but "good enough" suggests ample potential for difficulty and conflict. Our own experience in the psychoanalysis of neurosis is that the treatment (and results) are enriched by analyzing preoedipal as well as oedipal conflict.

Description of the formation of self and object images and representations out of identifications fulfills Rapaport's quest to establish how processes turn into structures. Identification establishes enduring mental images of experience with the object. These become structure with a slow rate of change.

To summarize:

- The neonate cannot differentiate self from object, nor internal from external sensations. Global thinking begins with relief from distress, and the at-first brief spans of alertness. Experiences are in the *coenesthetic* mode (Spitz). Identifications and object cathexes are indistinguishable one from the other. Images begin to be acquired and are internalized in undifferentiated form.
- The cry is an adaptive mechanism designed to ensure survival and relief from distress. At first the infant has no capacity to distinguish that mechanism from its effect—relief. This results in cathexis of the cry itself as a "magical" mechanism.
- The smiling response informs the observer that the existence of the external world has already been cognized, and is now being recognized affectively and with positive cathexis. That the smile is triggered by an

external source also informs that a level of differentiation has been achieved, but the child has a long way to go before he or she can clearly differentiate between object images and the self-image.

- The pace of differentiation accelerates and the existence of an object world begins to become clearer as interpersonal transactions, including a favorable balance of gratification and frustration, continue. Self-images that are somewhat separate from object images begin to form.
- Frustrating experiences—waiting, feelings of discomfort, hunger, pain, and the like, if not excessive, promote differentiation.
- As differentiation proceeds, "laws" or "rules" are laid down and assimilated. These include sleep patterns, feeding patterns, and all the elements that make up the affective climate.
- With differentiation, the self and object images are cathected with both positive and negative affect, and with varying degrees of intensity—that is, of value or importance.
- With the establishment of a cathected and constant self representation, reality testing begins to proceed more autonomously instead of being dictated by the perceptions of the object representations. The thrust toward autonomous functioning brings a measure of conflict with the external object, as well as with the object representations.

We have raised some questions about the nature of structure and the nature of conflict. Viewing the self and object representations as structural components interacting with each other and with the world at large clarifies a number of ambiguities about both ego and superego. We have used the following theoretical postulates:

1. Hartmann's concept that development takes place in a rhythm of differentiation (specialization of function) and integration of that specialized function into a higher and more complex level of integration.
2. Spitz's illumination of the process by which the psyche is organized.
3. Jacobson's thoughts about self and object representations and the relationship between them.
4. Mahler's research findings, which establish the importance of an adequate symbiosis and which illuminate the complex process of separation-individuation and the various subphases of that process.
5. Current neonatal research findings, in particular by Emde, which leave no doubt that object relations is the very matrix within which development takes place and which affirm Hartmann's postulate of innate

endowment and Mahler's stress on the importance of an adequate symbiosis for orientation into the object world.

The perspective we present uses the following considerations about structuralization:

- The nature and quality of the at-first merged self and object images acquired during symbiosis: Whether a sense of basic trust has evolved out of a preponderance of affectively gratifying experiences; whether the affective tone is intense or weak, positive or negative.
- The strength of the innately endowed separating thrust, when differentiation is well under way, which depends on whether it has been encouraged by the mothering person whose task it is to "nudge" the child out of symbiosis, much as the mother bird nudges her fledglings out of the nest; whether a father has aided the separating thrust by "luring" the child out of symbiosis.
- The strength of a sense of identity that begins to be acquired in the practicing subphase and how it has been sustained at this level of development by the necessary illusion of omniscient and omnipotent ever-present object representations.
- The degree to which the developing self representation can tolerate the normal pitfalls of daily life—the disappointments, frustrations, occasional humiliations, physical hurts, and failures in mastery. Competence in this regard would reflect a stable relationship between the self representation and the object representations in which the two sets of representations are cathected strongly and with equal positive value. Under such circumstances growth will involve the gradual transfer of function from the object representations to the self representation, leading to greater but always relative autonomy of the self representation from the object representations.

We have presented several ideas that are additions to existing theory, for example, that (1) the functions of the object representations are transferred to the self representation in the course of establishing autonomy and (2) the functions of the superego are to be found in the operations of the object representations. The nature of the relationship between the two sets of representations will reflect the degree of conflict or of relative peace between the two sets of representations. We believe these thoughts resolve some of the contradictions in the structural theory as it was first proposed.

We have also added a concept of object relations that derives from Freud and is extended by developmental theory. This object relations theory is more complex than theories of "attachment." We present a complex theory of interaction between internalized self and object representations that take place in early life. The resultants of those experiences make for fixed patterns of object relations that endure for life.

12

▼

Human Sexuality: An Object Relations Perspective

In the first edition the title of this chapter was "Special Forms of Ego Modification." Psychoanalysts once thought that pathological behavior can only be explained by alteration or "modification" of the ego. Now that we know so much more about structuralization and object relations, we realize that pathology of object relations can exist without the entire ego necessarily undergoing "modification." Where modification has occurred, one would have to search for causation in the innate endowment, the developmental process, and how those two factors combine. The subject of this chapter is sexuality and sexual pathology in terms of their object relations connotations. We shall not encompass all forms of sexual behavior in encyclopedic form. We present an overview that stresses the fundamental determinants of sexual problems.

Where there is pathology, one would have to look at whether the structure impairs or precludes normal sexual behavior. Ego capacities such as delay, impulse control and judgment are involved, for normal sexuality is not a simple matter of tension discharge. Where, when, and with whom sex is carried out are all cogent. So we speak not only of the form of behavior, but also whether self, other person, time, place, and suitability of the object are all taken into account. That suggests that we have to look for how far structuralization has proceeded, and especially at that part of the ego where the relationship between the self representation and the object representations exists within the totality of the psyche.

Sexuality, in the sense in which that term is used in psychoanalytic theory, begins at birth or before. In psychoanalytic parlance, sexuality has meaning far beyond the ordinary. Laypersons and physicians use the word *libido* as synonymous with *sexuality*, but in psychoanalytic terms libido is the force that seeks union. We know from sonograms that the fetus "unites" the mouth with the thumb. After birth, the infant's mouth roots for the nipple. From the beginning of life, the human being is pleasure seeking. That does not always mean pleasure in the ordinary sense of ecstasy or even enjoyment. It can refer simply to relief from tension, a meaning that extends far beyond sexuality in the narrow sense. When the neonate finds the nipple, the sensations are thought to be not only relief from hunger, but a totality of pleasurable feelings that include the sucking, the warmth of being held, the very closeness to the feeding person. We continue to refer to Spitz's studies on "Hospitalism" because they show so dramatically that feeding without the other sensations is not even enough to keep the baby alive in some instances.

Early psychoanalytic theory, in addition to being a libido theory, was a theory of transfer from one erogenous zone to another—the well-known progression from oral to anal to phallic to genital. That is a theory of psychosexual maturation. Freud thought that the drive, libido, has a source, an aim, and an object, another indication that psychoanalysis is not a drive theory only. Pleasure is derived from one's own body in contact with the object. At the beginning of life, that pleasure may be designated as narcissistic, not because it excludes an object, but because the object is experienced as part of the self. As differentiation proceeds and we experience ourselves and others as separate, whole persons, sexuality is the vehicle whereby we retrieve, momentarily, the bliss of infantile unity. The object becomes part of the self for a brief period before we recover identity. Some sex problems arise because the less-than-optimally separated person fears that regression will not be in the service of the ego—that is, reversible. Defense against unconsciously wished-for merger, and fear it will result in permanent loss of identity, may impair sexual functioning.

Human sexuality is complex for many reasons in addition to the fear of merger. A major contributor to the complexity is the uniquely human matter of diphasic sexuality. In the first phase, the human child, as contrasted with the lower animals, acquires sexual desire long before sexual capability, before physical maturation makes sexual union possible. This is compounded by the triadic nature of object relations and the incest taboo. The second phase of human sexuality arrives with physical maturity at puberty. Another complexity arises there because, although physically mature, the early adolescent is not ready psychologically for sex with another person; the developmental tasks of adolescence have first to be organized and consolidated. Sexual union, in an out-of-order sequence, impairs development.

Sexual need is biologically determined, powered by libido, the drive that seeks connection. The question of whether the drives are biological or psychological in origin is in a controversial area that we cannot pursue here. We can say, however, that use of the libidinal drive in human sexuality has both a biological and a psychological purpose. Biologically, it provides for the discharge of tension. We refer again to the historical fact that Freud enunciated two theories of anxiety. The first theory was chemical and biological—sexual energy, if not discharged, builds up accumulated toxins. Although largely superseded by the second theory of anxiety—namely, that anxiety is the result of intersystemic conflict—there are those, Rangell (1955) in particular, who believe that there is validity to the first theory as well as the second. In fact he would unite the two theories. In this context the biological factor is retained.

The theory of psychosexual maturation holds that bodily pleasure is not genital at first, but is preceded by the other zonal cathexes. The concept *genitality* refers less to a bodily zone and more to a psychological state. It came into the psychoanalytic vocabulary before object relations theory was explicitly annunciated. Yet it is an object relations concept, referring to the capacity to use the genital zone in conjunction with object love. With the attainment of genitality, the pregenital zones become subsidiary to *genital primacy*—that is, they play a contributory role—specifically, they are used in foreplay. This matter is pertinent to our discussion of sexual pathology because another aspect of pathology is the use of the pregenital zones in place of genital primacy. The aspect to which we have already alluded is fear of loss of identity in the regression of the sex act. These are not mutually exclusive. Failure to attain stable identity goes hand in hand with failure to reach genital primacy.

Autoerotic behavior begins as soon as the infant becomes physically mature enough to explore his or her body. It starts the child on the long road toward relative autonomy as it enables the child to depend less on the object for pleasure. Autoerotism takes many forms, from thumb sucking to rocking to bodily exploration to discovery that the genitalia are more pleasurable than the other zones. Autoerotism may be regarded as furthering the thrust toward separation-individuation. It would be erroneous, however, to conclude that the optimally developed individual has no need for an object. Once identity is secured, object need remains and can be gratified without anxiety. We use the term *sex problem* rather than the psychiatric term *sexual dysfunction* because the latter focuses on the symptomatology as though that is separate from the whole person. Sex therapy is limited in its helpfulness for the self and object relations reason that it is a mechanical adjustment. Even mechanically, the success rate for the milder dysfunctions are about the same as in psychotherapy, and less profound.

Freud "discovered" infantile sexuality in 1905. It shocked the post-Victorian world in which he lived because even the medical community chose to deny childhood sexuality. Freud commented that it was his fate to have discovered what every nursemaid already knew. When children find their genitals, that discovery exerts a powerful influence on their acquisition of gender identity. It would be unthinkable to believe that children do not become familiar with the total bodily self; that would impair acquisition of a self representation. This discussion of human sexuality is about what the human being does with genital discovery and how it can go awry, especially where the capacity to love is deficient.

Let us first deal with the taboos. The incest taboo is psychological, cultural, sociological, and religious. Its universality transcends vast cultural differences. It exists not only in our culture but in many disparate groups from the most primitive to the most civilized, although how incest is defined may vary from one group to another. In certain societies such as some Native American tribes, for example, incest extends far beyond what would be regarded as taboo in the European-Judeo-Christian culture. Even within Judeo-Christian precepts, what constitutes incest varies slightly from one denomination to another. Some forbid marriage between cousins, aunts, or uncles; others permit it. What is common to all religions and cultural groups is that sex within the immediate family is permitted only to the parents; it is taboo between parent (or grandparent) and child, and between brothers and sisters. Intergenerational sex, whether within or outside the family, is pathological. An exception is the initiation rites of some tribes whereby the adult initiates the pubescent child to sex. That, however, is performed ceremoniously, which makes the rather large difference that it is culturally sanctioned and the child experiences it as a rite of passage rather than as a violation.

This takes us to our first consideration of sexual deviation—violation of the incest taboo. The model of culturally forbidden incest, of course, is the myth of Oedipus as dramatized by Socrates. The story, well known to the ancient Greeks, was enacted over and over again as a play, a tragedy with dire punishment for Oedipus. It is said that ancient Greek audiences attended because they were gripped by the universality of the myth. We would add that they probably needed to have the lesson reinforced. The temptation of incest is great. And why not? We learn about love and sex within the family but are forbidden to practice sex there.

It is useful to distinguish between incest and oedipal strivings. We suggest that *incest* be used as the generic term, subsuming all else. That takes into account the possibility of sexual interest within the family before oedipal development, for bodily stimulation and reflexive response inevitably precede oedipal conflict and oedipal love. Distinguishing preoedipal sexual interest within a family from oedipal desire would help to clarify any confusion regarding polymorphous perverse sexuality and oedipal love. Although the Oedipus Complex can be promoted precociously by overstimulation, an out-of-order oedipal position is bound to be flawed because it encroaches on developmental tasks that must precede it in smooth development.

We rely here on the concept put forth by Rangell (1972) that the oedipal position is the fourth organizer of the psyche in the series proposed by Spitz. Spitz showed that the competence of each successive organizer depends on the satisfactory completion of the tasks of the preceding organizer. The fourth organizer, by this formulation, would be completely skewed if the first has influenced the second and the second the third in pathological directions.

Discussion of the incest taboo brings us to the first and perhaps most damaging of the several perversions—pedophilia. We shall describe several ways to define *perversion*. The one already mentioned is that the foreplay replaces the endplay. Here we propose a working definition of *perversion* as a sex act that harms the self or another. Foremost is pedophilia, whether literally incestuous or not. In a certain sense, all pedophilia is incestuous if we take into account that the child has unconscious incestuous wishes and fantasies. This is one of the innumerable instances in psychoanalytic thought when fantasies are normal when not acted on, and take a pathological turn when action occurs. In the child's unconscious, any adult may be a parent surrogate. Regardless of whether the adult is a relative or a stranger, sexual contact is damaging to the child, although the sense of abandonment and loss of safety feeling is likely to be greater with a relative who violates the trust of guardianship. The damage to the development of a child who is sexually assaulted by an adult is irreparable. The child is often damaged physically as well. So we would classify this as first among the perversions.

What makes for pedophilia? Absence of adequate object relations, fear of adult relationships, identification with the child, impulse discharge, all derive from a failure in structuralization at different levels. One pedophiliac may not know that a child is not a developed adult; another may not care. A third may be merged with the child who is used as a vehicle for enactment of narcissistic wishes; still another may be using the child in an unconscious reversal of a wish or repetition of a childhood experience. On the child's side, it does not matter whether the child has been seductive, likes what is being done, even seeks it out. Adults have a protective responsibility toward children, who are entitled to their fantasies. This also explains why it is damaging to the patient for therapists to engage in sex with their patients. It is not consensual even if the patient consents because, in the unconscious, the therapist is in loco parentis.

In defining perversion as we have, we deviate from the traditional psychoanalytic definition. Moore and Fine define pathological sexual behavior: "Fixed and urgent sexual behavior [is] considered pathological because it deviates in object choice and/or aim from the *accepted* adult norm of heterosexual genital intercourse" (1990:142; italics ours).

The "accepted adult norm" implies that foreplay eventuates in heterosexual genital intercourse. But we are left with, and shall be unable to answer satisfactorily, the question of who decides. Moore and Fine rely on the psychoanalytic position that foreplay that does not result in endplay is abnormal. We do not dispute that altogether, but we allow for the object relations factor. What do the two partners feel about it, and how does their sexual preference affect the totality of the relationship? What if one partner is ill yet it is desirable that the sexual part of their relationship is continued in any way possible? What about older persons who can no longer perform as they did when they were young? We cannot agree that whatever "deviations" such persons engage in are abnormal or perverse. With the sexual revolution some forms of sexual activity that were termed perversions are now accepted as part of an object relationship. Older physicians used to regard fellatio and cunnilingus as perverse. Now they are regarded as part of normal foreplay. Most laypersons, and even some therapists, use the global term *oral sex*. It is essential to the diagnostic picture, especially to assessment of the level of object relations, that the therapist ascertain more precisely the nature of the practice.

A woman in analysis reports her sexual practice with her husband. She is vaginally frigid, in itself a controversial term and issue these days. "Therefore," the patient says, "We have oral sex." The analyst asks her to be more specific, and thus learns that the husband performs cunnilingus and then penetrates her for his own pleasure. The question of whether this is object-related sex is to be explored in the analysis, not because of the analyst's value system but to learn as much as one can for diagnostic purposes. A good working hypothesis is that this is an arrangement of convenience for the husband who perhaps cannot spend sufficient time in foreplay. If he is narcissistic, or unable to tolerate delay, he would not find it worth his while to try to adjust his timing to the needs of his partner. It may be that with more interest in his partner, vaginal sex would be pleasurable to both. Since the analyst is treating the wife, the therapeutic issue becomes her willingness to accommodate to his narcissistic-like behavior. Hypotheses are always to be subjected to testing. But the treatment would not have gone even to hypothetically dictated exploration had the analyst been willing to accept a hazy term to describe the couple's sexual behavior.

The word *frigidity* is not well liked these days. Some would prefer to substitute *anorgasmic*. This is a residue of the feminist movement when so many objected to Freud's theories about female sexuality that even his terms had to be discarded. That the objection was valid is not in doubt. One can be absolute that many of Freud's ideas about female psychology and female sexuality were erroneous. It is not well-enough known that they are superseded in modern psychoanalytic thought. We shall discuss this in the section on female sexuality.

Fetishism

Fetishes change, literally, with the fashions. In Freud's time there were corset fetishes. That form has all but disappeared because women no longer wear corsets, but fetishism remains in other forms. Freud regarded corset (and shoe) fetishism as the consequence of the castration shock. The boy notices that his mother lacks a phallus and, by repression and displacement, unconsciously transforms the corset or shoe into a male organ. This is accomplished by splitting the ego; reality testing is abandoned in that one respect, while the remainder of the ego, including reality testing with regard to other matters, remains intact.

We review the history of the psychoanalytic consideration of fetishism because it is basic to understanding pathological sexuality. Fetishism is known as the "model" perversion—that is, the model for theoretical understanding of the structure of perversion. In Freud's time the central determinant of fetishism was castration anxiety. But as early as 1933 Glover noted that perversions have as their underlying purpose the patching over of flaws in the developing sense of reality. These early contributions by Glover are confirmed by the increasing knowledge about development that later investigations provide.

Bak (1953, 1956, 1965, 1968) and Greenacre (1953, 1955, 1959, 1969) write extensively about fetishism. Bak suggests that the etiology of fetishism is disruption of the body image because of some disturbance in the mother-child relationship during the separation-individuation process. This makes for a distorted phallic phase. The fetish undoes the threat of separation by substituting a thing for the object. Greenacre, whose work complements that of Bak, continues that theme—the fetish patches over flaws in the body image, flaws that can have their onset as early as six months of age in some instances, when genital confusion begins within a disturbed mother-child relationship.

The work of Bak and Greenacre demonstrates the gradual movement away from regarding perversion as determined exclusively by castration anxiety and toward inclusion of developmental vicissitudes broader in scope. At first Greenacre thought of the fetish as "the keystone of wavering genitality" (1953:94). Later she broadens her perspective to include more about ego functioning and object relations. She agrees with Bak that fetishism can result from problems in the separation-individuation process. She does not exclude castration anxiety as a factor in fetishism, but she believes that castration anxiety comes about at the phallic phase because of the already flawed body image. She says: "But this stern obligatory need to believe in the phallic mother must be preceded by disturbances in the first two years of life which drastically affect the progress of separation-individuation (Mahler 1968) and in consequence interfere with the developing object relationship and the orderly progress of the libidinal phases" (1968:55).

The fetish and the transitional object have qualities in common. Both are inanimate, chosen when differentiation of the self images from the object images imposes separation anxiety. The transitional object (Winnicott 1953), however, is a normal phenomenon, truly transitional. It is an adaptive measure that uses memory traces of gratification to perpetuate that gratification in order to cope with the anxiety brought on by awareness of a degree of separateness. The transitional object has the advantages of being constantly available, can be endowed with protective qualities, and is omnisciently responsive to the infant's needs. It forms a bridge between states of closeness with the mother and absence from her. It uses the tactile and olfactory qualities of the inanimate object to tide the child over temporary distress while new capacities for connection, such as visual contact and verbal communication, are developed and object representations are formed. Thus it protects from excessive separation anxiety in the transition to a higher level of internalization where separation is endurable. Then the magic of the transitional object ends because it is no longer needed. The fetish endures. Unlike the transitional object that retains the illusion of mother-child unity temporarily, the fetish is used in an attempt to repair a flawed body image. It inevitably fails; therefore, unlike the transitional object, the fetish is retained. Perpetuation of magic and illusion are essential to the "successful" operation of the fetish. Fetishism informs the therapist that there has been an early traumatic experience against which the mothering person could not shield the infant. In Greenacre's thought that experience was exposure to the female genitalia, or to blood, or to some other prephallic-like castration trauma. At that time fetishism was thought to be almost exclusively a male perversion. Now we do not think of it as specifically relating to castration anxiety in boys. Girls, too, experience castration shock and castration anxiety. For both sexes we now broaden the etiology to include separation trauma as well. This makes theoretical room for female fetishism, which undoubtedly existed before it was noticed and before theory could explain it.

Female fetishism has come to analytic attention recently (A. Richards 1989; L. Kaplan 1990). We believe it was hidden before because its subtleties were missed in the days when the shoe and corset fetishes were so blatant. There have always been subtle fetishes that have gone relatively unnoticed. Some do not come to analytic attention because if the fetish is a fortunate one the person is not troubled enough to seek treatment. The man who must have his wife wear a certain piece of lingerie if he is to be potent buys it for her, and she is flattered and pleased to comply, often without either of them realizing that it is obligatory for him.

It is the obligatory feature that is the sign of true fetishism. The individual, male or female, cannot carry out the sex act without it, or gets greater pleasure with it, or substitutes the fetish for sex with another person. The fetish also serves to create psychological distance. This suggests that the fetish has an additional function: it comes between the individual and the other person to reinforce the defense against wished for and feared merger.

The pornographic videotape is a modern fetish, used to enhance sexual excitement. Careful exploration is required to determine whether it is obligatory. The therapist might ask, "What is it like for you when you don't have it?" If it should turn out to be obligatory, then the therapist has to look to the childhood determinants, not as the arbiter of what is "normal" but because the therapist would not want to overlook the influence of inadequacies in the patient's early childhood experience.

Movies now have obligatory sex scenes and language that would not have been permissible only a few years ago. It is impossible, outside of analysis, to distinguish between the moviegoer who *must* have such movies from the one who tolerates sex scenes in order to see a movie. We cannot comment on the commerciality of the moviemakers.

It is impossible to provide a list of fetishes. Some are too subtle to detect, fashions change with the times, and unique creations are formed in the unconscious. New technology may bring new fetishes. We cannot predict what the psychological consequences will be of interactive television, for example, or of television telephones. A very common fetish these days is the use of words that used to be designated as four-letter Anglo-Saxon. Those words interspersed in every sentence, most often as adjectives, must carry a magical quality for the speaker.

Although fetishism is the model perversion, there are others of course. We shall not enumerate them here, in part because they, too, change with the times. There are single and multiple perversions—for example, sadism or masochism alone or together in the same person, or leather alone, or sadomasochism and leather combined. An encyclopedic listing and description of perversions would have to be updated annually. But the symptom is clearly not as significant as the structure and the level of object relations. Sometimes the symptom does matter—when the individual or another person or both are injured. Then the pathology takes on great importance because analysts are always interested first in safety and preservation of life. We say in our discussion of depression that our first obligation is to keep the patient alive, if we can. Next to life is concern for bodily well-being. The well-structured patient does not present such a problem for the analyst because such persons take care of themselves. But where a patient is injuring himself, herself, or others, the therapist must take measures to stop it. Sometimes this means assuming a more authoritarian role than the therapist might like. But respect for autonomy can never mean that patients are permitted to do as they wish if those wishes are dictated by unconscious pressures and are acted on without judgment.

Some forms of severe perversions involve the law. Patients are arrested, and then the role of the therapist takes on a new dimension. A therapist cannot protect a patient from legal responsibility. Law now requires that therapists break confidentiality to report child abuse, which makes for problems in the therapeutic relationship. It also makes for problems in definition. What is child abuse? In earlier times that which is now considered abuse was regarded as the opposite. Those who spared the rod spoiled the child.

When we hear about child abuse, whether in direct treatment or supervision, we insist that the patient provide precise details. A loving parent who slaps a child in an uncontrolled moment needs to deal with the inability to exercise restraint, but it is hardly in the child's interest to have the authorities intervene. Sexual abuse must also be defined precisely before a child is removed from the home. Therapists must ask themselves an almost unanswerable question. What, in the form of object ties, is the child being removed from, and to what is he or she being taken?

Voyeurism and Exhibitionism

Voyeurism and exhibitionism are thought to be two sides of the same coin and are normal forms of sexuality when exercised in attenuated form to conform with social and legal norms. Children are more primitive about it. They display their bodies and are inordinately curious about the bodies of others. But social considerations and normal shame set in early. A child may take his or her clothes off for guests at the age of two. That same child at age six will ask the guests to leave the room when he or she is undressing for the bath. In the intervening years normal shame has entered psychic life. With further development the wish to exhibit oneself does not disappear but takes on socially appropriate forms, such as adornment, which is of inestimable value to the clothing, jewelry, and cosmetic industries. Similarly, normal curiosity in children is naive at first but also changes with development, taking on new forms such as interest in learning.

Before sexuality is channeled into genital primacy, all children are polymorphously perverse. As is true of all pregenital sexuality, it has its place in normal foreplay. At issue, as we have made clear by now, are degree of structuralization, capacity of the ego to delay, and regard for the object. If the urges become so compelling that one must exhibit oneself in public places, the pathology is unmistakable. The key is the same as in fetishism—is the act obligatory and compelling?

We shall not discuss much about violent sex, such as rape. The same principles apply. Persons with adequate object relations do not violate others. Rape appears superficially as genital sex only because the genital organs are used. It has nothing to do with the psychoanalytic concepts of genitality or genital primacy, because it is not based on capacity to love and capacity to postpone gratification in favor of object regard. Criminal law considers only that a person has been violated. Psychologically, the criminal may not even know that a separate, whole other person is involved. We do not mean, therefore, that the criminal should go unpunished because public protection is the function of law.

Homosexuality

Again, we do not consider it within our scope here to offer an exhaustive presentation of homosexuality. We do believe that male homosexuality is different, dynamically, from the female form because of the usual circumstance that children of both sexes are mothered first by women. The identification process necessarily differs for boy and girl. Both have to identify *selectively* (Jacobson 1964) with the parents of both sexes, but the boy has a somewhat harder task. After identification with his mother to build structure, he has to *dis*identify (Greenson 1964) in order to reinforce his masculine identifications. We do not mean that he gives up so-called feminine traits altogether. He can retain tenderness, for example, and incorporate it into his masculinity. We shall discuss this further in relation to male sexual functioning.

We begin our discussion of some of the forms of homosexuality by considering how gender identity is acquired. It is acquired in three steps:

1. The chromosomal factor is decisive, except in hermaphroditism, which we must omit here.
2. The parental sex assignment is made at birth, sometimes before if the sex of the child is known by means of amniocentesis or other instrumentation. Where the fetal sex is known, that information reinforces the innate factor as the parents of the unborn child begin their object relationship with the child with fantasies and often with naming the child.
3. By the age of approximately eighteen months, children themselves note that there are two genders and assign themselves to one or the other.

The assignment may occur in identification with the parent of the opposite sex—a boy will identify with his mother, a girl with her father. A certain degree of such cross-identification is common to all, because everyone carries identifications with both parents. But that is different from acquisition of gender identity. We believe that much more will become known about heterosexuality and homosexuality when hormonal secretion and distribution in the embryo and fetus are better understood. It is reasonable to believe that estrogen or testosterone are not secreted in the same precise amounts in each individual. We think of a range of quantities of these hormones; a fetus may have a large, moderate, or small amount of the hormone appropriate to its chromosomal gender, and a proportionally smaller amount of the other hormone. Hormonal distribution would have an important bearing on the self-assignment of gender. Homosexual militants speak of "preference." That is not as conscious as it is believed to be; it is based on an intricate interweaving of factors, physiologically and unconsciously determined. Recently, research has turned to investigation of genetic factors and to the chemistry of the brain. It will take many years of investigation before science can provide answers to these questions. Claim to definitive answers are premature.

Homosexuality, then, can perhaps be genetically and chemically determined. But it can also be considered in developmental terms. We think there can be pathological homosexuality if the individual has gone astray in his or her gender identification at the age-appropriate time—the eighteen-month phenomenon. Pathology of object relations with reactive and hostile identifications is another possibility. Homosexuality could result from the absence of a parent of the same sex with whom the child could identify. And the very simple form, perhaps more prominent in female than in male homosexuality, is of a woman longing to be mothered by a woman. This does not always mean that a man who also wishes to be mothered by a woman is therefore in a true adult heterosexual position. He may make a fortunate connection with a woman willing to comply and thereby present the appearance of full heterosexuality. In psychological terms the man who needs mothering by a woman is in the same developmental state as the woman who seeks it from another woman.

Perhaps the most common form of homosexuality is that which results from the negative oedipal position. Freud thought that one loves the parent of the same sex before arriving at heterosexual love. But he also thought that the *negative oedipal position*, as he unfortunately termed it, can be a regression from the anxiety aroused by positive oedipal wishes. The formula is an address to the parent of the same sex: "I do not hate you; I am not your rival; I really love you." There is also a common form of regression to the preoedipal state of union with the preoedipal, protective maternal object representation because of fear of the daring of the positive oedipal wish. Often homosexual preference is to avoid oedipal anxiety.

Homosexuality may be defined validly as love for the person of the same sex, which renders it universal. To the extent that each parent was loved, we love others of that sex; to the extent that we all retain a certain degree of normal narcissism, we love persons who resemble us. That holds true even for those who live heterosexual lives. It is a matter of which is dominant. Persons who live heterosexual lives have friends of the same sex and engage in nonsexual social, athletic, and intellectual activities. They may also have homosexual fantasies within a normal range without acting on them.

Jacobson writes about so-called sexual deviation that can be integrated into a "comparatively consistent and coherent concept of self" where positive identifications with loving parents had occurred (1964:72). Moore and Fine say: "Many homosexual individuals appear capable of living well-adjusted lives and show no evidence of significant pathology" (1990:87).The most recent panel of the American Psychoanalytic Association on homosexuality was reported in 1987. The reporter summarizes a presentation by Charles Socarides: "He stressed that there are many types of homosexualities each with its discernible etiology, psychodynamics and therapeutic course. They originate in an object relations rather than structural conflict; incomplete self-object differentiation, failure in the developmental phase of separation-individuation" (173).

Isay (1985, 1986, 1987) sharply disagrees with Socarides. He objects to the value judgments imposed by psychoanalysts who attempt to direct homosexuals toward the "right" form of sexual orientation. He describes boys who fall in love with their fathers at an early age and who, as men, remain lovers of men. Unexplained is the nature of the oedipal configuration in those boys. He insists there is a genetic factor, but geneticists have not yet discovered one. We have already suggested that hormonal distribution in fetal development is not uniform, which might have an influence on acquisition of gender identity. The matter is not so simple, however, because many homosexuals, clear about their gender identities, nonetheless pursue homosexual object choices.

There is clearly a new trend of thought that has moved away from regarding the vicissitudes of the phallic phase as the sole determinant of homosexuality. It is the arrival of the developmental perspective (Blanck and Blanck 1972) that ultimately forced that restricted point of view to be amended. It is no longer tenable to attribute female homosexuality solely to penis envy and masculine strivings; similarly, the etiology of male homosexuality is no longer to be restricted to castration fear.

Bisexuality

Bisexuality, Freud thought, is biologically determined. He based this on anatomy; each sex has biological vestiges of the other. He did not yet know about hormonal distribution, which might have expanded his view. Whether biology alone accounts for psychic bisexuality is arguable. An individual may be described as bisexual by virtue of having loved both parents; again we take the very broad perspective as we did about homosexuality. That makes it essential to reiterate that ordinary fantasy life is vastly different from action. Children always fantasize about what it would be like to be a member of the opposite sex. And there is always narcissistic investment in one's own body. In homosexual choice, one seeks someone who resembles oneself; in bisexuality, fantasies are that one can be both; in heterosexual choice, the partner can resemble the fantasy of one's opposite gender self.

The reality of biological changes at puberty exert powerful influence on bisexual fantasies. Not infrequently, puberty brings disappointment. Children may retain the wish that they will change into the more desired sex at puberty. A girl who wishes to be a boy is severely disappointed when menstruation begins instead. A boy who wishes to be a girl sees his genitals grow rather than reduce in size. A woman patient had fantasies in latency that she would acquire a phallus at puberty. Instead she bled, which she took as a confirmation of the "reality" of castration. As these fantasies became conscious in psychoanalytic treatment, she was able to make peace with her biological destiny.

Genital Primacy

The concept of genital primacy comes into question because in earlier psychoanalytic theory it was based on orgastic capacity. Nathaniel Ross, referring to the orgastic component of genital primacy as a "solid bastion" of psychoanalytic thinking, spoke of "the stark clinical fact that many men and women achieve such genital levels without being capable of mature functioning, not only in the realm of object relationships, but in other areas of ego functioning. . . . It is an open question whether it is enough to correlate orgastic potency simply with mature object relationships, or to subsume other ego functions under a broader category of personality than the theory now encompasses" (1970:283).

Separating orgastic functioning from the object relations factor relieves theory of the ambiguities inherent in concepts such as the genital personality, a formulation closely tied to psychosexual phases but one in which the specific role and importance of the object was but an addendum to libido theory. The establishment of the concept of capacity to love another, which is only implied in the idea of the "genital personality," goes far beyond the physical aspect of genitality; it involves self and object constancy. We remind ourselves here that Hartmann defined object constancy as the ability to retain a mental representation of the object regardless of the state of need. Shakespeare said that more poetically in Sonnet 116: "Love is not love which alters when it alteration finds."

The concept of genital primacy, if one excludes the biological factor of orgasm, is still sound within a developmental object relations theory. It had to be reconsidered because female sexuality is so complex. Before we discuss that, we deal with male sexuality.

Male Psychology and Male Sexuality

Male sexual *dysfunction* is more accurately referred to as *impotence*. This alteration in terminology is the correlate of discarding *frigidity* as a term for political rather than scientific reasons. *Dysfunction* is no less global than *impotence*. Male impotence can range from total failure to attain an erection, to partial failure, to failure under conditions of anxiety, to premature ejaculation, to retarded ejaculation, to no ejaculation, to ejaculation without orgasm. First to be ruled out are physical causes, hormonal levels and the like, and certain drugs and medications that can cause impotence. The psychological causes have to be sought in the structure after organic causes resulting from cardiovascular, renal, pulmonary, endocrine, and other causes have been ruled out.

It was once believed that the sole psychological cause of impotence was castration anxiety, stemming from fear of rivalry with the father representation in the positive oedipal conflict. Developmental theory suggests other causes as well. There can be fear of the unconscious wish for merger with the preoedipal mother, fear of identification with her, fear of the female sex organs, fantasy of a vagina dentata, to cite the most common causes of one form of impotence. Excessive anger and hatred of women also must be considered.

Premature ejaculation requires special mention because it is the most common and most benign form of male impotence. It could involve unconscious fear of merger, of never getting out because of the unconscious wish to remain merged; fear of the vagina as a devouring mouth; unconscious equation of penis and breast with unwillingness to give the woman the "milk." Or it might be caused by inability to delay gratification, even though the end result is far from gratifying. It follows logically that treatment involves uncovering the fantasy and working it through. Sex therapy offers mechanical solutions, such as squeezing the penis to retard ejaculation. Although the claims of sex therapists is that success rates are high for this form of treatment, many men and their partners find it unsatisfactory. The objection of a developmentalist, of course, is that any form of "treatment" that fails to take the level of object relations into account is merely mechanical.

Castration anxiety is usually associated with oedipal conflict. But other developmental determinants precede it. We have alluded to the boy's need to *disidentify* from the mother who nurtures him in order to organize his masculine identity. Success varies from one boy to another. Probably it is never totally secure, and too great a feminine identification remains a danger for all men. The degree of danger or, in some instances, the strength of the unconscious wish to remain like the mother, determines how strenuously defense must be employed. The most profound danger is the unconscious wish to merge with the maternal object, a relic of the symbiotic or early separation-individuation phases. That leaves as its residue fear of engulfment and whatever defenses need to be employed against it. There are many symbols of this phenomenon, such as spider women and the vagina dentata.

The degrees to which these fears of unconscious wishes subside and disidentification succeeds are measures of the degree to which a man arrives at a comfortable appreciation of his own identity. Better structured men are less likely to need the defense of disparagement of the other sex. They can use the residual, partial feminine identification as a source of comfortable tenderness. It enables them to be good husbands, fathers, lovers. Men in the helping professions especially need to be comfortable with these qualities, in conjunction with a solid masculinity.

Other defensive arrangements are at work. Men who must deny homosexual tendencies have to overemphasize masculinity, often by comparison with the imagined inferiority of women. Some extreme group pathologies, such as skinheads and motorcycle gangs, overdo the masculine-like elements of their behavior. It is, in fact, a pseudomasculinity. Group "masculinity" denies homosexual wishes while gratifying them to some extent by the exclusivity of male clubs. Alcoholism may sometimes be another defense against unconscious homosexuality. The man who needs one more drink with the "boys" before going home to his wife may unconsciously prefer the "boys."

We have not emphasized hatred of women because that is based on a man's personal history and therefore differs in each case. That it can make for antifeminine bias and even violence is obvious.

Female Psychology and Female Sexuality

The history of psychoanalytic thinking about female psychology and female sexuality is not a distinguished one. But taking into account the mores of his time, it is to Freud's credit that he was at least ambivalent about some of his attitudes toward women. After all, he held some of his women colleagues and pupils, including his daughter Anna, in high esteem. Ambivalence is notable in some of his writings. Although he is disparaging in many places, he tries to be objective in others. As the founder of psychoanalysis, it is perhaps remarkable that Freud was sometimes aware of his bias but not of the psychological reasons for it. That, of course, was because he was discovering fundamental features of theory and technique; it remained for his heirs to evolve developmental theory, which clarified this essentially masculine defense.

Freud's effort to be objective appears in his lecture on "Femininity" where he says: "The ladies, whenever some comparison seemed to turn out unfavorable to their sex, were able to utter a suspicion that we, the male analysts, had been unable to overcome certain deeply-rooted prejudices against what was feminine, and that this was being paid for in the partiality of our researches" (1933a:116).

After acknowledging that he is indeed prejudiced, Freud concludes that lecture with a recommendation for more research. One gets the impression that Freud did not much like the subject and preferred to leave it to his women disciples, principally Ruth Mack Brunswick and Helene Deutsch. They did a very poor job of it. Mack Brunswick (1940) affirmed Freud's ideas; Deutsch (1944) added that women are intrinsically masochistic. Karen Horney (1967), who dissented from Freud because of his omission of cultural factors from his larger theory, also showed how Deutsch extrapolated from pathology to present a distorted picture of femininity.

Much political outrage has been expressed about the concept of penis envy. Feminists scoff at it, but child observationalists see the eighteen-month-old girl's dismay in vivo. This does not mean that it endures for life, however. So young a child wants everything that another child has, and is not yet able to comprehend human anatomy in its totality. In some educational circles it is advocated that the girl be told that she has "something" too. To tell a little girl that she has a vagina can only bewilder her, because the vagina is not visible. What, then, should she be told? It is best to avoid casting the issue in terms of compensation. Girls are different—equal, not similar or better. One little girl asked her mother, who was in analysis, about this. The analyst suggested telling her: "You are exactly the way you are supposed to be." There is no single answer that settles the issue for the child. The answer this analyst suggested was designed to begin a dialogue between mother and daughter that could go on for years and to add more intricate explanation as the child becomes older and better able to comprehend more. The mother who all too quickly says, "But you have a vagina," is anxiously trying to be compensatory.

Freud believed that psychoanalytic therapy of a woman reaches "bedrock" when she accepts her anatomical "shortcoming." This idea is rejected by contemporary psychoanalysts. It is suggested (Grossman and Stewart 1976) that "penis envy" is not to be taken literally. It is a metaphor that expresses dissatisfaction in concrete form. We (Blanck and Blanck 1986) elaborate on this out of our experience with persons who have been deprived of emotional supplies at the time of life when affects cannot yet be verbalized. The girl, still at the stage of concrete thinking, observes that the boy possesses something she does not have. Were she able to express her thoughts, she might say that she lacks not a penis but love, maternal attunement, and similar abstract psychological necessities. We remind ourselves once again that a series of traumatic incidents is usually remembered as a single event. The continuous trauma of emotional deprivation is more difficult to designate, and so one seizes on something concrete to convey the feeling that something is missing. Perhaps boys are less fortunate in that regard, and perhaps much castration fear represents fear of loss of emotional supplies as well as of the phallus per se.

Girls who have had a good enough psychological start in life do not grow up to be bewildered, distressed, and envious women. Out of our clinical experience with adult women, we have come to a tentative hypothesis that the girl has an additional road to recovery from the so-called castration shock. She employs masturbation to heal and to provide a sense of intactness. It has long been believed that masturbation serves as a vehicle for discharge of oedipal fantasies, and that remains correct. But child observationalists, Spitz in particular, suggest that autoerotic activity at all levels serves development. Although masturbation serves both boy and girl in the struggle for autonomy, we suggest that it serves an added function for the girl. The experience of orgasm through masturbation in early childhood unifies and organizes the sense of self, including the bodily self. In this manner it may serve to conquer "penis envy." Clearly, this is a matter for further investigation. For both sexes, we have said, autoerotic activity at appropriate levels of development promote the separation-individuation process. Because of the sense of bodily intactness despite castration fears, we speculate that boys do not require the unifying experience of orgasm to the same extent as girls. In his studies of male and female sexuality, Kinsey (1948, 1953) did not investigate this factor.

As a biologist Kinsey could find no physiological support for vaginal orgasm. This is in sharp contrast to Freud's insistence that the measure of maturity in women is the transfer of sensation from clitoris to vagina. The so-called transfer theory was disproved by the investigations of Masters and Johnson (1966). They found that not one part or another of the complex female apparatus, but all of it acting in concert, is involved in sexual arousal. We regret that they used their enlightening biological research findings to venture into sex therapy.

We are left with questions about "frigidity," of why the total response is inhibited in some instances. For the answer we have to look not to biology but to contemporary psychoanalytic psychology which has corrected Freud's erroneous ideas about female psychology. In addition to correcting the "transfer theory" and the concept of penis envy, the matter of frigidity also has to be thought about in terms of developmental theory. In well-structured women it may well be caused by oedipal fantasies against which strong defense has to be employed. In understructured women, there may be factors similar to those we saw in understructured men—fear of merger and fear of the "little death," as the French refer to orgasm. Some cannot permit the regression.

Clinical experience finds that the less structured woman, who has direct (undefended) avenue to discharge, is likely to be more easily orgastic. This is believed to be so because she is unencumbered by oedipal conflict and defense. At a lower level of object relations, the sex partner matters less to her, or not at all. In contrast, the structured woman retains residual oedipal wishes against which unconscious defense operates.

The sexual partnership remains to be discussed. One of the more valuable discoveries of the Master and Johnson physiological investigation is that all women can be orgastic with adequate stimulation. Often frigidity can be shown to be false if we examine the behavior of the partner, as we have done from one angle in our case illustration. Men and women have different timetables for arousal. Often it takes much accommodation for sex partners to adjust to one another. Benedek (1968) suggests that a woman can adjust to a man's more rapid discharge if she uses fantasy to accelerate her timing. The male partner, at the same time, needs to find a way to employ delay of discharge. Couples in long-term relationships can arrive at mutually satisfying accommodation.

Part Two

Technique

13

▼

Descriptive Developmental Diagnosis and the Fulcrum of Development

The medically accepted form of diagnosis is to match the patient's symptoms with the criteria in the *Diagnostic and Statistical Manual–III–R*, which is the third, revised edition. This manual is used universally for statistical and administrative purposes. Since it is atheoretical by design in order that therapists of all orientations may use it, the manual does not of itself provide a guide to treatment. The form of treatment is left to the decision of the therapist who acts according to his or her theoretical orientation.

The method of diagnosis of the manual is based mainly on symptomatology, which fails to recognize that the same symptom can exist in different structures. For example, obsessive symptoms can be present in obsessional neurosis as a true compromise formation, in borderline structures as a defense against decompensation, or as organicity to be treated by medication. Thus far, emphasis of the DSM system is on diagnosis by symptoms. Sometimes this results in mistaking the symptom for the pathology. One hears of obsessions, phobias, sexual dysfunction, and other symptoms as though they are the illnesses. There are even forms of therapy that purport to treat them. In a developmental diagnostic scheme, the pathology lies not in the symptom but in the structure.

We (Blanck and Blanck 1968, 1974, 1979) have been evolving a diagnostic scheme, and we have used metaphors boldly. We are aware that they usually fall short of precision, but they can be extraordinarily helpful in enabling the diagnosing therapist to visualize the structural strengths and deficits. In our first attempt (1968) we thought it would be useful to present developmental criteria in the form of a chart from which the diagnosing therapist could draw a graph that would depict the pathology. Much can be said for providing that kind of pictorial view. In 1979, however, because of Mahler's 1975 discovery about the importance of the rapprochement subphase, we were impressed by the dramatic quantitative and qualitative leap in development that takes place around that subphase. We then saw that the rapprochement subphase is the focal point of development around which further development proceeds. If there is severe failure in the developmental task of rapprochement, there will be borderline pathology at best. The rapprochement subphase, therefore, is a fulcrum. It is the place in development where structuralization and internalization take a major turn. We use Mahler's discovery to change our diagnostic depiction from a chart to one that we designate as a Fulcrum of Development.

We continue refining even that newer scheme. The Fulcrum of Development may be visualized as a balance scale on which to "weigh" the developmental features as they become known to the diagnosing therapist. Diagnostic information falls on one side or the other of the balance scale. A preponderance of features that tilt the Fulcrum to one side indicates borderline development, while features that indicate structuralization tilt the Fulcrum to the other side to indicate neurotic development. This, then, becomes a rough guide to treatment. Of course, the minutiae of the individual features in each case play a determining role in how the treatment is to proceed. Using the Fulcrum helps the therapist know which form of treatment to institute—psychotherapy and structure building for borderline pathology, psychoanalysis for neurosis. Never can it be expected that all, or even very many features of development will be detected even in a prolonged diagnostic evaluation. Also, much may alter as treatment proceeds, either because new features are revealed or because, as is appropriate, treatment alters structure.

One would think it scarcely needs to be said that diagnosis precedes treatment, for it is the diagnosis that dictates the form of treatment to be undertaken. Nevertheless, we often find that treatment is begun without diagnosis. How can that be? Mainly, we think it is because therapists are compassionate. Most patients arrive in pain, and so one tends to begin by attempting to alleviate their pain. Without an adequate diagnosis, this can be hazardous and usually exacts a price later in the treatment. It can, for example, impair the transference; it can hold out the promise of painless treatment which, because this is impossible to fulfill, will lead to later disappointment.

A second and somewhat better reasoned tendency is to begin treatment prematurely. Some therapists advocate that the first encounter should provide a therapeutic experience, a "taste" of what therapy has to offer. This, it is argued, will capture the patient's interest and ensure that he or she will want to continue. Overlooked there is that the first meeting with a therapist is an experience in and of itself. We do not have to strain to provide it; it is built into the very arrangement. We call this arrangement the *benign climate*. It provides an experience different from all others. A therapist listens to a patient respectfully and is there solely in the patient's behalf. Psychoanalysis has been described as an impossible profession, for it uses one's own personality, affects, unconscious, in addition to the skills one acquires in training. This applies to psychotherapy as well. Regardless of how much or how little enjoyment the therapist derives, he or she is there solely for the patient in a way that is not demanded of other professions. Only in psychotherapy and psychoanalysis are we obliged to keep our appointments on time, to listen with evenly suspended attention, to refrain from imposing our own needs, interests, moods. Nor can we befriend and socialize with a patient we like, as is permissible in other professions.

The diagnostic process is most desirably undertaken by the therapist who will perform the treatment. We do not advocate diagnosis by an intake person who will turn the patient over to a treating therapist, although we recognize that this is administratively necessary in some settings. The advantages of diagnosis and treatment carried out by the same therapist are that a beginning therapeutic alliance is established in the course of the diagnostic process; the patient learns about his or her role, which is to provide material and, in many instances, to extract developmental, structure building responses from the therapist. Some persons are excellent extractors, some need to be helped to know how to extract, some cannot do so, even with help. These factors also contribute to the prognostic implications but are not the whole of them.

At the initial consultation, it is the patient's task to provide the therapist with diagnostic information. Haste to relieve pain is neither the most compassionate nor the most rewarding course of action. At any rate, our ability to do so is limited, especially when we are operating in diagnostic darkness. Freud was a most compassionate therapist, yet he offers good reason for delaying treatment until the case is well understood. He reasons that the discomfort, or symptom, constitutes the motivating force that keeps the patient in treatment.

Is that our objective, to keep patients in pain so they will continue in treatment? Not at all. If a therapist can solve a patient's problems in one or two sessions, why not? Freud avoided symptom relief for the most compassionate of reasons. It was not his purpose to keep the patient in treatment to gratify the therapist's need or greed, but because symptom relief is temporary. Symptoms return, either in the same or in mutated form. Freud did not want to throw a pebble at a giant.

There are brief therapies that resolve some kinds of problems. Usually, these therapies deal with practical matters that can be changed by altering behavior or environment. Such therapies are particularly apt in situations in which prolonged therapy is not likely to be useful, or where there is a crisis that will result in permanent damage if it is not dealt with quickly. The outstanding example of such a crisis is, of course, a suicide attempt. There the therapist moves to save the patient's life before all else.

In the long run most patients can benefit only from structural change. Treatment short of that is usually stopgap and does not endure. Alteration of structure is a long and profound task. Freud's work was altogether devoted to structural change, to altering the relationship among ego, id, and superego. That matter has become even more complex now that we have added the object relations factor, the relationship between the self representation and the object representations. Structural change calls for big guns.

Freud's big gun was psychoanalysis—long term, expensive for the patient, demanding of both patient and analyst. He was, after all, the discoverer of psychoanalysis and the innovator of its technique. Therefore he treated patients who had reached a high enough level of structuralization to render them capable of enduring the analytic process. He had no techniques for other types of problems, those we would designate today as borderline or psychotic.

Within the last thirty years or so, techniques have evolved for the treatment of these understructured patients. This makes diagnosis far more necessary than when psychoanalytic treatment was for neurosis only. Now therapists must choose. They can engage in brief therapy to alleviate an immediate problem. They can decide, on the basis of diagnosis, that they are dealing with an understructured personality, in which case psychotherapy is called for. They can, also on the basis of diagnosis, find that there is sufficient structuralization for psychoanalysis to be the treatment of choice. What we must not do is allow the patient to dictate the form of treatment. Patients have been known to ask for "only a little help" or to say they want to come once a week or to place other demands and restrictions before the therapist. After diagnosis, it is the responsibility of the therapist to tell the patient the indicated and desirable form of treatment. We describe this stance as "taking charge of the case." Medically trained therapists perhaps do this better than those who come from other disciplines because it has been part of their basic training that the doctor knows what form of treatment is indicated once the diagnosis is made. Therapists from other disciplines sometimes have to train themselves to take charge. We are not advocating an authoritarian stance, but an authoritative one. As we have been maintaining throughout, we are devoted to promoting the patients's autonomy. In fact, we regard attainment of autonomy as the very goal of treatment. But it is not an autonomous act on the part of the patient to demand a form of treatment in ignorance. That the patient's friends attend only once a week or that the patient does not have more time are not autonomous reasons. We take charge because that is our responsibility. Moreover, it reassures the patient to find that we know what we are doing.

We are arguing for sound diagnosis and versatility of treatment options. In order not to place the patient on a Procrustean couch, the therapist should be versatile enough to provide the best form of treatment for the individual patient. A structured patient is best treated by psychoanalysis. It cannot be emphasized enough that it is a disservice to the structured patient to provide psychotherapy precisely because such patients can benefit somewhat, but not optimally. It gives them half a loaf.

With some understructured patients, structure may be built to the point where the treatment can be shifted from psychotherapy to psychoanalysis. The psychotherapist who is qualified to conduct an analysis would then shift the form of treatment. Those who are not also psychoanalysts would then refer the patient to an analyst.

Psychoanalysis does not currently enjoy great popularity. Otherwise educated persons know only vaguely what psychoanalysis is. Having barely heard of it, and usually in a negative vein, they believe it to be some outdated, Victorian idea. To many, even some in the mental health professions, Freud's work has passed into history as a huge mistake.

The mistake is the tendency to throw out the baby with the bath water because Freud was not uniformly correct on all issues. Many of Freud's errors have now been corrected, especially his psychology of women which has been the bête noir of the feminist movement. Ego psychology has contributed in no small measure to the elaboration and modernization of Freud's theories, some of which indeed have needed updating. Freud himself was the principal revisionist of some of his own theories. It would have taken two lifetimes for him to have revised all his work, and it would have detracted from going forward with new theory construction. Revision is rightly the obligation of his successors.

Ego psychology provides the most useful revision of Freud; it elaborates, as well as revises. It has led the psychoanalytic community, among other gains, to knowledge of how to treat the understructured personality, a matter that baffled Freud. Freud used a trial analysis to arrive at a diagnosis. In approximately twelve sessions, which in his day occupied two weeks, he was able to determine whether the structure could tolerate the analytic method. If it could, he continued the treatment. If it could not, he dismissed the patient as unanalyzable.

A trial analysis is a rather crude form of diagnosis in light of our greater knowledge today about development and why it sometimes falls short of full structuralization. The Fulcrum of Development uses that which is known about development and structuralization to enable us to determine the degree of structuralization of a given patient. Further, it dictates the nature and course of the treatment. Before describing the Fulcrum of Development in detail, let us deal with the practical aspects of undertaking a developmental diagnosis.

The practical aspects include the duration of the diagnostic evaluation, whether it should be accomplished in the first consultation, whether a diagnostic period of several sessions during which the case is evaluated is preferable, and whether one should use psychological testing to augment the clinical exploration.

Our answers are largely in the affirmative. One should take as long a time as necessary to arrive at an evaluation that indicates where to address treatment. A course of treatment should not be undertaken before the diagnosis is clear. Diagnostic testing is helpful if the diagnosis is so puzzling that a psychological report will help clear up certain murky matters. Testing is particularly useful in cases of low-level borderline structures to rule out psychosis and to assess the potential for growth. In such cases it is especially important to guard against regression.

What does the therapist do during prolonged diagnostic exploration? The therapist thinks, while the patient's story unfolds. We advocate a combination of unstructured and structured sessions—unstructured to allow opportunity for the patient's unique style of approach to unfold, structured where certain facts need to be elicited if they have not come through in the patient's account.

The therapist is aware that a transference of sorts exists even before the first consultation. A telephone contact has been made to arrange the appointment and, no matter how brief, the patient has formed some impression based on a preexisting pattern of object expectation and object need. When the patient arrives, a tenuous transference is elaborated, still on the basis of need and of established patterns of object expectation and object relatedness. It is useful to observe the approach behavior and to make some tentative hypotheses about the object relations pattern. The style of presentation provides diagnostic information about defense as well as about level of object relations. How much is the patient able to reveal to the therapist who is still a stranger? Patients are expected to depart from normal reserve because of the need for treatment. Is this done with or without discomfort? A degree of discomfort may be a sign that defenses are in operation, whereas free and easy revelation of intimate matters may be indicative of thin ego boundaries.

Diagnosis of neurosis is based on the assumption that the neurotic patient has reached the oedipal level developmentally, is capable of enduring conflict and of dealing with it by means of defense and compromise formation. On the object relations side, neurosis includes having reached the level of self and object constancy. Anxiety, in neurosis, arises from structural conflict and is experienced in attenuated form as a signal for the deployment of defense. Compromise between the conflicting forces allows token gratification to both sides of the conflict. Since the structure of neurosis is intersystemic, structure does not require building as the main therapeutic objective, as with the understructured personality. Rather, treatment of neurosis involves redistribution of the relationship among id, ego, and superego. Ego psychology adds, as its unique contribution, that intrasystemic relationships, between the self representation and the object representations, also require therapeutic attention. This is especially pertinent now because, although psychoanalytic theory has long held that attenuation of the harsh superego is a prime objective of the treatment, we have added (chapter 11) that the superego is formed out of object representations. Psychoanalysis is the treatment of choice for neurosis because these intrapsychic transactions are not usually amenable to psychotherapy.

The neurotic has reached the oedipal level and has the capacity to endure analysis of the conflict. Again, the unique contribution of ego psychology is that, in addition to the sexual aspect (drive theory) and the rivalry with the parent of the same sex (object relations theory), one is concerned with such character traits as ambition, healthy narcissism, and whether the separating thrust is favored or disapproved of by the object representations (developmental theory). At the oedipal level, affect is not restricted to hatred, hostility, and parricidal wishes; also included are love, admiration, gratitude (affect theory), and identification with the parent of the same sex.

The metapsychology of neurosis has long been known and accepted in psychoanalytic thought. That is not true with respect to the borderline conditions. Here we find several sometimes competing theories. As a result, both diagnosis and treatment can be viewed in several different ways. It is hoped that consensus will be reached as experience in dealing with these structures accumulates. Yet that seems distant now because the theories are so divergent that they may not be reconcilable. The best outcome would be that accumulation of experience will result in retention of whatever proves to be sound without regard for partisan loyalty to one theorist or another.

A Diagnostic Scheme

Ego psychology includes classical psychoanalytic theory and a theory of development of self and object relations by means of differentiation, followed by integration at the next higher level, followed again by differentiation, and so on. The fetus is part of the mother's body. With birth physiological connection between child and mother is severed. Having lived together for nine months, both must adapt to the physical separation.

The mother has developed during her own girlhood and adulthood, integrating her feminine identity to include the prospect of future mother-hood. With pregnancy she fantasizes about the unborn child. By the time the child is born, he or she is already established in the mother's mental representations. We pointed out (chapter 11) that the interaction between mother and child results in a connection that is considerably more pro-found than a bond. Both have to overcome the altered physical circum-stance brought about by birth (differentiation) and to enter a new quality of relatedness on a higher level of integration. Differentiation and integra-tion proceed apace in the early months of life. But a profound qualitative change for the child takes place at the rapprochement subphase. That sub-phase is critical because its success or failure determines how further devel-opment will proceed. It is then that the major turn to the internal world takes place if the rapprochement movements are accepted. The mother's tolerance and attunement cushions the child's discovery that return is not really possible, and the child will have to move on developmentally. This must be what Milton meant by paradise lost. If rapprochement fails, par-adise, the merged mother-infant state, is forever sought; that search is, of course, doomed to failure.

To put it less poetically, physical maturation and structuralization have proceeded to the point where they bar the way to the interpersonal life of infancy. The child who has experienced rapprochement disappointment seeks to return to the interpersonal life of infancy even though some struc-turalization has begun. We know of no better description of the develop-mental failure of the borderline patient than that he or she is left in search of the merged state that is no longer attainable. Because there is some structuralization such persons escape psychosis, but they cannot move on developmentally to form more separate self and object representations.

For these reasons we regard the rapprochement subphase as a turning point in development, as the time when the separation-individuation process has produced a qualitative change of major significance. We use the metaphor of a balance scale to describe these events. As the diagnosing therapist listens to the material and formulates hypotheses, aspects of development are sorted out in the therapist's mind as they are detected. Progressive features of development are relegated to one side of the scale, while features that connote arrest or regression are placed on the other side. Whether the patient is structured or understructured is decided by where the preponderance of developmental features lie, how the balance scale tilts.

It is useful for the diagnosing therapist to have a clear picture of the ideally structuralized patient to use as an instrument against which the patient's pathology is measured. This is analogous to the baseline of perfect health against which a physician measures an illness. The criteria of structuralization are:

Drives

- Drives are channeled by a competent ego.
- The libidinal drive seeks connection.
- The aggressive drive serves to sever connection.

Ego

- Thought is used as trial action.
- Secondary process predominates.
- Ego controls delay of discharge of affect and impulses.
- Ego possesses the capacity to tolerate frustration, anxiety, and conflict.
- Regression operates in the service of the ego.
- There is capacity for self-observation.
- The self representation is relatively autonomous, i.e., relatively independent of the object representations.
- Functions of the object representations have been transferred to the self representation.
- On a neurotic level the ego can be in conflict with the drives; on a postneurotic level the ego is relatively conflict-free.
- The ego has the capacity for organization and reorganization.
- Ego functions are relatively consonant with innate endowment.
- Both autoplastic and alloplastic modes of adaptation are used flexibly.

Defensive System

- Anxiety is recognized as a signal.
- A competent defensive repertory employs resistance in the analytic situation.

Self and Object Relations

- The representational world is established.
- Self and object representations are relatively differentiated, with occasional dedifferentiation in the service of the ego.

- Self and object constancy are established.
- There is capacity to distinguish between present reality and internalized patterns of negotiations between the self and object representations.
- The capacity to engage in transference has replaced the search for replication of early object need.
- Triadic object relations have replaced dyadic ones, making it possible to tolerate the complexity of the oedipal conflict relatively unimpeded by the persistence of dyadic need.

Affects

- There is evenly distributed, preponderantly positive cathexis of self and object representations.
- Ambivalence is tolerated within the context of self and object constancy.
- There is a relatively complete and differentiated affective repertory on a spectrum with many shadings, replacing the global all good and all bad. The shadings appear as depression, dejection, sorrow, sadness, low-keyedness, and the like; as elation, ecstasy, happiness, joy, contentment, and the like; and as hatred, dislike, rage, anger, and the like.
- Moods are relatively even and stable, with appropriate modulation.

This list describes the ideal person, structuralized beyond what is realistically possible in any individual.

In approaching the diagnostic process the therapist seeks out the combination of innate endowment and life experience that make for each individual's unique development. Always to be kept in mind is that an adult, no matter how severe the pathology, has developed beyond the phases and subphases of early life. As we have said, ongoing organization incorporates the developmental failures but does not halt development and maturation along other lines, all of which become parts of the total organization.

Despite the differences between individuals, many features of ideal structuralization are characteristic of neurotic structure. Therefore structured, neurotic patients present a relatively stable and reliable set of features that lie within narrow limits and can be relied on as constants that do not require therapeutic attention but, in fact, support the therapeutic effort. Principal among these is that identity is intact, that self and object constancy obtain. That means that the individual experiences self and others as separate, whole persons and can therefore form a true transference.

In contrast, understructured patients present wide variations in almost all the developmental features enumerated. The diagnostician-therapist has to evaluate such matters as degrees to which identity formation and so many other features of development have been approached, features that are more rather than less uniform and stable in neurotic structure. Methods of diagnosing the understructured patient include seeking out those symptoms that help the diagnostician arrive at a decision. *DSM–III–R* lists eight symptoms in relation to borderline pathology. If the patient presents five out of the eight, the presumptive diagnosis is borderline. That may or may not change in *DSM–IV*. The method may be useful in some diagnostic situations, such as a crisis in which a quick decision must be made about hospitalization or medication.

The weakness in relying solely on symptoms for diagnosis is that identical symptoms may present in different structures. Evaluating structural factors is more difficult but also more accurate. The method we describe is more time-consuming. It assumes the patient is ambulatory, voluntary, and presumptively capable of engaging in a diagnostic process that may involve more than one session and of undertaking continued treatment if indicated.

This method does not require that a decision be made in the first consultation. The diagnostic process can continue over several sessions if need be. On relative completion of the diagnostic process, both therapist and patient usually know whether treatment is to be undertaken and, if so, the kind of treatment needed, and even where to address treatment in terms of developmental level.

We present two clinical illustrations of the diagnostic process. The first is of a structured personality, the other of an understructured personality.

A forty-year-old professional man began treatment with the presenting problem of anxiety about his work. On the surface he was successful but not well liked by his colleagues, who called him a worrier. He said in the initial consultation that he could never relax.

He had been married for ten years when he came for treatment and had two young children. He tried to enjoy them because he was a do-the-right-thing sort of person. He became especially anxious when they had their minor illnesses or even when they became ordinarily cranky. His relationship with his wife was also determinedly good. He wanted to have a model family.

To walk through the diagnostic process: He appeared anxious to make a good impression. The word *anxious* is used correctly here. It was not possible to put him at ease. He told his story obediently, trying to be a good patient. The descriptive word for him is *good*. The diagnosing therapist had to seek out the price he was paying for his "goodness."

He was the older of two boys. His father was a small-town dentist in the Midwest. The boys were expected to go to college and professional school. His brother went overboard in the 1960s and dropped out. Our patient followed the straight path and went to college and law school.

His parents had remained together in an unhappy marriage. Father was cold, remote, demanding of obedience. Mother was unhappy most of the time, probably depressed. The patient had school friends and engaged in athletics without distinction. He dated in high school, met his wife in his sophomore year at college. He was relieved that she could put up with his anxiety. They married after college. He did moderately well at college and automatically enrolled in the state university and graduate school. He came to New York because he was recruited for a job.

The therapist had to ask about sex. He said it had never been the big deal it is made out to be. He found it more of a chore than a pleasure. He did get pleasure from masturbation. The therapist asked about his fantasies, for both masturbation and intercourse. The intercourse fantasies were about beautiful women, movie stars, who adore his body and perform fellatio. They ask nothing of him. His masturbation fantasies were always the same. He is in a hotel, lying in bed. A maid comes in to make up the room, sees him there and offers a massage. It results in a more powerful orgasm than in intercourse.

The therapist also had to ask when he first had intercourse. He had tried once or twice on dates in college, but it didn't work. The therapist noted silently that this was beginning to go uphill. He did not explain what did not work. Consciously he wanted to be a good patient, but he was not forthcoming with information without prodding. The decision at this point was to test it out a little longer.

The therapist then had to ask why sex had not worked and learned that he had become so anxious that he lost his erection. The young woman who later became his wife was patient with this, and after many tries he succeeded. But it remained a continuing problem to this day. Each encounter was fraught with anxiety about whether he would be successful this time.

By now the therapist must begin to think that masturbation is probably easier for him because no one was asking anything of him. This matched the patient's behavior with the therapist. He wanted to meet the requirements of the interview situation, that is, to tell his story. He got off to a fair start and then had trouble keeping it up! The therapist also noted that he had begun with a generalized anxiety that now appeared to be more specific. A hypothesis suggested itself: He was trying earnestly to be active and masculine against the tide of an overwhelming passivity.

The first interview was coming to an end. To get him to think about his past, the therapist said that next time we would talk about his early life. This had a purpose beyond the obvious one that the diagnosing therapist needs to know about early life. One does not hope to learn much because it would all be conscious. Nevertheless the information would provide some facts and, more important, some continuity. Exploring a patient's early life has more value for the patient than for the immediate diagnostic inquiry. It gets the patient to think about himself, to connect himself with his past. It seeks to determine whether he thinks of himself as a continuous person. This is an important diagnostic matter because the person who cannot remember his childhood lacks a continuous self representation.

He came to the next session having thought about himself, as the therapist expected. It is not always desirable to assign homework. In this instance, however, the therapist made use of his consciously obedient behavior and, at the same time, left room for him to counteract unconsciously. There was a risk. It is not desirable to establish a pattern of telling the patient what to do. The therapist took that risk because of the hypothesis about the conformity-oppositional conflict. It appeared that when he tried to conform, the unconscious tendency to oppose would become more prominent as his conscious efforts encountered his unconscious oppositionalism.

It was not easy for the patient to speak spontaneously for any length of time. He tried. He began with his school years, logically enough. This met his need to be conforming, yet at the same time intellectual, organized, and unlikely to get into affect-laden areas. Despite his effort his account of his school years was sparse. He did well enough in school. There were no outstanding events.

The therapist tried to lead him into some of the more affect-laden areas by asking whether he remembered starting school. He remained factual. He started kindergarten at age five. He acknowledged with shame that he had been fearful and that it had taken him a long time to get into activities. This alerted the therapist to look for evidence of separation anxiety but was not enough for the therapist to draw a firm conclusion. What one can know is that he regarded feeling fearful as undesirable and unmanly.

Now the therapist is faced with the dilemma of whether to continue with the question-and-answer format. While this patient would have welcomed it, it sets a tone that precludes the patient's working participation. The diagnosing therapist who will go on with treatment, if that is decided, is in the difficult position of needing diagnostic information but must not obtain it in a way that will jeopardize the future treatment process. Here the therapist decided to risk one more prod for the sake of a firmer diagnosis, after weighing the possibility that to continue to prod this patient would be undesirable.

At this point summarizing what is known about the patient and what the therapist is still in the dark about might be useful.

Known

1. He is firmly in the secondary process. However, he lacks the flexibility to regress in the service of the ego. Is there anxiety lest the regression would not be reversible?
2. His gender identity was established but remained shaky. Although he knew he was male, he had considerable anxiety about losing his masculinity. Was this because he had not succeeded in disidentifying from the maternal object?
3. His principal defense mechanisms are isolation, repression, reaction-formation.
4. His object relations pattern is to be obedient and passive. Is this for the purpose of pleasing the external object or the structure (superego)?

Unknown

1. Whether the psychosexual level is anal or phallic?
2. Whether he is at an arrested or a regressed position?
3. What is his sexual development, both physically and psychologically? When did he reach puberty? How was he prepared for it? What did he know about gender differences? Who was his informant? What was the emotional climate in which he received his information?

In this case, the diagnostic process had to end without full information. Guardianship of future treatment dictates that the therapist not continue with questions and answers. A psychotherapist probably could do this productively by making the patient aware that he did not answer fully and alerting him to the conflict that determines that form of behavior. However, this appeared to be an analyzable case. Therefore one would not want to proceed in a way that would preclude analysis. Borderline features did not emerge, despite some indication of separation anxiety. He appeared to have reached the phallic level, in which case the separation anxiety would resonate with castration anxiety. He is relatively separated, as noted by his dealing with the therapist as a separate, whole other person.

His defensive system appeared sound, with defense mechanisms well established. The primary process is perhaps too well bound. His object relations pattern appeared to be based in an anal struggle, with reaction-formation—oppositional tendencies concealed by an appearance of being pleasing. On the oedipal level, he wished to appear nonthreatening. His tendency toward passivity suggested that the approach to the oedipal conflict was made timidly, perhaps burdened by a fearful practicing subphase (G. Blanck 1966).

We present this case to illuminate the diagnostic process in some detail and to show its limitations if the same therapist is to perform the treatment. The therapist forgoes eliciting certain information if seeking it for its own sake would impair future treatment; in any event, one can never find the answers to all the diagnostic questions in a diagnostic study of this kind. If sufficient evidence to tilt the balance to one side or the other is elicited, one can proceed with treatment with some confidence that one is dealing with either a structured or an understructured personality. This enables the therapist to plan treatment accordingly.

A therapist who acts only as a diagnostician and is not going to continue treatment can be more intrusive and evoke more anxiety. The advantage of learning more, and more quickly, is outweighed by the continuity provided when the diagnosing therapist continues the treatment. The therapist learns somewhat less at the outset; needed information will emerge later.

Our second clinical illustration of the diagnostic process is of a patient with a borderline structure.

John was a thirty-two year old programmer who came for treatment because his wife was threatening to leave him. The trouble began when John and Jane, married eight years, had their first child. Jane became involved with the baby while John felt left out. Nevertheless they struggled along for two or three more years. At first they fought. Later John withdrew in silent anger and mild depression. The crisis came when Jane wanted another baby. John became enraged. Jane then wanted to terminate the marriage if he refused to comply. John felt alternately angry, despondent, depressed, and withdrawn. A friend suggested he see a therapist.

He was not spontaneous in telling his story. He waited for the therapist to begin, while the therapist waited for him to begin.

One notes the passivity, but cannot allow the silence to go on too long in the first meeting. Later, in the therapy, the therapist might not move in too quickly because it will be up to the patient to take on his therapeutic task. Here the therapist had to move in. It is not desirable to ask "How can I help you?" because that question contains a promise of help when in fact the therapist does not yet know if help is possible. A good intervention might be "I want to listen to what you have to tell me about yourself." This is better than "Tell me about your problem" or "Tell me what brings you here." The therapist wants to know the total person, not restrict the question to the problem or to the immediate presenting request. Therefore the intervention should be phrased in the broadest terms. The narrow features will emerge as the patient tells his story.

The person's behavior with the therapist in what has been called the *here and now* is most informative. It tells much about the nature and quality of the self and object relations. John was passive and wanted the therapist to do all, and perhaps to know all even before being told. Even this early in the evaluation, one may make a presumptive guess that the separation-individuation process was incomplete because John appeared to expect that the therapist was part of him, knew what was on his mind. This is most tentative so early in the process and must not be held too rigidly. One must explore further and look for evidence that will either confirm or refute each diagnostic hypothesis. John's response to "Tell me about yourself" was "I want you to keep her from leaving." This was oblique in relation to the therapist's request but very much to John's point.

One still does not leap to a conclusion. A well-structured man also would not want his wife to leave. But he probably would couch it differently. He might say, "I am here to find out what has gone wrong and what I can do to repair the rift." Obviously, that is a far more active stance.

The therapist then asked, "What do you think I can do?" His response was "I'd like you to see her." Thus he took himself out of the picture. In fact he was not in it. His adaptation was rigidly alloplastic. The world (his wife) needed to be changed, not he.

By now it appeared that pressing him would only result in his retreat into further passivity. The therapist has to get into a position that will appear less demanding. Now might be a good time to ask for history: "As long as you are here, tell me how all this came about." This defuses the situation. It does not challenge John on his wish to have the therapist "fix" his wife, to make her over to his liking. Such a challenge might propel him out the door. A request for history might provide information and, perhaps more important, might provide a clue that would give the therapist an opportunity to engage John in way that would not challenge his passivity. In listening to his history one looks for something that troubled John about himself rather than about his wife. At the very least it would forestall an impasse.

This also illustrates the advantages of a partly structured and partly unstructured diagnostic approach. If structured too tightly, the therapist loses the opportunity to observe the patient's characteristic object approach, the patterning of self and object relations. If structured too loosely, valuable time may be lost in the patient's wanderings. One may want free association later but that depends on the form of treatment decided on. At this point the therapist needs the secondary process insofar as the patient is able to engage in it. If the patient is not able to engage in secondary process, that reveals itself rather quickly and suggests a low level borderline problem or regression caused by excessive anxiety.

History taking is important because the therapist, expecting distortion, needs to know about the patient's life as the patient sees it. As we have already advocated, the value of the history lies in the fact that it gives the patient a task and a new view of himself and his past. It introduces him to the developmental approach in a way that does not instruct him in so many words that "your behavior is the product of your transactions between your self and object representations in the past."

As a patient thinks about himself, he acquires continuity. Some severely understructured patients do not have a continuous identity. That, too, would become apparent by this method. Presenting the patient with a task can be looked upon as placing a burden just a bit heavier than the patient can carry, or thinks he can carry—a test of whether the ego is elastic enough to be stretched. The measurement is delicate. Too little a burden infantalizes, while too great a burden discourages. Yet we have no instrument beyond the therapist's intuition to aid in measuring. Especially in this case, which appeared to be so rigidly unworkable, it was especially useful to test out the extent to which the patient could stretch when given the unchallenging task of telling his life story.

He described the quarrels with his wife and said that he had lost interest in sex. On questioning he acknowledged that he had never had much liking for intercourse. His preferred form of sex was fellatio. The therapist noted (silently) that this was probably a reversal of an unconscious wish to be given the breast. Jane no longer wished to continue satisfying him in that way. She insisted on intercourse in order to become pregnant. John refused and reluctantly acknowledged to the therapist that he became impotent in the face of her demand.

John was an only child of a lonely mother. His father, although living at home, was involved with his business and traveled a great deal. Mother was John's sole companion—or we can put it the other way around: he was called on to be her companion.

It is not possible to elicit information about early development from an adult patient because those events have been subjected to normal amnesia. (With a child, the parent can provide information, but distortion and defensiveness need to be taken into account there.) With adults, one can detect behavioral patterns emanating from early life because the patterning of self and object relations, established then, are used in relationships with secondary objects. That is why we use the here and now. It is also useful in the treatment process because the patient interacts with the therapist in accordance with those patterns and indeed, in many cases, alteration of maladaptive and inflexible patterns is at the core of treatment.

John had a most difficult time in his first year of college. He had not been away from home before that. Although miserably unhappy he was a good scholar. Absorption in study helped him fight his depression and loneliness. Eventually he met an equally lonely young woman and they clung together. That had the superficial appearance of repeating union with his mother, but that would be an oversimplification that overlooks the fact that a nineteen-year-old college student has developed beyond the level of a toddler. We repeat: Organization does not cease when there is an affront to development but continues to become more complex, incorporating the consequence of the affront in its onward march.

John and Jane married at the earliest possible moment. It had the external appearance of a perfect match because each had the same needs. But precisely because of that, the one could not satisfy the other. It resembles, but is not the same as, two toddlers who cannot give one to the other because both are at the same state of need.

But the real problem arose when a baby came. Predictably, and to a large extent appropriately, Jane became involved with the baby. It was then that John became angry, despondent, depressed and withdrawn. He also had headaches and digestive upsets. They quarreled over trifles, neither one knowing what the real issue was. The crisis came when Jane wanted another baby. When John refused, she threatened to end the marriage. It was because of this that John sought help. By this time he was a presentable but very sad and withdrawn man of thirty-two.

Now let us begin to weigh some features in this case and compare them with the ideally structured personality. One need not use every feature of structuralization. Indeed, that would hardly be possible. The therapist selects the features that are revealed in the diagnostic evaluation and places each on one side or the other of our imaginary balance scale. The scale will tilt to the understructured or to the structured side, depending on which "contains" the heavier weight. This helps the diagnosing therapist arrive at a decision about whether the patient is borderline or neurotic and thereby decide on the treatment of choice.

The following are the diagnostic criteria that emerged through examination of this case: The libidinal drive seeks connection with an object that John appeared to perceive as part of the self representation. We speculated that the aggressive thrust had been suppressed because he felt disapproved of when he used this thrust to power separation-individuation. Below we explore further the diagnostic criteria in this case.

Ego. John had completed college and could work at a high level job. This suggested both good endowment and that not all his ego functions were bound up in conflict. What conflict existed was not between the ego or superego and id but between the self and object representations—that is, the self representation is unable to wrest free of the object representations in the service of establishing autonomy and identity. There was organization, but capacity for reorganization appeared feeble and was probably dormant. It would be worthwhile to try to start it up in the treatment process. A few promising indications emerged in the diagnostic exploration—that John could be encouraged to work harder in the service of his own development and that his secondary process appeared relatively intact. However, his ability to tolerate frustration and his capacity to delay were not well developed. Regression was not in the service of the ego. He had poor capacity for self observation. Adaptation was largely alloplastic with little flexibility.

Object relations. There is insufficient differentiation between the self and object representations, making for a nonautonomous self representation. There is, however, a modicum of awareness of an object world. He appeared to have failed to reach self and object constancy. He uses a rigid preestablished pattern of self and object relations inflexibly in disregard of present reality. In other respects, however, reality testing is intact, a feature which distinguishes borderline conditions from psychosis.

He had not attained triadic object relations as indicated by his inability to assume the role of father. Instead, he is a rival to his baby. Although that has the flavor of oedipal rivalry, it appeared as though he envied the infantile supplies the baby was receiving.

The functions of the object representations are not sufficiently transferred to the self representation. Therefore he felt he needed the ministrations of the object in almost the same degree as a baby does. This was far from absolute and, if treatment were to be undertaken, it may be one aspect that could be addressed in terms of making him aware of more advanced capacities than he believed he possessed.

Defense. John's anxiety is on the level of separation anxiety rather than signal anxiety. The major defenses are regression, projection, and reversal. There was evidence of splitting of the object representations into all good and all bad. His wife was a good object who threatened to become a bad object by leaving. This also demonstrates the use of reversal. The therapist speculated that his disapproved of self-image derived from identification with the disapproving object during the separation-individuation thrust. Now his wife threatened to be "bad" in the same way, that is, to separate.

Affects. The superficial affect was flat, with an undercurrent of rage that John handled by withdrawal. Moods fluctuated somewhat, but were mainly on the depressive side.

The "weights" on the balance scale tilted the fulcrum very much to the understructured side, indicating that psychotherapy rather than psychoanalysis is the treatment of choice. There are hopeful prognostic signs if he could be helped over the initial hurdle of wanting his wife changed and be moved to wanting treatment for himself. Optimally, he should attend therapy sessions three times per week, but there are resistances to be overcome before he could be expected to accept that. The principal difficulty is that he projects the problem onto his wife.

Treatment. In beginning treatment the best approach would be through John's affective state. He is depressed and might respond to the therapist's desire to help him feel better. But that could not be the first move. One needs to buy time. Therefore one might say, "I think it might be better to postpone seeing your wife until I know you better." If he were to accept that, an alliance would develop out of his object need. Then one could approach the depression, which appeared to be caused by a fear of object loss and a negative, "bad" self representation because of disapproval of the separation thrust, now pervading the self representation.

The therapist must seek out cautiously whether some of the burden of therapy could be turned over to John. The most likely immediate outcome would not be compliance but rage that the therapist did not gratify him by taking over his functions. The rage would not be overt; it would first manifest itself by withdrawal. It will be no easy task to elicit it openly because John's object need is so great that he would find it hard to risk fantasized destruction of the object. It might take a long time for him to begin to believe that the therapist will be there for him despite his rage. If this were to succeed, however, his depression would lift.

In John's early development, it appeared that he had no choice about employment of the aggressive drive in the service of separation because his mother needed him to remain tied to her. Object need takes precedence over autonomous striving. By not taking over his functions in therapy and not acting as though he and therapist are merged, the therapist elicited his anger. But in so doing he was enabled to proceed to a more autonomous state.

We have said that termination of the treatment of an understructured personality can take place when the self representation becomes relatively independent of the object representations (Blanck and Blanck 1988). In the most favorable cases, structure builds to the point where the ego can tolerate conflict, first intrasystemic and, in the most favorable outcome, intersystemic as well.

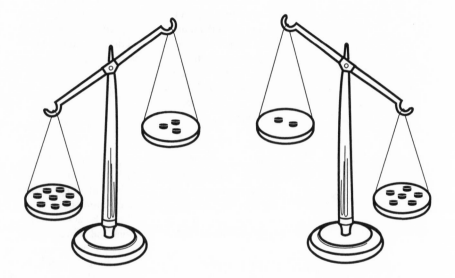

	Differentiation	*Ego Functions*
Early Life	At the beginning of extrauterine life neonate and mother are separated physically but not yet psychologically. During the early part of the first year the boundary between the individual and the mothering person is blurred. Ego functions such as motility, comprehension, memory organization, and the like promote boundary formation.	An undifferentiated matrix exists at birth with potential for unfolding ego functions. These include memory, perception, motility, anticipation, object comprehension, auditory capacity, and the latent ability to speak, among others.
Rapprochement	At approximately eighteen months of age distinctions between self and other have begun to be made. The formerly fleeting images become stabilized. Now they are referred to as mental representations.	The practicing subphase, which precedes rapprochement, provides for vast expansion of ego functions because of locomotion and attainment of the upright position, a new perspective from which the child views the world. Reality brings about rapprochement when the child realizes that she is very small in a large world.
Psychological Birth	The self representation had been differentiated from the object representation.Ego boundaries are clearly established.	By the time of psychological birth the child has a full repertory of ego functions—conflict-free, adaptive, and creative.

of Development

Affects	*Identity*	*Soothing*
Affects are total. That which brings comfort is experienced as good; that which is frustrating is projected outward.	The neonate has no identity but is involved in a dual unity with the mothering person.	Subject to organismic distress, the neonate is incapable of self-soothing. However, thumb sucking is known to begin in utero.
With recognition of external objects who bring gratification or frustration, objects are cathected with "good" and "bad" affects.	The process of establishing a distinct identity has gone forward. This includes attainment of gender identity.	The object's soothing function begins to be internalized to become part of the object representation.
Not only is there a wide spectrum of affects, but also, aided by verbalization, the affects are discriminated and named.	There is relatively clear identity with differentiated and constant self and object representations and evenly distributed positive cathexis of the two sets of representations.	Soothing has been transferred from the object representation to the self representation. The child can self-soothe.

	Transference	*Frustration Tolerance*
Early Life	The infant is at one with the object; the concept of transference is not applicable.	Relief from distress must be instantaneous because fear of annihilation is dominant. Tolerance for some frustration begins gradually if frustration has been experienced in tolerable doses and if predictable gratification follows.
Rapprochement	The object relations level that later develops into the capacity to engage in transference has not yet been reached. The representational world is still being formed. Without internal representations the child is still vulnerable to object loss. Arrest here results in inability to engage in true transference.	Frustration tolerance has been increasing gradually, but the toddler cannot yet tolerate the ambitendency that is part of the rapprochement crisis. Therefore there are affect storms.
Psychological Birth	Self and object constancy are attained. Under the duress of need, such as in the therapeutic situation, present may be confused with the past, but the transfer that does take place is of feelings, attitudes, and behavior that originate toward separate, whole, other persons, now displaced upon the analyst.	Now sufficiently positive cathexis of both the object representation and the differentiated self representation exists. Frustration and disappointment remain within the overall affective climate and are better tolerated than previously.

# of Development

Defense

Defense is a function of
the ego. Since the ego is
not yet developed in the
neonate, only the primi-
tive form of defense is
possible—turning away
from unpleasant stimuli,
projecting unpleasant sensations outward.

Splitting

At first the child has no
object world. As soon as a
world outside the mother-
infant unity exists, it is
experienced in totalities—
all good when it pleases,
all bad when it frustrates.

Signal anxiety is not yet
attained. Anxiety about
object loss can reach overwhelming proportions.
Since the object is experienced in some degree as
part of the self, defense is
designed for object retention, and somewhat later
for retention of the
object's love.

Splitting persists well into
the second year of life.

The neurotic person
defends more competent-
ly. Anxiety is now largely
intersystemic—conflict is
between agencies of the
psyche. Signal anxiety is
operative. There is no
longer fear of object loss
or loss of the object's love
but that the superego will
be displeased and will
punish.

The formerly good and
bad perceptions of the
object have been fused
into representations of a
single whole other person.

	Body and Mind	*Object World*
Early Life	In the beginning of extrauterine life self and other and psyche and soma are not differentiated. The infant lives literally in the body. Inside is not distinguished from outside. Responses to stimuli, whether from inside or outside, are total.	No object world exists at first. The level of object relations is that of a dual unity without a boundary between self and other.
Rapprochement	At this midway point in the process of differentiation considerable psychic development has taken place, especially beginnings of the inner world. The child begins to "live" more in the mind than previously.	The level of object relations is largely that of use of the object for gratification of need.
Psychological Birth	The likelihood of somatization is less because psyche and soma are relatively differentiated. The bodily self, however, remains an important part of the self representation.	Stable and constant self and object representations now exist. The object is valued regardless of the state of need.

Tension Discharge

The need to discharge tension is immediate at first. In a short time, with experience that relief arrives, the infant begins to develop a capacity to wait.

Triadic Object Relations

At first only the dual unity of self merged with the object exists.

Interaction

With no boundary between self and other, the neonate cannot engage in interaction.

Frustration tolerance has begun to build but is far from complete or effective.

Now the object world has expanded considerably. There is no longer only the dyad. Especially where two parents have been present, object relations has become triadic and the toddler establishes a new relationship with the father, no longer as an alternative need gratifier but as a person in addition to self and mother.

Interaction is between the self-image and the not yet clearly differentiated other person, who is still experienced in some degree as part of the self.

The child has a competent ego that can mediate between need and appropriateness of discharge and can decide the form that discharge will take. Because of a well-developed sense of time, postponement is possible. The ego can even decide in some situations to dispense with gratification altogether.

Triadic object relations include erotic interest to form the Oedipus Complex.

Interaction is intrapsychic, between the self representation and the object representations.

	Levels of Anxiety	*Representational World*
Early Life	Anxiety at first is at the level of fear of annihilation. This is an adaptive mechanism designed to ensure survival. Obviously, this is entirely dependent upon the cry of distress being heard by another person.	There is no representational world for the neonate. Mental representations are to be built from experience.
Rapprochement	As differentiation proceeds and the object is experienced as no longer part of the self but still necessary for survival, the level of anxiety shifts to fear of loss of the object. Somewhat later the quality of anxiety changes to fear of loss of love of the object.	Considerable images of self and other have accumulated, with ever increasing degrees of differentiation.
Psychological Birth	Now anxiety is experienced as a signal. The level of anxiety becomes fear of the superego.	Stable self and object representations that approach reality are the hallmarks of psychological birth.

of Development

Thought Processes

At first, thought is in the primary process.

The shift toward secondary process thought has begun.

Secondary process thought dominates in the waking state.

14

▼

Differences Between Psychoanalysis and Psychotherapy

Two interrelated factors influence whether the treatment of choice is psychoanalysis or psychotherapy: the structure of the personality and the goal of treatment.

In dealing with neurotic structure, psychoanalysis is clearly the treatment of choice; with borderline and narcissistic structures, psychotherapy is indicated. After structure-building psychotherapy, some borderline patients can become analyzable; we shall discuss that further. In those instances the differences between the two forms of therapy tend to blur. There is no consensus on these issues. Some draw a sharp line between psychoanalysis and psychotherapy, some regard the understructured personalities analyzable with modifications in technique, and some would analyze all patients regardless of structure.

If one considers *psychotherapy* the generic term under which psychoanalysis and other forms of therapy are subsumed, then of course psychoanalysis is a form of psychotherapy. That is academic, however, because common usage has it that one form of treatment is *psychotherapy*, another *psychoanalysis*.

It is commonly believed that psychoanalysis is the superior form of treatment. Freud regarded analysis as pure gold in danger of being alloyed by the copper of suggestion. Glover, too, believed that all that is not psychoanalysis is nothing more than suggestion. But that was another era. Matters are more complex today, made so by the accretion of theoretical knowledge about how the ego develops.

In the early part of the twentieth century, many patients suffered as a result of the fallacy of ranking psychoanalysis above psychotherapy. "Not analyzable" was tantamount to a sentence of a lifetime of untreatable psychopathology. Some understructured patients were analyzed nevertheless, with mixed results; some were treated without the advantage of a disciplined approach to the psychotherapy of the borderline states because none existed yet; others were dismissed as untreatable. It was not until the 1950s that the structure and treatment of the borderline and narcissistic conditions received serious consideration. In the 1960s Kernberg began to offer a series of papers that presented a systematic approach to those pathologies (see chapter 9).

Psychotherapy that is not psychoanalytically informed includes suppression in addition to suggestion in the belief that some patients are better served if material is kept out of awareness. In psychoanalytic psychotherapy suppression is supplanted by supportive (ego-building) techniques that seek to strengthen defenses. Patients whose defenses are weak cannot tolerate exposure of unconscious conflicts and fantasies. While suppression attempts to keep them under cover, ego building strengthens the ego's defensive function.

Supportive psychotherapy still has a place in psychoanalytically informed thought (Wallerstein 1989), now influenced and modified by ego psychological considerations. The belief commonly held by lay persons and nonpsychoanalytic psychotherapists is that support consists of doing for, advising, praising, and encouraging. Such devices are not helpful because they fail to promote ego autonomy. We refer to them as the *good neighbor policy* because they consist of nothing more than what a good neighbor, relative, clergyman, or other nontrained person of good will might do for another.

Support of defense means strengthening the ego in the interest of ego autonomy, which is qualitatively different from unending reliance on another person's good will. Good will is comforting but rarely, and certainly not reliably, can good will be internalized to become part of the individual's self-esteem and defensive system. *Ego autonomy*, on the other hand, defined as relative independence of the ego from the drives and of the self representation from the object representations, frees the individual from dependence.

On the contemporary scene Kernberg and others would distinguish supportive psychotherapy from expressive. Expressive psychotherapy is applied in instances where psychotherapy short of psychoanalysis is deemed to be the treatment of choice. The choice is usually made on the basis of expediency. It seems obvious to us, although some might disagree, that a person capable of engaging in expressive psychotherapy is analyzable, especially if one is guided by the criteria of the "widening scope" philosophy (Stone 1954), which implies that some persons with developmental failures are nevertheless capable of enduring conflict.

Expediency usually means that the patient is unable to attend a full-fledged analysis because of external factors such as time, geographic distance, and money. One may question whether psychoanalysis should be compromised in that way, especially by the less experienced analyst. Undoubtedly, in the hands of a well-trained and experienced psychoanalyst, expressive psychotherapy is a challenging art.

What makes psychotherapy more difficult than psychoanalysis? Primarily it is the structure of the patient, and secondarily it is the state of the art. The psychoanalytic patient has reached a degree of structuralization that brings several built-in, reliable factors to the therapeutic endeavor. Such a patient has experienced a more favorable first round of development and, although there may be developmental lags, the structure is basically sound. Self and object constancy, and distinct identity exist; the core conflict is oedipal; the capacities to endure conflict, to tolerate the frustration of abstinence, to regress in the service of the ego, and to engage in true transference are relatively intact.

Transposed to the everyday working analysis, this means that the psychoanalytic patient regards the analyst as a separate, whole, other person, can abide by most of the rules of psychoanalysis with minimal or no acting out, can engage in a therapeutic alliance, and can maintain an observing as well as an experiencing ego. The analytic work is directed primarily toward uncovering and resolving major conflicts.

The psychotherapy patient is in a different state. Once again defining the borderline and narcissistic conditions as caused by failure to have completed the separation-individuation process and to have attained psychological birth, the matter becomes one of degree. The major diagnostic difficulty in psychotherapy is attributable to the fact that no two borderline or narcissistic patients present the same degree of developmental failure. The pathology varies far more widely from one patient to another than in neurosis. Patient A may be lost in the primary process, in fantasied merger with the maternal object, lacking identity, barely structured, unable to transfer from past to present, unable to experience the therapist as a separate, whole, other person. Patient B may be capable of enduring conflict, may present many neurotic features, and can almost be analyzed as a neurotic were it not that regression is too rapid and not easily reversible when there is anxiety. Patient C may fall somewhere in between these two extremes. Patient D may be involved in a narcissistic union with a fantasied part of the self representation and thereby unable to form a transference of any sort. The matter is made even more difficult because these states are usually not static. Patient A may sometimes be in an advanced position that appears more stable than it is. Patient B may regress in a state of anxiety because the defensive system is weak. Patient C may appear sometimes more regressed, sometimes more advanced. Patient D may at times appear more object related than truly obtains, because narcissistic patients who are intelligent have learned to simulate object relatedness as a method for getting along with other people. This says that these cases are difficult to diagnose as well as to treat.

As for the state of the art, despite serious attempts at systematization, the methods of psychotherapy are not as clearly established and universally accepted as those of psychoanalysis. In psychoanalysis the patient attends four or five times per week, lies on the couch, voices all thoughts, observes as well as experiences, regresses in the service of the psychoanalytic work and recovers after the session, accepts the task not only of providing the material but also of working on it with the help of the analyst, engages not only in transference but sometimes forms a transference neurosis—that is, an artificial neurosis within the psychoanalytic situation.

On the analyst's side of the endeavor, rules were established by Freud (1912a, 1912b), Glover (1955), and Fenichel (1941), among others. Although not always adhered to, they remain guides. "Do not deflect associations" is probably the most universally accepted rule. Interpretation of resistance before content, although no longer universally agreed on, is still a reliable guide. Interpretation of transference is not much in dispute, although the timing of such interpretation is at issue in some quarters (Gill 1984).

Some psychoanalysts object to "rules," probably because they feel it suggests superego constraints. That objection can be satisfied by substituting the word *moves* to conform with Freud's analogy of the psychoanalytic process with the opening gambit and end point in a chess game. Far more important than whether they are rules or moves is the influence of modern theory, that is, of ego psychology, on the so-called classical maneuvers that were established in the early part of the twentieth century.

Before ego psychology it was thought that the goal of psychoanalysis was to make the unconscious conscious, that is, to expose the content of the id in its conflict with ego and superego. The reliable ego of the psychoanalytic patient, once confronted with the heretofore repressed infantile material, would reprocess it in adult terms and thus absorb it into the adult structure. Much has changed about the nature of the therapeutic action of psychoanalysis. Perhaps the greatest area of controversy is whether the psychoanalytic process provides a new experience. The strict classicist remains as opposed to this today as when Alexander and French (1946) introduced the idea of a *corrective emotional experience*. They were forced out of institutionalized psychoanalysis for their apostasy. This is not to say we agree with them. They realized there is something "corrective" in the therapeutic experience, but they did not have the tools of modern ego psychology to discipline their endeavors. They were led, therefore, to propose artificial devices, such as manipulation of the transference, to provide correction. We do not advocate artificial arrangements of any sort because, aside from being ineffective, we believe that a sine qua non of the therapeutic endeavor is that the analyst or therapist present absolute integrity. That is probably the newest part of the experience for many patients who felt deceived by significant persons in their lives. Manipulation tends to be false and to undercut the therapist's credibility. Also, since our objective is internal change, this can only be brought about by therapeutic address to the structure.

The strictest view on the issue of whether the therapeutic experience provides newness still has it that the person and personality of the analyst have no bearing on the analytic process; the analyst is a blank slate. If that is so, it is a requirement no human being can meet. We doubt that a patient can be treated by an analyzing machine. Patients need the human qualities that a disciplined professional can bring to the therapeutic endeavor. The question is how the analyst can perform that task in a truly disciplined manner that serves the patient. The blank slate philosophy is sometimes confused with neutrality. *Neutrality* is defined as remaining equidistant from id, ego, and superego.

Some are loathe to acknowledge that there is newness in the therapeutic experience. To us it is obvious that the newness is intrinsic. We refer only to the very arrangements of the analytic situation. The analyst keeps appointments reliably and on time, is there solely in the interest of the patient, listens without judgment. These are new experiences for most, perhaps all, patients. At issue is not whether they are new, but whether they have a therapeutic effect. We would answer in the negative. The arrangements set the stage for therapeutic action but are not an intrinsic part of the action.

We are indebted to Loewald (1960) for conceptualizing the therapeutic action of psychoanalysis. To the well-known effect of interpretation of conflict within the transference and transference neurosis, he adds the object relations dimension of a "therapeutic differential" that has an impact late in the treatment. He notes that at some point the patient realizes and has to deal with the often painful recognition that there is a difference between the analyst and the primary object. This transcends the better-known interpretation of transference. Loewald clarifies that the patient has to struggle to accept and process this difference. The "differential" forces the patient to recognize that the analyst does not fit the established pattern or program of object relations. This spells out Loewald's concept and adds that the objective is not only to promote recognition of difference but to render the object relations pattern more flexible. We are describing a process that takes place in the ego of the patient and is quite different from deliberate *provision* of a new experience. Here, not much that is new is provided except the already described reliability. What the analyst does provide (not directly to the patient), in addition to reliability and integrity, is knowledge about ego psychological object relations theory. The analyst uses the theory to guide the patient's move in the direction of reorganizing the formerly rigid pattern of object relations.

We shall deal with one more aspect of psychoanalysis before going on to the more complex matter of modern psychotherapy. Until 1967, when Greenson set out to add a two-volume text to the literature on the technique of psychoanalysis in order to introduce the ego psychological point of view, there had not been a text since Menninger (1958). Unfortunately, Greenson died before he could complete the second volume. Thus we lack a unified text on contemporary technique, although many papers are scattered throughout the literature that deal with one aspect or another, along with one of two new texts that lack the ego psychological perspective. The consequence is that the impact of ego psychology on psychoanalytic technique has not yet been systematized. We shall not attempt that here because it warrants a text in itself. It is appropriate, however, to mention a few ego psychological concepts that alter the so-called classical view of psychoanalytic procedure.

The most traditional view of the roles of analyst and analysand is that the analysand is the provider of material while the analyst is the interpreter. Of course it is not so simple. The analyst has adjunctive tasks, principally that of noting resistance in order to help the analysand keep the associations flowing. Ego psychology dictates that activity be promoted by exercise of function. This stance dictates recasting the roles of analyst and analysand. The traditional activity of the analyst remains: to listen from a stance of neutrality with evenly suspended attention, to encourage the flow of associations, to note when resistance constitutes an impediment, to aid in clarification for the purposes of enabling the analysand to bring material from the unconscious to the preconscious—that is, to bring it into an interpretable position.

Now the analyst is also required to encourage exercise of function, to forgo using her or his ego in favor of allowing the analysand to perform certain reorganizing exercises. For example, after free association has developed a theme, the analysand might be asked to consider the meaning of what has been said, or at least to describe the theme. Resistant analysands are inclined to protest that they are obeying the rule of free association and to object to being held to account. This is a form of abuse of free association. It takes a small degree of persistence on the part of the analyst to convey an attitude that assumes that such responsibility can be taken. This describes that the analysand is required to fulfill all the traditional tasks of free association and, in addition, to work actively in the treatment to the extent that he or she is able. Ability increases as the ego exercises its functions.

To illustrate the changes in technique wrought by ego psychology, we use Sharpe's (1950) description of analysis of obsessional neurosis. She believes the analyst is helpless in the face of the cyclic nature of obsessive thinking and can only sit by while it wears itself out. Eventually, of course, it enters the transference, but even there Sharpe has no choice but to wait it out. This is because such patients are totally absorbed in an intrapsychic "debate" between ego and superego, leaving no avenue for the analyst to enter. The ego psychological approach asks the analysand's observing ego to scan what has been said. Looking back over one's associations for the purpose of understanding them, if presented to the analysand as a task, becomes rote after awhile. Then the obsessive patient can note that some associations go round and round, and can begin to appreciate that this is a symptom of the neurosis rather than true free association that would lead to insight.

Clinical examples of the way in which the patient begins to take responsibility for the treatment or, to put it differently, begins to exercise more autonomy is found in the questions that the patient asks. No longer "What do you think?" but questions addressed to himself or herself. "What am I getting at?" "What am I talking about?" "Why have I made that slip?" "Where am I heading?" "What is the identity of that figure in my dream?" "Why have I forgotten yesterday's session?" Analysands have many latent ego functions that can be encouraged. If the analyst does not preempt them, there is much to be gained. Not only do functions become activated, but belief in the analyst's omniscience diminishes as the analysand begins to appreciate his or her own functional capacities.

Now to psychotherapy. Random psychotherapy has been conducted in some form over the ages. Before the mid-twentieth century, psychotherapy was practiced where the individual analyst realized that psychoanalysis was not appropriate. Yet the "unanalyzable" patients were always with us—the psychotic and borderline patients who could not respond to the analytic method. Before the mid-twentieth century, analysts were forced to invent their own techniques, which ranged from "wild analysis" to disciplined and creative interventions. We have recorded the history of the gropings that have led to the establishment of guidelines for the practice of psychotherapy. In its more primitive days it was acceptable to do "anything that works." It took a long time for a more disciplined approach to the problem to begin to be worked out. In the psychoanalytic community, this was effected through a series of symposia that proceeded progressively over a period of years. Slowly, psychoanalysts have worked at evolving a systematic psychotherapy. Three points of view are now extant. One is that there is no difference between the two modalities and that properly conducted psychoanalysis can benefit all diagnostic entities. A second position, to which we have adhered in the past, is that there is a sharp difference between the two modalities. A third view is that of the "widening scope of indications for psychoanalysis" (Stone 1954), which holds that some pathologies short of neurosis proper can be treated psychoanalytically.

Our position is a first cousin to the "widening scope." We find that many patients who begin treatment with inadequate structure can be helped by making structure building the very heart of the psychotherapeutic endeavor. Often such patients become gradually more and more analyzable as structure accrues. The difference between this and our former position is that we drew a sharper line between psychotherapy and psychoanalysis, arguing that psychoanalysis can begin only after psychotherapy has had an effect. (See the case of Mr. Baker [Blanck and Blanck 1974]). Now we see the process as the one modality blending into the other more gradually and less sharply demarcated. That is especially applicable in those cases where there is a borderline structure with some neurotic conflict. The technical problem in those cases is that the ego is not capable of dealing with the conflict and has to be strengthened before true analytic work can begin.

A female patient was the oldest of three children in a chaotic household. Her two brothers were excessively seductive toward her, as was the father toward his only daughter. Both parents were moderately alcoholic, and the mother was probably addicted to barbiturates as well. The mother was out of the picture so far as maintaining discipline was concerned. The brothers used the patient for sexual exploration and exhibited themselves freely. She had little opportunity for smooth progress through the separation-individuation process even before her brothers were born because of the mother's unreliability as a developmentally attuned partner.

In treatment, which began as psychotherapy, there were oedipal dreams. The therapist did not avoid them but tested whether the patient could endure interpretation of conflict and ceased when the responses showed this was not yet tolerable. Each such session resulted in moderately severe regression, which had to be repaired before treatment could move forward. (This illustrates the advantage of daily sessions.) After approximately two years, while structure building occupied center stage in treatment, the patient became able to tolerate interpretations of triadic object relations. Only after she became thoroughly convinced of the therapeutic differential—that is, of the availability of the (female) analyst despite rivalry and matricidal wishes in the transference—could the oedipal conflict be tolerated as a step toward its resolution. The psychotherapy moved gradually to a more psychoanalytic stance.

This case also shows that the object relations dimension is of prime importance in analysis of conflict as well as in the promotion of development. One factor that prevented the patient from dealing with the oedipal conflict was the conviction that there would be object loss. In this case, as in perhaps all cases, there needs to be absolute certainty that the transference object, unlike the real object, will not be offended by the hostile wishes. Also illustrated is the corrective experience in the treatment, but applied with precision and as part of the therapeutic posture rather than as a deliberate *provision* of something new. The oedipal child's death wishes toward the parent of the same sex are fleeting, but at their height, there is fear of the parent's retaliation. The "newness" in the therapy is that we do not treat our patients with counterhostility.

Those who hew to the sharpest lines of demarcation distinguish not only between psychoanalysis and psychotherapy but make distinctions within psychotherapy, between the supportive and expressive forms. In our present view the lines are not quite so sharp for reasons already given, principally that structure builds before our very eyes and the patient can sometimes be ready for expressive procedure, where only yesterday supportive measures were in order. To maintain a sharp difference between those two forms would deprive the therapist of moving flexibly from one to the other as the material dictates. It is best not to be so boxed in that one fails to allow "expressive" procedure if one has already decided to be supportive only or, conversely, to fail to apply support if one is determined to employ expressive techniques. It can be argued that all therapy, including analysis, is supportive as well as expressive if one always keeps in mind that support involves support of the highest level of functioning. In that sense, the well-structured psychoanalytic patient needs less support than the arrested borderline patient, but support as a philosophy of honoring ego autonomy is inherent in the ego psychological approach in all modalities.

It is hardly possible to practice psychoanalytically oriented psychotherapy without psychoanalytic training. We advocate such training not because we value psychoanalysis over psychotherapy, but because there is no way to practice psychoanalytically informed psychotherapy without being psychoanalytically informed.

It was once believed that psychotherapy contaminates the transference and that, therefore, a patient whose ego, through psychotherapy, becomes competent to endure analysis should be transferred. That is rarely practiced any longer. It is a relic of the days when psychotherapy was undisciplined and, in the interest of promoting a "relationship," the psychotherapist tended to enter into an interpersonal exchange. Now the professional stance is maintained regardless of modality and, therefore, there is no danger of "contamination." The psychotherapist who is also a psychoanalyst can shift modalities and, in fact, there is much to be said for maintaining the existing transference rather than subjecting the patient to forming one with a new analyst. The needs of the structure, however, must always dictate the treatment. If the therapist is not competent to perform psychoanalysis when that is indicated, of course transfer is the only recourse.

Much is sometimes made of the frequency of attendance and the physical position of the patient, as though such external factors as whether the patient is lying down or sitting up defines whether treatment is psychotherapy or psychoanalysis. Fenichel (1941) commented that these are superficialities and that analysis can be conducted whether the patient is sitting or lying. We do not believe, however, that analysis can be conducted less frequently than three or four times per week. In practice, psychotherapy is often conducted as infrequently as once a week, but that does not dictate that it should be so. We have heard of psychotherapy on a less frequent schedule, every two weeks or even once a month, but these would be unusual and the circumstances would have to justify such infrequent contact. We can imagine that a patient who lacks capacity for further growth might need to be maintained on an infrequent schedule. Where long distances have to be traveled, psychoanalytic patients sometimes attend "double" sessions one day, stay in town overnight, then attend another such session the next day. This, too, is an expediency that bends the method. Whether such arrangements can be effective often depends on the talent, motivation, and resistances of the patient. Some use such unusual arrangements well; others allow the resistance to make use of them.

Freud conducted his analyses six days per week. When analysis came to the United States, the American five-day work week prevailed. Five days a week is still optimal; some make do with four or, as mentioned, even three. Something is lost with less frequency. Freud encountered resistance even on a six-day per week schedule, the so-called Sunday crust. We have to think that the greater the interval between sessions the harder the crust becomes because resistance (re-repression) has greater opportunity.

The purpose of frequent sessions in psychoanalysis is to keep the analysis moving. That means allowing a transference and transference neurosis to develop, remaining in touch with the daily life, dream life, fantasies, and free associations of the patient. Especially important to dream analysis is that the material of one session constitute the day residue of a dream reported in the next session.

Why the couch? Myths and even jokes abound. Freud said, with some levity we believe, that he did not like to have patients staring at him all day. This has been blown out of all proportion as though that is the sole reason for use of the couch. In fact, the reasons are more profound. The couch allows for regression and fantasy. Regression in the psychoanalysis of neurosis is always in the service of the ego and therefore desirable in order to arrive at material not readily available to the adult, well-structured patient who functions in the secondary process. Primary process can be approached in the psychoanalysis of neurosis without fear that the foothold in the secondary process will be lost. With many psychotherapy patients, one has to be more cautious. In addition to promoting free association, the couch facilitates fantasy production and development of transference and transference neurosis because the analyst is not seen.

Those are also reasons for being selective about whether to place an understructured patient on the couch. The criterion here is whether reality testing is intact enough to distinguish reality from fantasy, whether the patient has a foothold in secondary process thought, whether regression can be in the service of the ego. This states that psychotherapy can sometimes be conducted with the patient on the couch. Deep regression used to be feared more than today because it was not yet known that, with adequate attention to the functioning of the ego, one can guard against undesirable irreversible regression. As an example, we are clearer today about the difference between the gibberish of the primary process and true free association. The former is not to be confused with free association and is not to be encouraged. With such safeguards, the physical position of the patient is of secondary importance.

Frequency in psychotherapy is not as clear in terms of rationale. The phrase *usual and customary* has been inserted by insurance carriers. But one cannot formulate a treatment plan for the convenience of the insurance carriers. For them, usual and customary is one time a week, with some concession to twice a week. It is to the advantage of the insurers that the patient not have treatment at all! A more rational criterion is that which is based on object relations theory. We can almost present a rule of thumb here. If the objective of the therapy is to promote higher levels of object relations, then certainly twice and preferably even three or four times per week is indicated even if the treatment is deemed to be psychotherapy rather than analysis. It is relevant in this regard to distinguish between capacity for transference and search for replication of experience with the primary object (see chapter 17). The usual borderline or narcissistic patient is not capable of elaborating the kind of transference that we take for granted in the better-structured patient. More likely, he or she is seeking to reestablish the relationship with the primary object. We think a narcissistic element is present in all borderline cases and that the therapist is therefore likely to encounter a rather rigidly fixed object relations pattern with the real or fantasied object from the past. These are not easily altered, even in frequent contact, and are not likely to alter at all on a once-a-week basis.

Psychoanalytically informed therapy depends heavily on object relations, that is, on the capacity of the patient to form a transference. Most psychotherapy patients, if the therapy is based on diagnosis, are unable to form a true transference because they experience themselves in some degree part of the other person or, if narcissism predominates, part of a fantasy object. When such a patient becomes capable of transference, the therapy may be at an end because the objective of differentiation between self and object representations has been reached. Therapy ends where true transference can begin, that is, where self and object representations are more fully differentiated. This is theoretical. In practice, there are wide variations and, therefore, some psychotherapy patients form a transference while others do not. Or, the object relations levels can fluctuate progressively and regressively, so that sometimes there is transference and sometimes search for replication of object need.

Therapy based on object relations and on an object relationship with the therapist eliminates certain forms of therapy that are not psychoanalytically oriented. It can readily be seen that therapy conducted jointly with another person, a spouse for example, or in groups, evokes different forms of transferencelike phenomena and limits full address to object relations patterns. We distinguish between object relations and relationships. The former refers to internalized forms of relations between self and object representations, the latter refers to the relationship formed with another person. Thus there are therapies—marital counseling conducted in joint sessions, for example, that set out to repair or improve relationships, but have little or no impact on the intrasystemic patterning.

The traditional techniques of psychoanalysis are well established. To recapitulate, they are

1. The patient attends four or five times a week.
2. The patient lies on the couch.
3. Free association, designed to loosen cathexis to the secondary process, is encouraged to allow primary process material to come through.
4. Dreams are analyzed almost invariably. Those that are used as resistance are subjected to resistance interpretation.
5. Especially in the beginning, the analyst intervenes only for the purpose of keeping the associations flowing and building the transference.
6. The setting: couch, frequency of sessions, free association, and the analyst's nonintervention all encourage regression as well as transference.
7. It is hoped that transference will evolve into a transference neurosis, although this does not always occur.
8. Usually, the first interpretation is of a transference resistance.
9. Interpretation is the prime tool.
10. Time is allowed for working through of interpretation.
11. The oedipal conflict is uncovered, reworked within the transference, and worked through.
12. Termination is appropriate when the ego is relatively freed from involvement in intersystemic conflict.

In psychotherapy these techniques are applied where appropriate but many of them have to be modified, and some that are not applicable to psychoanalysis are added:

1. Ego building devices are used. In the main, these consist of enabling arrested development to proceed by promoting differentiation between self and object representations.
2. Preverbal experiences and affects are brought into the verbal realm.
3. Dreams are sometimes used for growth promotion rather than interpretation of conflict.
4. Greater attention has to be paid to the level of object relations.
5. Transferencelike behavior must be distinguished from search for replication of early object experience.

15

▼

On Beginning the Treatment

The title of this chapter is borrowed from Freud's paper on technique. Had he had the theoretical underpinning that is available to us now, he would perhaps have altered it to read, "How to Enable the Patient to Begin the Treatment." The patient's task, as we have shown, is far greater than Freud thought in 1912 when, in true post-Victorian practice, the authority of the analyst as interpreter overrode the role of the patient.

On the other hand, Freud was not as rigid as he would appear. He "opposed any mechanization of the technique" (1913, *S.E.* 12:134) because of "the extraordinary diversity of the psychical constellations" (*S.E.* 12:123). That leaves much room for elaboration on technique by later contributors.

One of these is Ella Freeman Sharpe, whom we designate as a "premature ego psychologist." Her writings on technique stress guardianship and promotion of the patient's autonomy. She says: "If we are anxious to 'cure' instead of to 'analyze' which leads to cure, we shall give to symptoms an emphasis of attention instead of directing it over a wider field of observation. We have to orient ourselves afresh to each individual. We have never seen his or her like before" (1950:24), and "Our purpose . . . is not to find out his complexes, but to help him to find out why he *feels* like this, why he *does* that" (1950:25). Sharpe also writes: "The person on the couch has his own problems, and it is not for us to envisage any result of the analysis in accordance with our particular sense of values and desirabilities (1950:25–26). She adds: "Only as we can bear the unknown, only as we are not 'hot for certainties' shall we be able to let the patient alone" (1950:26).

Ego psychology conceptualizes much about technique that Freud and Sharpe already knew, and adds to it. We have presented our idea about the analyst's role as catalyst of the patient's curative potential, which follows the theory of Hartmann and Mahler and Emde that many capacities rest with the individual who is our patient. Freud used the analogy of the French surgeon whose response to praise for his skill was, "I dressed his wounds, God cured him." We use our skill to propel the patient in the direction of healing rather than perpetuation of the compromise formation that keeps the patient at a standstill. That applies to the psychoanalytic situation. In psychotherapy, disciplined flexibility is even more necessary.

In both modalities the curative role is assigned to the patient. What, then, is the therapist's role? The therapist is the catalyst of cure. We use the term *catalyst* almost literally—a necessary presence without which action would not take place, and yet not an active participant in it, since the "action" takes place in the internalized structure. To be able to function as a catalyst means that the therapist must be free of his or her conscious and unconscious need to become involved in the action. This requires that the therapist be relatively free of bias and blind spots. Most therapists follow Freud's suggestion that they subject themselves to analysis in order to assure that they will function in the patient's best interest. Inevitably, because psychoanalysis is imperfect, some blind spots remain.

Each individual is unique and different. Professional knowledge and technical skill can alert the therapist to more generalized lines of inquiry. Only the patient can perform the task of identifying his or her unique pathway to the cause of the difficulty for which the patient seeks help. That attests to the immense value of free association in psychoanalysis. In psychotherapy, where the therapist does not often rely on free association, the therapist is directed to the developmental failures by the guidelines of normal development against which the deviations are measured.

Participation is not assured until the person truly becomes a patient. We may not assume that simply because a person comes to see a therapist that he or she is ready to enter treatment as a participant. Therefore, beginning the treatment consists of finding ways to help the individual become a patient—that is, enlisting his or her curiosity about the problem and ultimately enabling the individual to explore the unconscious processes.

To enlist the person's interest, the therapist listens in a special way. Freud designated this as listening with *evenly suspended attention*. It means that therapists suspend their own value judgments, sense the affective tone, and listen to the manifest content in order to hear the clues that would lead to the latent content. This manner of listening avoids our focusing on the familiar, lest that prevent us from hearing something new. This is a special kind of listening, not used in ordinary conversation. It has sometimes been referred to as the *third ear*. It requires training analogous to the ear training that a musician must cultivate.

This way of being heard is new to most patients because they have not been listened to in that way before. The therapist has to be available to the affect as well as the content, to the clues to unconscious material, to new information. It is not as simple as it may appear to hear all that is being conveyed. One must catch undertones as well as overtones, resonances, illogical gaps in the verbalizations, and the appropriateness of the affect.

This form of listening also keeps the therapist alert to material that suggests alteration in the initial diagnosis, which is always to be thought of as tentative and subject to change. As the therapy deepens, material usually emerges that was not patent in the diagnostic evaluation. Initial diagnostic hypotheses are to be modified, sometimes even discarded, as the material dictates. We have said that the very purpose of treatment is to alter the diagnosis for the better. Therefore we may expect changes that do not necessarily mean that the original diagnosis was incorrect but, rather, that the treatment is going well.

Also involved is *neutrality*, a concept sometimes misunderstood as a stance devoid of interest on the part of the therapist. The true meaning dictates that the analyst or therapist remain equidistant from id, ego, and superego in order to avoid imposing his or her standards and values and to be able to exercise evenly suspended attention.

Thus begins a *therapeutic alliance*, a situation in which, except for the necessary resistances, the patient is allied with the therapist in the common goal of defeating the tendency of the illness to repeat. This also alludes to the *benign climate*, a circumstance within which the therapist's reliability and interest in the patient becomes ever more evident to the patient. More specific techniques that apply to the entire treatment process are discussed in chapter 23.

Rapport is not discussed much these days. That is because the fashion has changed. The new word is *empathy*. Although not synonymous, one has overshadowed the other in popular usage. One does not need to extend oneself to "create" rapport; it comes about naturally if one is aware of the necessity for establishing a benign climate. As for empathy, we repeat that it is a personality characteristic of those who would practice psychoanalysis and psychotherapy; it is not a technique.

The therapist always remains in charge of the treatment and determines the most appropriate arrangements. Respect for the patient's autonomy dominates. We assume that an ambulatory patient is capable of some autonomous functioning, and we wish to build on that. This never means that we accept pseudo-independence, especially if it is acted upon, for that would abandon the person whose judgment has not yet developed optimally to engage in self-destructive decisions, and possibly action. There is a decisive difference between accepting autonomous functioning, insofar as that has developed, and mistaking willfulness for autonomy. Proposed action on the part of the patient must always be examined to determine whether it is in the patient's best interest.

When analyses were far shorter in duration than now, Freud instructed his patients not to make life decisions for the duration of the analysis. His reasons are still valid today, although we cannot impose the same strictures. He could ask a patient to postpone marriage, for example, when an analysis took six months. Now that it takes so many years, that would not be reasonable. However, the unconscious motivation in a patient's choice of a partner should always be examined. Similarly, such life decisions as a divorce or a career change should be examined, but any opportunity for patients to better themselves is not to be forfeited. The therapeutic attitude is different in the case of motherhood. We never advise a woman not to have a child, for this would violate her femininity and biological destiny. That does not mean that we fail to examine, as carefully as with other matters, the unconscious motivation and even the timeliness. Where a woman's "clock" is running out, it may be better to let nature take its course without interference, even if it should later turn out that motherhood was not the ideal choice for her. Just as we do not want to allow irreversible choices where they may be postponed, we do not make irreversible choices for the patient.

There is a "laundry list" of prohibitions that therapists sometimes impose at the beginning of treatment. We do not advocate presenting a long list of what not to do, some of which would not even occur to a given patient. Some therapists, for example, announce a total "policy" regarding fees, not only the amount but the method of payment, responsibility for missed sessions, vacations, illnesses, and the like. At the outset these regulations are likely to be overwhelming. It is far better to take up such matters as they arise in the course of treatment, within the context of the transferential state at the time. This has the added advantage of "tailoring" them to the patient's unique situation and therapeutic needs.

We have alluded to our extension of Mahler's discovery that the lion's share of adaptation rests with the infant to dictate the therapeutic technique: the lion's share of the therapeutic task rests with the patient. This does not relieve therapists of their part in the endeavor; it merely clarifies that we cannot do the patient's work. Therapists have their own work to do, however. The therapist's task may be compared to the problems facing those who sailed the seas before the advent of steam power. They depended on the movements of the seas and the wind. The therapist depends on the patient's motivation and must learn to put every ebb and flow to therapeutic advantage.

Patients fall roughly into three categories of "extractors." Some have only a minimal capacity to extract, and therefore the prognosis is guarded. Some are excellent extractors with whom the work goes relatively smoothly. Most patients fall somewhere in the middle range; they have a good enough capacity to extract, but it has not been sufficiently encouraged or exercised. Therefore one of the first tasks of therapy is to establish the roles of the two participants. This is not done in words. By the therapist not doing too much in the form of taking over the patient's functions, the patient will come to understand his or her own role. Doing too much for the patient exercises the therapist's ego functions and skills, while infantilizing the patient. The therapist remains always ready to be "extracted from."

Glover (1955) compartmentalized psychoanalytic treatment into "phases," as though there is a beginning, a middle, and a termination phase. That division may have some heuristic value but, on the whole, it is artificial. Although we are dealing here with how a therapist begins, we do not designate the beginning as a phase. We get into the thick of treatment as soon as the material lends itself to it; it is never the same for any two patients. The middle, if it can be said that there is one, blends with the beginning and the end. Each intervention is made with a dual objective in mind. The immediate objective, of course, is to move the case forward. The long-range objective is the ending of treatment. Therefore an intervention is to be worded with an eye to the effect on the future. Thus the beginning and end exist simultaneously.

Treatment begins. With very few exceptions we allow the patient to begin the session. This is not to be understood as dictating the entire course of the session. The patient begins because we need to know the patient's current situation before we impose our own ideas. We want to know what has transpired in real life between sessions, what were the dreams and fantasies, and whether there is continuity—that is, whether the beginning of a session is a continuation of the preceding session. Most often the beginning of a session is marked by normal resistance. The events of real life overshadow the therapeutic situation. Only after some time has gone by does the patient get to the material that the therapist will select to work with. Moving in too quickly would eliminate the resistance, not always honored as something we need to know as much about as the other matters. Although Anna Freud said as far back as 1936 that the functioning of the ego (defense) is as important as the material in the unconscious, sometimes therapeutic zeal forces the therapist to move in and override resistance. If we could state a rule it would be to listen first and then choose the material to be dealt with. We hesitate to make that a hard and fast rule because we wish to allow for the many exceptions that cannot be taught except as they are guided by the therapist's knowledge and skill. The most common form of initial resistance is recounting the events of the day, or some personal encounter outside of therapy. We enter these only in psychotherapy cases where we have made a considered decision to deal with these matters rather than with internal affairs. That would apply to low-level, understructured patients with poor prognosis for structure building. In the psychoanalysis of the structured patient, regression on the couch takes over after the initial resistance of detailing the events of the day, so the analyst needs to do nothing more than wait for free association to lead to primary process material.

The therapist makes a considered choice, too, when it comes to which material to "pick up on." There are four choices, all related to timing. The therapist must decide when to deal with the present and when with the past, when to deal with affairs outside the therapeutic situation and when within the transference. Transference is always present, but not always patent. Under optimal conditions the transference is chosen above all else because it is there that one captures the object relations pattern as well as the intersystemic conflict in vivo.

Designation of the problem is the simplest part of the task, often performed by the astute layperson in the form of confrontation. Confrontation from the outside is useless when we are dealing with an ego syntonic matter that troubles others, including the therapist, but not the patient. Rendering a problem dystonic is not simple, but made easier by developmental object relations theory. As the object relations pattern unfolds in the transference, the differences between assumptions arrived at in the past and the behavior of the therapist in the present highlight the problem for the patient.

Much that we have discussed raises the issue of whether the therapy is a new experience. We imply that the benign climate, taken alone, is always in itself a new experience because we devote the session to the patient's best interest without imposition of our own needs. Beyond that, the concept of alteration of the relationship between the self representation and the object representations requires that there be some sort of new experience. The nature of that experience is delicate. Reparenting is an undesirable and unworkable way of providing experience because structure, no matter how pathological, exists to bar the way. In other respects, "newness" of the therapeutic experience can no longer be denied.

Alexander and French (1946) introduced the term *corrective emotional experience*, thereby raising a furor in the psychoanalytic community. Then the differences between psychoanalysis and psychotherapy were not so clear, and the authors had neither the theoretical underpinnings nor the technical tools to support their position. Therefore they had to resort to devices such as manipulation of the frequency of the sessions in their attempt to attenuate the intensity of the transference. We do not advocate artificial devices, nor do we find need for them. They can only undermine the patient's confidence in the therapist's reliability. Alteration of the relationship between the two sets of representations provides a new experience that is largely intrapsychic, with the therapist as surrogate, first experienced as representing past objects, and later as a partially new set of object representations.

The following cases illustrate some of the technical challenges in beginning treatment:

A patient begins the first session with "I only want a little help." To focus on the manifest content would lead the therapist to ask why the limitation. The therapist needs to hear that it was anxiety that dictated "only a little." Then one would hear, "I want help" and respond to both the anxiety and the wish for help.

Another example is of a man who begins with "I blew it again. I got so angry with my wife, I bit her head off." In this way he presents the therapist with guilt and remorse. These must not be exacerbated. "When you blew it, you were unable to find another way of dealing with your anger. We have to find out why no other way occurred to you then." "I hated her then." The therapist asks, "Do you hate her always?" The man replies, "Of course not, I love her."

This alerts the therapist to search out whether and why splitting appears to be in the picture. First one has to help with discharge of affect; it may take some time before one can deal with the split object representations, and the therapist does not want him to "blow it" again while working on it. One does not yet know why the "all good" and "all bad" object representations have not fused into representations of single, whole, separate object, or whether this split in the object representations is regressive. If it is regressive, the task is to find what anxiety caused it. If it is a developmental failure, we have to rely on its coming into the transference where the therapist will see it firsthand. A therapist can do what no other person can because, having no stake in how the patient behaves in the therapeutic situation, one can keep countertransference at a minimum by devoting oneself to the needs of the patient. In this case, if it should turn out that the problem is a developmental rather than a regressive phenomenon, the patient will alternately project "all good" and "all bad" attributes on the therapist. The therapist accepts the projections without counterattack. After awhile the therapeutic differential will rescue the situation and fusion of the object representations will take place. As the object representations become both "good" and sometimes not so pleasing, the self representation will benefit as well. Because the sets of representations always operate in concert, "good" (positively cathected object representations) "rub off" on the self representation as well. In simple terms, the patient will feel better.

A woman begins treatment with "My husband says I'm hostile, and I've begun to think he's right." Treatment is doomed if the therapist accepts that at face value. What we are dealing with here is excessive compliance and low self-esteem. "Then that must leave you feeling awful," is an empathic response that does not accept the manifest statement, but connects with the affective state and the level of self-esteem. Treatment can go forward only if we do not accept her husband's "diagnosis," or her own. Much later the therapist will have the opportunity to explore why the wife had to agree with her husband's "diagnosis," but then that will be worked out on neutral ground.

Another patient begins: "I'm so terribly anxious all the time and feel so awful that I will do everything you tell me to do to feel better." If the patient means this literally identity formation is deficient, as evidenced by the absence of resistance, abandonment of autonomy, and the attribution of omniscience to the therapist. An appropriate response from the therapist would be: "Tell me about yourself. As you do, we will search for the reasons why you are so anxious." This draws the patient into the treatment first by joining him with "*we* will search" and then by lending oneself immediately to the painful affect. Note that the therapist makes no promise to "make" him feel better. "We will search," demonstrates that the therapist will work for him, *with* him, while eschewing any promise of a cure before knowing if a cure is possible.

We have offered some thoughts about beginning treatment that may differ from other ideas on the current scene. We believe that our ideas follow Freud's suggestions about beginning the treatment, which we have modified and brought into conformity with contemporary developmental theory. We have especially stressed that the therapeutic alliance is a partnership, unequal to be sure, the first objective of which is to transform the person who seeks our help from applicant to participant.

16

▼

On Beginning the Treatment:
Practical Considerations

The arrangements for treatment are decided by the diagnosis, as we have already emphasized. Such arrangements are always tentative, as diagnostic impressions change as the patient gets better and as the patient's real circumstances alter.

In chapter 14 we discussed how frequency of sessions differs in psychoanalysis and psychotherapy; here we add that arrangements for treatment, especially those made at the outset, are always subject to change. The therapist, after deciding with the patient that treatment is indicated, also specifies the optimal frequency as determined by the diagnosis. Ideally, that will be the accepted manner of beginning. Often patients are unable to undertake three, four, or five sessions per week for psychological, financial, or geographic reasons.

The psychological reasons are a form of resistance that may have to be honored and worked out. The understructured patient who is fearful of unconscious wishes to merge with the other person will try to limit the contact, and the therapist will then undertake to work with the patient on that issue until the perceived danger diminishes. The financial reasons are more difficult because they have become extrinsic now that third-party payment and managed care interfere with professional decisions. We shall discuss that shortly when we describe the fee structure of the therapist in private practice. Geographic reasons are real and are usually dealt with by double sessions. This is not ideal, but far better than settling for contact that is too infrequent to keep the treatment flowing.

Arrangements are to be regarded as an agreement for the beginning of treatment, not as an inviolate contract. Analogous to the beginning relationship between neonate and mothering person, patient and therapist need to find how to fit together. This takes time and there will inevitably be changes. It happens more often than not that, as a solid therapeutic alliance is built, patients who have undertaken to come once or twice a week begin to regret the time lapse between sessions and ask for more frequent sessions. If they do not ask, the complaints about the intervals between sessions provide the therapist an opportunity to suggest greater frequency of attendance.

A word of caution: we are speaking only of those patients with good prognoses. It would be a disservice to offer frequent attendance to a patient whose capacity for change is limited. In those instances we do our best to keep the person functioning, but to ask such a person to attend more frequently implies a promise that cannot be fulfilled.

We are often asked about those therapists who work in a clinical setting where the administration determines the frequency, fee, and other policy matters. In that setting, the therapist has to abide by what the administration establishes. But in a well-conducted facility, staff discussions allow therapists some input. The therapist then has a professional responsibility to educate the administration as well as fellow therapists to the policies that best serve the patient.

Policies that serve third-party payers and managers are not designed with the patient's best interest in mind, but only the best interest of the insurance carrier. Such third parties exert an unfortunate influence on the patient, who is likely to tell the therapist, "This is what my insurance will pay" or "My policy calls for one session per week for twelve weeks." We have to remind prospective patients that the insurance carrier would prefer that they have no treatment at all, for the plans are arranged to save the carrier money, not to serve the patient in the best way possible. The ideal manner of dealing with this is to assume that insurance is a contract between the individual and his or her carrier, not between the individual and the therapist or the carrier and the therapist. It is most desirable to remain outside the third-party system. This can be done by informing the patient that we will sign whatever forms are required, but we do not accept payment from the carrier. The patient pays for the sessions and is reimbursed by the carrier for whatever amount the contract calls for. Almost invariably this is less that the therapist's fee, and provides for less than the optimal frequency of attendance.

Third-party involvement introduces a new form of resistance. The patient will behave as though he or she can follow only the dictates of the carrier. This is to be dealt with as a resistance because reason alone will not always decide the issue. Reason may be used, of course, to inform the patient that the policy contract was not written with his or her specific therapeutic needs in mind. But the therapist should be prepared to work with the hurdle that the patient may seize upon as a resistance.

Freud's rules regarding attendance and responsibility for the fee were established with the neurotic patient in mind; we still use those rules with the well-structured patient who has the capacity to tolerate frustration and especially to function at that level of object relations that assumes automatic awareness of reality and the needs of the other person. Thus when Freud advocates that the therapist expects a fee, he relies on the neurotic's structured level of object constancy, including appreciation for the therapist's need to earn a living. We can make no such broad assumptions in deciding on practical arrangements for the treatment of the less structured patient. Some can abide by the terms of agreement between patient and therapist; some are at a lower level of object relations and have such poor reality testing that therapists are speaking another language if they hold rigidly to these demands; some begin treatment unable to fulfill such ordinary requirements as regular attendance. It becomes a high-water mark in treatment when patients do become able to abide by some of these requirements. In no other aspect of therapy is the versatility and flexibility of the therapist put more to the test than in determining how demanding to be, for it is as detrimental to patients to ask for less than they can do as it is to ask for more.

The fee, however, is an exception. This is the one area, if the fee proves to be a problem, where the therapist must ask the understructured patient to function beyond his or her level of object relations. Some such patients have little or no understanding of the other person's needs and of the fact that, in our economic system, one pays for service. Physicians and others in the helping professions encounter a similar problem. Because the service is not tangible and concrete, some patients have difficulty appreciating that it cannot therefore be given away. Only a therapist can deal with this in terms of object relations. The situation may be used to recognize that the patient is troubled by this requirement, and that it is part of the total problem. In that way greater regard for the object is held out, and the matter is used as a therapeutic objective; when the level of object relations improves, so will the capacity to know that the separate, whole, other person has needs. This is not to say that we waive or even reduce the fee. What is likely to improve is *willingness* in the mind of the patient.

The fee must be paid even when appointments are missed, whatever the reason. The therapeutic task is to firm up and maintain ego boundaries. One of the several techniques for accomplishing that is to be clear that what happens to the patient is to be borne by the patient. Patients are responsible for the time allocated for therapy even if the session is missed through no fault of their own. For the therapist to make up for events in the patient's life would be infantilizing. In the unconscious, therapy is equated with mothering. It should be clear in the therapist's mind that the objective is to promote growth, not to represent oneself as a better parent. Also, empathy for the patient's suffering must not lead the therapist into overlooking that corrective experiences can be effective only where development has proceeded to the level of capacity to reorganize structure. Certain aspects of structuralization—such as the period of coenesthetic reception—cannot be repeated or relived therapeutically.

If an understructured patient adamantly refuses to pay for missed sessions, to the extent of jeopardizing the continuation of treatment, the therapist is wise to sidestep confrontation by being flexible. Payment may be postponed in order to buy time to work on the problem. Never is payment to be waived. It is far better to invoke the patient's capacity for organization and reorganization to the extent that it exists, for that is the means by which one can promote advance to ever higher levels of structuralization. This stance is the most effective way to avert transference psychosis.

For that reason, among others, payment for missed sessions is only one of several rules that may not be abrogated. We have heard some therapists say, regarding not only fee for missed sessions but other practical matters as well, "*My* policy is . . . " There cannot be individual policy, for that is idiosyncratic. The patient is likely to feel, rightly in many instances, that such a statement is a matter of the therapist's whim.

In many parts of the country physicians as well as therapists charge their established fees, which patients pay regardless of what they are reimbursed. This puts a financial strain on some. Often one is well advised to explore other resources, such as relatives who can help, additional work one can take on, and the like. Some prospective patients will protest that they do not want to be dependent on relatives, especially parents. They express the wish to be "independent." This, of course, is a pseudoindependence, for we have by this time made it clear that independence or autonomy is a psychological state, not a financial one. If the patient is proposing to be subsidized by the therapist instead of by the parent or other relative, that hardly constitutes independence.

The duration of the session is a good example of sound professional stance. When the time is up, the session is over. The patient may want it to go on, but we do not ordinarily extend the time. This, too, calls for flexibility. If the patient is experiencing unusual and extreme distress that is not a regular occurrence, the therapist might try to allow a moment for the patient to recover. But ordinarily time is no more under the control of the therapist than of the patient, and it is desirable to demonstrate that time is a reality. Conveying the impression that the therapist can control the passage of time presents a false aura of omnipotence.

In his discussion of fees Freud (1912–14) relies on the theory he had developed up to that time, namely, libido theory and the phases of psychosexual maturation. He attributes withholding to the anal phase, using the unconscious equation of money and feces. This still holds true but is only part of the larger picture. Adding the object relations dimension does not refute that the wish to retain, to refuse to give to another person, is based in anality. But even in the anal phase, when the child believes that the feces are demanded while he or she regards them as a personal possession, it is an object relations struggle as well as a drive manifestation. The proper timing for use of this important theoretical information is when the manifestation arrives in the transference. Before then, to emphasize that the patient has the wish to withhold constitutes scolding rather than therapy.

Raising fees for ongoing patients more often than not turns out to be difficult. It is desirable to say at the outset, "This will be the fee *for now*." That informs the patient that the fee will not be the same for the duration of therapy, which can take many years. If the patient's economic circumstances improve in the course of therapy (sometimes as the result of the therapy), we do not pounce. Waiting for a fee increase without too much eagerness or greed can sometimes result in the very desirable offer on the part of the patient to increase the fee. If this does not happen, the therapist is obliged to take it up in therapeutic terms, to consider whether this, once again, is an object relations problem combined with anal with-holding.

The state of the economy is a consideration. With inflation, fees need to be raised from time to time. Again, the patient at the level of object constancy appreciates this. But it remains a problem for many, for reasons already discussed—ego boundaries, object relations levels, wish for better parenting, withholding, and the like. Refusal to increase the fee when it is logical to do so introduces the danger of a negative countertransference reaction in the therapist. Therapists should never allow themselves to be exploited. Countertransference is not always undesirable. In its positive usage it can instill feelings in the therapist that provide important clues to how the patient is feeling or how the patient wants the therapist to feel. But a real reason for the therapist to feel negative, angry, or deprived is to be avoided. Altruism is often credited with being a virtue when it is sometimes a pathology.

There is the corollary. What to do when the economy takes a downward turn? Shall we then reduce the fee? That seems to contradict our own dictum that what happens to the patient is happening to him or her. But we must be realistic. These decisions can only be made on an individual basis. There is a difference between a temporarily unemployed person who will soon be working again and one who is not likely to get a job for a long time. In the final analysis, we cannot treat without a fee; if the patient cannot pay, treatment must come to an end. It is no service to the patient to blur ego boundaries.

We do not advocate accumulation of debt. Normally the fee is to be paid regularly. In unusual circumstances we might waive this rule, but cautiously and selectively. Never allow a debt to become so great that there is little chance that the patient will be able to make it up. It is antithetical to the therapeutic role for the therapist to become a creditor of the patient. The patient, with the therapist's help if need be, is to be encouraged to explore other sources for seeking loans.

We were once confronted with an intriguing complication in a workshop we conducted. The patient sought treatment in a clinic for his problem in paying bills; accordingly he anticipated that the clinic fee would be subject to his disability. Therefore he asked that payment be deferred until he was cured. The "treatment" could never have succeeded under such circumstances. In this instance the patient had to live with the fact that paying his bill was as important as his very coming to the clinic for treatment. Any other course would have produced an irremediable resistance. This is another example of a situation in which the patient must be asked to function above his psychological capacity of the moment.

There is the special situation of those therapists who have signed up as providers for Blue Cross, Medicare, and Medicaid. In those instances the fees are strictly circumscribed. This is not a matter with which we can be of much help. If the therapist deems it in his or her best interest to become a provider, then of course the conditions have to be met.

We can help with such decisions in another way, however. Few therapists take into account that the private practitioner has to include in the fee: overhead such as rent, utilities, and insurance; vacations and sick leave; and pensions for one's old age. When these are factored in, fees that the patient and others may consider quite high are often too low.

We prefer not to promulgate "rules" because that appears contrary to reasonable flexibility. "Guidelines" allow therapists to use their judgment in individual situations. This is of special value in the developmental point of view that we advocate because it takes into account the patient's degree of structuralization. We offer the following guidelines:

1. The therapist maintains a professional stance.
2. The therapist abides by the established times of the sessions.
3. There is to be no contact outside therapy.
4. The therapist does not touch the patient except to shake hands.
5. The therapist's personal life is not part of therapy and is not to be revealed to the patient.
6. The patient is not there for the therapist's gratification. If the therapist likes the work, that is a gratification in itself. Some sessions, especially where the negative transference has to be dealt with, are not likely to be pleasurable. The therapist's pleasure and entertainment are to be sought after hours.
7. The countertransference is not to be revealed to the patient. It is to be used in two ways: (a) for self-analysis if feelings are troublesome, to ascertain whether they are a factor of the therapist's personality, or (b) for understanding whether the patient is trying (unconsciously) to induce a particular feeling in the therapist, in which case it becomes a matter of determining whether or when to interpret.

8. Gifts are not ordinarily accepted. This is one of the matters that calls for thoughtful flexibility. For the neurotic patient the matter is not at issue. There the fee and the healthy narcissistic gratification of working effectively remain the only gratifications the therapist receives. In working with the understructured personality, gifts sometimes arrive and must be dealt with differently. There, too, they are not, or should not be, for the gratification of the therapist, but it is not always desirable to refuse them. They may be reflections, in adult form, of attempts to repair developmental failure. In fact they may even inform the therapist where the developmental failure may lie.

We present two examples. The child, toward the end of the first year of life, begins to become aware of the partner in a new way. By reversal, and because of narcissistic belief that the mothering person needs exactly what the child needs, the child begins to relate reciprocally. An everyday example of this is that of the child who seizes the feeding spoon and tries to feed mother. If this developmental thrust is rejected, there is a narcissistic injury that can be lasting. Another delicate developmental locus is the rapprochement subphase. Here the child might bring things to the mothering person in an attempt to reestablish contact after the relative independence of the practicing subphase. Severe and enduring narcissistic injury can be inflicted if there is a rapprochement disappointment. For these reasons the therapist of an understructured patient sometimes accepts gifts, while the psychoanalyst of the neurotic does not. The therapist looks upon these, not as against the rules, but rather as an adaptive attempt to repair early injury. Of course, mere acceptance of the gift is not therapeutic. The reasons behind the patient's need to offer the gift are to be understood. Rarely can this understanding come about at the precise moment the gift is presented. In a progressing treatment the therapist might store the information for use with the patient at a later time within the context of the transference. The gift per se is sometimes accepted, therefore, and the act of giving is absorbed in the normal flow of the process, whether accepted or turned back. If the gift is durable, it should be set aside until returning it would not constitute repetition of traumatic rejection. That comes about when the patient, through treatment, reaches a higher developmental level, no longer needing to "feed" the therapist or "return to home base," but appreciating, out of a greater degree of separation and higher level of development, that the needs of patient and therapist are not the same.

Common sense enters here. We have heard of a therapist, remaining rigidly within psychoanalytic rules, whose patient arrived with two ice cream cones, one for each of them. We leave the solution to that challenge to the creativity of the reader. There are solutions, but each therapist might arrive at a different one.

9. The therapist neither gives gifts nor makes loans. One can be excessively rigid about that too. The philosophy that what happens to the patient has happened to him or her must be applied with thoughtful flexibility. We know of one situation where the patient arrived for her session during a snowstorm and discovered she lacked ten cents toward a subway token for her return home after the session. The therapist held to the rules, forcing her to walk some ten city blocks while it was snowing. A small loan is more humane in such a situation, leaving for the next session exploration of why she put herself in that position. Another therapist was having some architectural repair to her office and the patient's washroom was not functioning during the alterations. This office was in the therapist's home, but she refused to allow the patient to use her own bathroom because that would be an invasion of her privacy. These kinds of rigidities have no place in the treatment of any level of structure.

Therapists are subject to all the vicissitudes of human life—they have transportation and parking problems, they become ill, or their children or other dependents become ill. A therapist may even have a memory lapse, forget an appointment, or accidentally make two appointments at the same time. Obviously if such lapses occur frequently, then the therapist has a problem to be worked out. But having had a reasonably successful analysis does not assure that the therapist is free of the "normal" psychopathologies of everyday life. Spitz remarks that "normalcy" is rare; probably it is nonexistent. We are required to be reasonably stable; to aspire to more than that approaches narcissistic grandiosity. It is not a catastrophe if the therapist arrives late for a session, if that is infrequent, although some patients may experience it as catastrophic. Usually patients recover. Although we never advocate arranging an artificial situation, one can make use of those that happen accidentally. When the therapist is late, it can be useful to elicit the fantasies the patient inevitably has about the reason for the lateness. Very often this is how unconscious death wishes come to light.

On the part of the therapist, a word of regret suffices, together with an attitude that considers the matter minor. The therapist apologizes, but not profusely. The importance and meaning to the patient is always to be explored. The fantasies about why this happened are to be elicited only where reality testing is sound. If reality testing is poor, the therapist does not want to lend an aura of reality to the fantasies. Often the reaction to an error on the part of the therapist reflects a need to preserve parental omnipotence.

A therapist had a trustworthy secretary prepare the monthly bills. As happens, that secretary left and then there was a succession of secretaries. The therapist realized that this would not do because too many secretaries would get to know the identities of the patients. She began to prepare the bills herself, making errors frequently but never deliberately. Some patients found narcissistic pleasure in correcting her. Others had extreme reactions of dismay in the obvious failure of omnipotence.

Vacations provide the patient with an in vivo experience that often illuminates separation-individuation problems. Some patients react by having to leave first, or vent their anger and displeasure by deciding to terminate altogether. If the therapeutic alliance is solid enough, these wishes to reverse can be worked through. One should not rush into an interpretation of the wish to retaliate even though that is often the case; therefore one interprets the patient's act as an attempt by demonstration to let the therapist know how it feels to be left. This brings the action into the verbal realm and defers interpretation of destructive wishes until object constancy is secured.

The therapist who, on returning from vacation to find a letter or telephone message announcing termination, must try to help the patient return. This provides an experience in which the patient's distress receives a careful and respectful hearing and understanding; the feelings about being abandoned can be talked about rather than acted on. It demonstrates the therapist's object constancy, something that patients who have been disappointed in the past do not expect. This awareness of the discrepancy between the object expectation and the therapist's different behavior is the "therapeutic differential," as the patient begins to recognize that the therapist's level of object relations is not the same as was experienced with objects in the past.

The first weeks after the therapist's return from vacation may contain much useful material about the patient's capacity to deal with separation. In most, or all, understructured patients the relationship between the self representation and the object representations is not one of evenly distributed positive cathexis. The therapist's vacation brings on anger, anxiety, and defense. This is because the object representations are unreliable; therefore the object expectation is of unreliability. Therapists have personal reasons for absences aside from vacation, such as illness, attendance at conferences, or personal emergencies. These are best kept private. While the patient may press for the reason, or even become anxious about it, most often a simple statement—"It is better for your therapy if we do not get you involved in that"—will suffice.

The patient is a special guest in the therapist's office, entitled to some, but not all, of the usual courtesies. One of us (RB) has opened doors for women most of his life and would not easily be able to change this habit. We heard at a conference that some therapists regard these courtesies as power plays. That, we believe, is a most superficial understanding of male-female relationships. One behaves naturally, and we hope we are not being too old-fashioned in holding to those niceties. GB always precedes a male patient into the room because that makes him more comfortable than going before her. She allows a woman patient to precede her.

We offer certain courtesies to guests who are not patients that would be antitherapeutic if offered to a patient. It is desirable, at the outset, to set a tone that does not lead the patient to regard the visit as a social call. Food, cigarettes, coffee, or other refreshments are never served. Many patients bring their own cigarettes; some bring containers of coffee, even sandwiches. We do not accept the patient's offer to share these, but we refuse politely. The outset of treatment is usually not the time to raise the question about why the patient needs to be fortified with oral supplies. Later it is of central importance to explore and interpret this, but only when the therapist is certain that the patient has become curious about his or her own behavior. Beginning therapists sometimes ask what is wrong with serving coffee. The only answer is the psychoanalytic one. A clinic where we did in-service training had a coffee pot and cookies in the waiting room for the patients to help themselves. In a discussion the staff argued, "What is wrong with oral gratification?" Using the psychosexual progression as value free, we asked, "Would you allow anal gratification or phallic exhibitionism?" We are there to reverse regression, not reinforce fixation.

Today of course the situation regarding cigarettes is vastly different. Patients are no longer permitted to smoke in the consultation room, not only for their own sakes but also because therapists must demonstrate careful guardianship of their own health. This, too, can be done with the most careful appreciation of the difficulty it poses for some patients. With one patient who was having enormous difficulty in postponing smoking, the therapist began by employing simple steps such as asking her to see how long she could hold out. Then, as she started to reach into her purse, the therapist suggested she just hold the purse for a while; then she was asked to hold the cigarette in her hand without lighting it; then she could put it in her mouth, still unlit. In this fashion the session could go by and could constitute a practical experience in helping her delay impulse discharge.

Therapy is conducted in optimal fashion when patient and therapist meet only in the consultation room. In analytic training institutions this cannot be sustained, as patient and analyst will be thrown together much more often than in other situations. Common sense must prevail. Artificial avoidance is awkward. Contact should be held to simple, brief, and friendly greetings rather than to awkward avoidance or excessive formality. A therapist encounters patients in unexpected places, even in a city as large as New York—on the street, in restaurants, in department stores, at art galleries, in the theater, even at parties. The most appropriate behavior is to greet the patient politely, perhaps shake hands, and go one's way.

The therapeutic "hour" was fifty minutes for many years; now the trend is toward forty-five minutes. The session should be unhurried and unpressured, whatever the length of time. We have experimented with double sessions for selected patients, those who well understood the patient's tasks in the therapeutic endeavor. But this must be done carefully and selectively; it cannot become a general practice, especially in psychotherapy.

Accepting referrals a patient makes requires that the impact on the patient be carefully considered. Sharing the therapist with others is hard enough when the "others" are other patients whom the patient sees in the waiting room. To share the therapist with a friend can prove to be too difficult, and is often best avoided, even when the therapist has open time. The most usual reason a patient has for making a referral of a friend is to provide a repetitive experience with a sibling. This is grist for the therapeutic mill, most often not to be acted on. There can be exceptions. Here is another place for exercise of flexibility.

We do not advocate treating husbands, wives, children, or siblings of patients concurrently. This is one of the aspects of technique that differs markedly from treatment that is not psychoanalytically oriented. The principal and, in our opinion overriding, reason for this rule is preservation of the transference as a prime tool in treatment; a relationship with any other member of the patient's family will inevitably impair it.

Arguments can be made on the other side. One of the most convincing ones is that the therapist who sees both spouses learns much about their interaction. This cannot be disputed. We are concerned, however, with what the therapist does with such knowledge. One can confront the patient, in the presence of the spouse or at another time, with his or her behavior and its impact on the other person. But the ego psychological approach observes that confrontation from without informs the patient of something the patient already knows and cannot change—namely, that his behavior is unacceptable to others. The painfulness of such knowledge is increased by the fact that the change demanded is usually beyond the patient's developmental level: "You have no consideration for your husband," no matter how tactfully stated, is meaningless to the woman on a low level of object relations. It is analogous to telling a two year old to have consideration for his or her co-occupant of the sandbox.

The chief argument against concurrent or conjoint treatment is, as we have said, preservation of the transference and of the therapeutic alliance. It is essential that the patient feel that the therapist is there altogether for him or her. Some therapists believe sincerely in their own objectivity. But if they also believe in the subtle, unconscious operation of the repetition compulsion, they will be cautious about undertaking arrangements that contain inherent danger to the therapy. Working in the medium of developmental object relations theory requires most careful consideration of the nuances that go into all interpersonal relationships that reflect the existence of patterned (internalized) forms of interaction. Identification of the early affective experiences that have shaped the relationship between self and object representations is already a demanding task with a single individual and probably impossible in groups.

These considerations are also to be applied flexibly and to be related to the capacity of the ego. For example, married couples often ask to be seen together. If the reason is only that they think this is the preferred method of marital counseling, then it is usually easy for them to accept the suggestion that they come separately. Those couples who are symbiotically bound together, however, are likely to be unable to accept any arrangement that separates them. One might ask, "Do you think you will be able to talk freely with your wife present?" If the answer is something like, "Oh, yes, we always share everything," then there is little to be gained by trying to treat the symbiosis mechanically by refusing to see the couple together at the outset. There will be time, later in therapy, when such a joint problem can be treated interpretively with a view toward proposing individual treatment, preferably with different therapists (Blanck and Blanck 1968).

Therapists need to be available for emergencies. Even with the overindulged patient who has not developed an adequate capacity to wait, therapy is not advanced by being rigidly unavailable. In many years of practice we find that patients do not tend to abuse the telephone. If some do, it is better dealt with on an individual basis than to hold to a hard and fast rule. Some patients who are in need find it difficult to telephone. We do not ask, "Why didn't you call?" because that has undertones of both criticism and challenge. A better way of going about it is to explore what thought deterred or prevented the call from being made. Often valuable material emerges—the nanny resented being called; the primal scene will be interrupted—to cite but two of many possible underlying reasons for the inability to ask for help.

In this electronic age there is audio and video tape recording of therapy sessions, usually for research purposes. Those who do it say that after a while neither patient nor therapist remains aware of the machine. But that is not the issue. Technology has not, and perhaps never will, reach the point where the patient's withheld material, the therapist's thoughts, the unconscious of both patient and therapist, and especially the unspoken affective tone of the interaction, can be recorded. Use of such technological tools diminishes the affective tones of the therapeutic relationship that is the very medium within which the work is carried on.

This touches on the issue of confidentiality. It is understood that the patient's material is confidential. But what does that mean? Patient's material is used for supervision, for presentation in seminars, for publication in books and journals.

Supervision is a legitimate use of otherwise confidential material, for there is no other way of learning. We do not advocate tape recording for supervision, not simply for the already stated reasons but because supervision is a process with its own rhythm. The detailing of the patient session by the therapist inevitably introduces information from the therapist's conscious and unconscious feelings about the patient that are an indispensable guide for the supervisor. There are two philosophies of supervision. One proposes that it is the case that is supervised. Here the supervisor is undertaking some responsibility for the case. The other position assumes that the therapist is an independent practitioner who, by undertaking such work, is responsible for his or her own case. The therapist who is under this second kind of supervision is there to learn how to perform therapy. There the case material is used to help the therapist develop generic skills that are applicable across the board. Obviously we favor this second type of supervision. Taped sessions would be detrimental to the purpose because we want to hear the therapist's version of the session. Those who want the recorded "whole truth" are, we believe, placing too much credence on legalistic precision, and too little on the undertones that reveal much about patient and therapist.

Case material is also used in seminars, conferences, and other teaching situations. There, wherever possible, it is desirable for the presenter to disguise the case if that can be done without altering the basic features. As for publication, we never use patients' material without permission.

17

▼

Transference: Interpretable and Uninterpretable

I t has been said repeatedly that transference is ubiquitous. Like infantile sexuality, it existed through the ages before Freud "discovered" it. Only Adam and Eve had no past, no childhood, and therefore no storage of object relations patterns to eventuate in transference. Transference is a replay—an old game played on a new field.

The field may be anywhere, not only in the psychoanalytic situation, but in everyday relationships as well. Attitudes and interactions with friends, colleagues, spouses, children, and others appear real to the players. Only in psychoanalysis does one person on the field know that it is a replay, and knows also not to react as though it is real—as Fenichel (1941) put it, not to play the game.

In psychoanalysis a transference interpretation, made at the proper time and in the proper therapeutic context, alerts the well-structured patient to the confusion between transference and reality, enabling the patient to make the distinction. That the understructured patient is unable to understand that difference and to use interpretation of transference has been known since Freud (1912). His well-known distinction between the analyzable transference neurosis and the unanalyzable "narcissistic neuroses" was made for precisely that reason.

We struggled over many years for a way of describing and designating more accurately the difference between the analyzable and unanalyzable transference phenomena. Analysts no longer dismiss patients suffering from "narcissistic neuroses" as untreatable, although these patients may indeed be unanalyzable. But what is to be made of the fact that they elaborate a different kind of "transference"? Our answer is to try to understand the degree of structuralization, and this tells us that those patients are understructured—that is, they have not completed the separation-individuation process. Need for union without adequate drive-modulating capacity causes the understructured patient to perceive past experience as present reality. This misperception occurs with the structured patient too, of course, but we have shown that that can yield to interpretation. With the understructured patient, however, that is usually not so.

In its strict definition, transference is the *transfer* of feelings, attitudes, and behavior toward a person from the past onto the analyst in the present. Transference and transference neurosis are understood as being powered by the repetition compulsion, which brings feelings and attitudes that originated in relation to past objects and displaces and projects these feelings and attitudes on objects in the present. Fenichel parsimoniously and tersely defines transference as mistaking the present for the past.

Some use the concept of transference more broadly, to refer to everything that pertains to the therapeutic relationship. That, we believe, covers too much ground and deprives us of the advantage of specificity, of knowing precisely whether one is dealing with transference phenomena or something in the real relationship with the analyst.

We propose an expansion of the classic definition of transference. Ego psychology, or developmental object relations theory, provides the theoretical tools that enable us to make explicit that which has always been implied and included within the classic definition. We articulate it this way: transference deploys the individual's established object relations pattern. By bringing it into present-day relationships, it obscures the object relations aspect of reality by dealing with present object relationships as though they are the same as those in the past. That pattern, laid down in childhood, becomes part of the character and operates in all relationships. The level of structuralization determines whether the repetition remains rigidly fixed or whether better capacity to distinguish present reality from past experience makes a more flexible response possible. It is that flexibility that enables the patient with a high degree of structuralization who loses the distinction in the thick of a transference reaction to respond to interpretation.

That transference is the manifestation of the established pattern of object relations raises important questions about transactions and affective attitudes toward other persons. Is love, as Freud (1905) says, the refinding of a lost object? Is the new love object merely an old department store dummy dressed in new clothes? Or does a person in love, as the Bible would have it, abandon past objects in order to cling to a new person and become one flesh? It appears at first glance that the Bible advocates that we abandon our primary objects in favor of a new object, but is this so? When looked at from the point of view of ego psychology, both Freud and the Bible suggest there are no new love objects. The "new" object of the Bible is one flesh, which we interpret to mean a symbiotic partner. This is refinding at a very early level of development. Are all persons fixated at that level?

The matter is not so problematic if we extend our thoughts about the affective dimension. Then we no longer speak of object, but of object need. This recasts the issue. Whether the object is new or "old" is determined, not by who the other person is but by the level of need, which also rests on degree of structuralization. The neonate is totally helpless; the infant and child are in a state of intense object need that slowly diminishes with structuralization accompanied by physical maturation. The well-enough structured adult finds a contemporary love object by bringing into a new relationship internalized representations from the past and, at the same time, by adapting to the reality of the new person. The new relationship, then, is not simply a "refinding." By combining one's own object relations pattern with the reality of the other person, a new and unique relationship is created.

Freud discovered transference because he was courageous enough to venture where Breuer feared to tread. A patient fell in love with Breuer, who was so disturbed by it that he fled. Freud recognized that a patient's love for him had nothing to do with the charms of his person, just as the negative feelings did not reflect his evils. Both kinds of feelings, his genius informed him, had to do with the past, not with present reality. And so analysts today, with the sophistication of having studied the vast literature on transference, having experienced it in their own analyses, and having worked with the transferences of their patients, do not feel flattered when the patient expresses positive feelings and do not feel wounded and retaliatory when the feelings are derogatory.

Freud also distinguishes between the ubiquitous phenomenon of transference and the transference neurosis that can only be brought about in the analytic situation. The concept of transference neurosis and the technique for dealing with it rest on the assumption that an infantile neurosis lies embedded in the personality. The core of that neurosis is the Oedipus Complex, with which the structured patient deals by means of defense and compromise formation. By encouraging regression in the service of the ego (Kris), the analyst bares the infantile neurosis in the form of the transference neurosis, to revive it in the present in order to have it become "alive" in the treatment. Correct and timely interpretation informs the ego of the well-structured patient of the displacement and projection on the analyst of feelings toward past objects.

Those ideas about transference neurosis preceded developmental theory. Early on, it was believed that psychic structure is established in childhood and remains fixed for life. Neurosis was thought to be formed by the age of five or six as a compromise formation, the consequence of the first round of the oedipal conflict. Bornstein (1945) reports on her treatment of a child, "Frankie," conducted under the assumption that she could cure his infantile neurosis and thus free him of neurosis for life. In 1966 it was revealed that Frankie, as a young adult, had returned for analysis of a compulsion neurosis. That disclosure led analysts to realize that child analysis does not cure once and for all. Especially because a child is at an accelerated pace of development, and because development continues through adolescence and beyond, one can only treat a child by bringing him or her to the age appropriate developmental position. Bornstein took the child Frankie as far as possible developmentally. It seems simple now to realize that Frankie as a young man had developed beyond his "infantile neurosis," and that he sought treatment for his adult neurosis—that is, the neurosis that evolved as the result of the telescoping of the residua of childhood developmental flaws, infantile conflict, adolescent development, and adult compromise formation. This throws a different light on the concept of infantile neurosis and also raises question about transference neurosis.

"The extraordinary diversity of mental constellations" (Freud 1913, *S.E.* 12:123) establishes that transference phenomena are far more complex than first thought. By 1956 Zetzel began to question whether transference is the sole feature in the relationship with the analyst. She made a distinction between the transference and other aspects of the analytic relationship, suggesting that there is also a *therapeutic alliance*. Greenson (1965), too, found that there is something "real" in the analytic relationship, terming that the *working alliance*. Greenacre (1959) preferred to refer to *active neurotic transference manifestations* because she thought this a more accurate description of what takes place in an analytic session. She observed a fluctuating quality in the transference, not only from session to session but even within a given session. She was also much interested in the importance of guardianship of autonomy in handling transference phenomena, because she recognized how readily they could lend themselves to misunderstanding and misuse. Because she wrote in the era of explosion of knowledge about ego psychology, she also calls attention to a matter new at the time—that transference phenomena evolve out of the mother-child dyad.

Especially at the beginning of interest in treatment of the so-called borderline conditions, transference neurosis had no meaning for such patients, since they did not have an infantile neurosis to be reproduced. In the gropings of early, as-yet unsystematized psychotherapy for the borderline patient, transference and transference neurosis were regarded as impediments to be disregarded, avoided, or diluted. The theorists of the 1950s believed that psychotherapy should focus on real-life issues, and the therapist was advised to avoid aiding in the elaboration of a transference (Tarachow 1963; Murphy 1965).

Even in psychoanalysis proper, controversy enters regarding the use of transference (Friedman 1984; Gill 1954, 1984). More recently, questions are being raised about whether there is or can be a true transference neurosis (Shaw 1991). The early definitions of transference neglected to make explicit that transference is the employment of the characteristic pattern of object relations in the treatment situation. That was always implied, but it was not until we began to know a great deal more about structure formation, including how object relations levels alter with development, that one could be more specific about the interrelationship among those several factors and how they influence the form the transference takes. Looking at transference in object relations terms, contemporary theory confirms what Greenacre merely sensed—that transference is a phenomenon that emanates from the very earliest period of life. Jacobson, too, using the theoretical terms of her day which did not include the object relations theory available to us now, had the concept but not the language. She says: "In adult patients we must not confuse transference processes based upon displacement from one object to another, such as from the mother to the analyst, with projections" (1964:17).

Emde's investigations confirm Greenacre and Jacobson by providing observational data. He says:

> Early relationship styles and patterns later become internalized by the individual in the progression from infancy to early childhood (Stroute and Fleeson 1985; Stern 1985). To put it another way, relationship aspects become internalized by the individual, continue as strong influences in development throughout childhood, and are activated in similar relationship contexts throughout life (1988:28).

We suggest there is a factor, not much considered in the vast literature on transference, that influences how analysts regard transference phenomena, which is that transference manifestations are disquieting. They disrupt attempts at coherent organization. They range over a wide spectrum, from simple manifestations to violent eruptions and, while they follow a logic, the logic of the primary process is difficult to define and follow because it is so disorderly when looked at with secondary process logic. The delusions and paranoid ideation of the psychotic reflect the presence of infantile fantasies untouched by developmental processes of differentiation of self representation from object representations and by reality testing. And the uninterpretable or barely interpretable "transference" manifestations of the understructured personality inform us that, although development has proceeded beyond the psychotic border, it is still deficient in terms of differentiation and reality testing. Most disquieting of all is the recognition that the "normal" individual also functions within transference modes to a far greater extent than we knew until now.

We know now that continuing development does not fully transform infantile ideation. At best it provides better mechanisms for coping with them. This becomes more understandable as we look again at the origins of transference in the developmental process.

We shall recapitulate developmental theory, this time emphasizing those origins of transference. Increasing degrees of separation-individuation take the child into the world of his or her own reality, which is different from that of the mother. As the child begins to "read" reality in his or her own way, the two sets of representations come into conflict. This is a formidable developmental step for the child. It calls for capacity to tolerate disillusionment and to withstand a kind of object loss—because differing with the mother means losing the all-omniscient object. In good enough circumstances, this is not only tolerable but is essential to further growth. For only when a degree of independence from the object representations is attained can new situations be assessed accurately and be distinguished from past experience with primary objects.

The innate striving toward ever greater autonomy leads the toddler to begin to investigate the wider world and to try to fit together with a larger and different reality. Where development is proceeding favorably and is encouraged by the partner in the dyad, the conflict between the two sets of representations is well enough tolerated. In poor circumstances, that conflict can lead to abandonment of one's own perception in favor of object retention. The "transference" manifestations of the understructured personality are so different from those of the structured personality because object retention in the former dominates and thereby obscures present reality more rigidly. Need for autonomy and mastery conflicts with the need for safety feeling, which still rests with the external object and with the object representations as they begin to be internalized. By the time of psychological birth, the child is aware of his or her own identity, including sexual identity, has incorporated his or her physical endowment into the self representation, and is possessed of a sense of self as a growing developing individual. Simultaneously, reality testing informs that the caregivers are also *caretakers* of a small child in a huge world.

As the self representation continues to differentiate from the object representation, the affective relationship between the two sets of representations is established and solidified. Positive cathexis arises out of gratifying experiences and negative cathexis arises not only out of whatever inadequacies existed in the relationship but also out of essential frustration that promotes growth. These cathexes form a pattern of affective relationship between the self representation and the object representations. In excellent circumstances, there is an evenly distributed cathexis between the two sets of representations (Jacobson) which may be described as a healthy narcissistic balance; both the self representation and the object representations are valued. There can be narcissistic imbalance. The self representation can be overvalued at the expense of undervaluing the object representations. The opposite can occur—the object representations can be overvalued, thereby impoverishing cathexis of the self representation.

What kind of balance can be achieved between the burgeoning self representation and the still authoritative object representations in a field of so many conflicting forces that include tidal waves of affective experience from the past, both conscious and unconscious? Each child has to thread his or her own way through the confusion of positive and negative affective forces in the continuing process of defining ego boundaries (separation), has to find his or her own unique qualities (individuation), and yet has to maintain libidinal connections (safety feeling). Ultimately, in normal development, some state of balance is achieved among the forces involved. These include the intensity of cathexis of both self and object and their mental representations, and the degree to which positive or negative affective balance is reflected in the internalized resultant. In such a fierce contest of fluid and conflicting emotions, defensive organization is of paramount importance.

Our own views about transference have moved with the newer theoretical discoveries. In 1974 we attempted to distinguish between those with established object representations whose transferences could be interpreted and those whose object representations were less clearly differentiated from the self representation, and who could therefore not achieve a therapeutic—that is, viable, interpretable—transference. At the time object relations was considered to be but one of the many ego functions, a function that pursues a pathway from primary narcissism to relations on a need-gratifying level and finally to object constancy. The transcendent position of object relations in the actual process of structural development emerged only slowly.

True transference involves *transfer* in its literal sense—from past to present. And here lies the rub, for it assumes that all persons have attained a developmental position where the other person is appreciated as separate and whole. In 1977 we distinguished the transference object from the real object, accepting the positions of Zetzel (1956) and Greenson (1965) that the therapeutic relationship involves more than transference alone. And we moved toward suggesting another term for the kind of therapeutic relationship elaborated by the understructured personality. In 1979 we termed this phenomenon *replication of early object need* or, in its abbreviated form, *object replication*. Our search was for a way of explaining why the therapist in such situations is perceived more as a real object than as a transference object. While the difference between psychotic "transference," whereby the therapist is experienced as the primary object, and true transference as displacement, was always understood, there remained this murky middle ground of what truly is elaborated by the borderline and narcissistic patients.

By 1979 we thought more about the borderline patient who feels himself or herself to be part of the other person, and of the narcissistic patient whose object relationship is with a fantasied "perfect" object. We termed their relationship with the therapist, perhaps awkwardly, as *search for replication of early object experience.* Our purpose was to be descriptive rather than to add a new term to the already difficult vocabulary of psychoanalytic theory. Our preference would have been for a term other than *transference,* but that would have taken us too far from the arena of communication with the therapeutic community. Since, whether called transference or something else, the understructured patient's therapeutic relationship, operationally, cannot be interpreted to the patient in the same way as to a neurotic, structured patient, we termed it *uninterpretable transference.*

Why is it not interpretable? The child in the early weeks and months of life is in the beginning of the process of developing a structure within which self and object experience will become internalized. Therefore the developing child deals with the object in interpersonal interaction. There is an apparent paradox here. The object, before completion of the separation-individuation process, is experienced as part of the self, but in ever-increasing degrees of differentiation. Even in very early infancy, the baby has a dim awareness of an external object. So two systems are at work simultaneously—the self-object unity alongside a growing awareness that an outside "something" also exists. Gradually, as an internal world is built, interpersonal interaction becomes subject to intrapsychic transactions. This is the turning point, the *fulcrum of development,* where development takes a qualitative and quantitative leap.

Our greater appreciation that adhesion to the omnipotent object creates an inertia enables us to add now that the early-in-life intermingled self and object representations do not differentiate easily, even with relatively smooth separation and individuation. That is why, in later life, self and object representations are easily confused to become difficult-to-interpret transference manifestations even in a neurotic structure, and uninterpretable in borderline structures.

We also added considerations about internalization of object relations that illuminate how transference potential lies latent for life, to emerge when triggered, especially in the therapeutic relationship where the arrangement provides fertile ground for it. It remains for us to clarify that replication of early self and object relationships is not necessarily the same as transference. The issue revolves around whether the replication is of a state in which psychological birth has been reached so that the patient has come to regard other persons as separate and whole, or whether developmental lag leaves the individual still experiencing the other person as part of the self representation.

To interpret to an unseparated patient that the present is not the same as the past cannot be effective because retention of the omnipotent object constitutes a barrier to perception of present reality. This means that the ego function of reality testing in the understructured personality is not defective, as in the psychotic; rather, it is intact but impeded. It might be said that it is a prisoner of object need. The technical dictate is thus made clear. Structure building to free the patient of lingering confusion between self and object representations has to precede interpretation. Late in the treatment of the understructured personality, when greater differentiation has been achieved, the therapist may gradually and gently help the patient become aware that he or she is not exactly like the primary object.

This is a delicate aspect of the technique of structure building. It brings about, belatedly in the adult, a developmental leap that normally takes place in childhood. For the normally developing child, as we have said, this leap comes out of recognition of differences between self and object representations and involves a measure of disillusionment and object loss. The adult patient who had been unable to take this developmental step in childhood, takes it in therapy in the context of a benign climate that includes careful timing.

To clarify that the therapist is not dealing with true transference in the understructured patient, we described it as replication of early object experience or object need. To return to the beginning, the person plays this out on any field available. In the therapeutic situation, we can use this to understand that this is not a transference phenomenon but, rather, the individual's characteristic way of dealing with others. In real life this can lead to interactional difficulties where the other person knows he or she is other, while the understructured person does not. Where both parties are understructured, the difficulties are compounded. What we have termed *uninterpretable transference*, then, is not truly transference but persistence of object relations patterns, inflexible and unaltered by development of reality testing in other areas.

Defining transference as the displacement and projection of past object relationships onto the present, it is logical to assume and to note in the clinical situation that the person who has not yet come to experience self and other as two separate, whole persons cannot *transfer* from one person to another even though primary object experience and experience with the analyst are separated in time. There cannot be *transfer* where the first round of the separation-individuation process had not been completed to the point where differentiated object representations exist to transfer from.

Because of the historical accident that psychoanalytic theory evolved before there was interest in and understanding of the understructured personality, we are far more familiar with what we have termed *interpretable transference* than with the rigidly fixed patterns that do not represent *transfer* from past to present but, rather, object relations patterns that remain fixed as though time has not intervened between childhood and adulthood.

It need come as no surprise to find that so much of what has been "discovered" can be found in Freud:

> Now our observations have shown that only a portion of those impulses which determine the course of erotic life have passed through the full course of psychical development. That portion is directed towards reality, is at the disposal of the conscious personality, and forms part of it. Another portion of the libidinal impulses has been held up in the course of development, it has been kept away from the conscious personality and from reality, and has been prevented from further expansion except in fantasy or has remained wholly in the unconscious so that it is unknown to the personality's consciousness.   (1912a:100)

Let us review the materials out of which basic transferences are formed, the fixed assumptions created early in life, the intaking processes of the period of coenesthetic reception. Spitz (1965:204) referred to these as the "mute, invisible tides" that were formed during the period of symbiotic union and exert an unconscious influence throughout life. At that early time of life, capacity to determine whether they are self generated, object generated, or jointly generated is blurred. Experience is registered affectively more than cognitively. Affect-laden experiences lay down neuronal channels that can be summoned to action later in life.

As the self representation becomes more clearly demarcated, a tension develops. Response is no longer determined by interaction or by early experience alone. Where there is good enough structuralization, visceral response is tempered by more advanced processes, such as selective rather than total identification, and by judgment that may become increasingly independent of reliance on the reality testing of the object. Such incremental expansion of the capacity for reality testing produces the psychological ingredients necessary for the purpose of casting doubts about some fixed assumptions. Ideally, this capacity creates potential for comparing current events with past events and noting their differences.

This may be an unrealizable ideal. Regression and progression are in flux throughout daily life. Anna Freud, Hartmann, and Kris thought that normal mentation comes about through detour and regression rather than in a straight line. Reality testing also fluctuates in each individual, depending not only on the level of structuralization but also on the momentary affective state that may trigger unconscious connection with early object experience. Analysts accept that behavior is dictated by unconscious determinants, in optimal circumstances tempered by sound reality testing, judgment, capacity for delay, and use of thought as trial action. We have added the proposition that the ubiquitous nature of transference phenomena is determined by patterns of experience formed very early in life that exert powerful unconscious influence on perception that differs widely from one individual to another, depending on the level of structuralization.

Persistence of early object experience is an automatized phenomenon that exists in all persons even in our moment-to-moment activity, subject only to the structural capacity to differentiate self from object and thereby present from past. This explains why transference is ubiquitous. Where the structure is adequate, there is true, interpretable transference, as Freud described so long ago. We have made yet one more attempt to clarify why not all transference is interpretable.

18

▼

Resistance: The Unmotivated Patient

In the first edition the title of this chapter was "The Unmotivated Patient." We have retitled it to include the more familiar forms of resistance, as well as the special problem of the unmotivated patient. Of resistance Freud says: "The length of the road over which an analysis must travel with the patient, and the quantity of material which must be mastered on the way, are of no importance in comparison with the resistance which is met with in the course of the work, and are only of importance at all in so far as they are necessarily proportional to the resistance" (1918, *S.E.* 17:11–12).

We discuss resistance in its historical context, describing Freud's struggles with it, because we believe it is best understood as Freud's difficulties with it are appreciated. The historical route also highlights that one does not learn how to be a therapist by accumulation of knowledge only, important as that is. Also involved is a developmental process in which one grows in professional skill.

Freud's changing attitudes toward resistance are interesting to follow. He was able to abandon hypnosis when he found that it bypasses the ego and thereby the resistance. In reporting on Elisabeth von R in 1895, he notes that his attempt to put her under deep hypnosis failed. It occurred to him to try applying pressure to her head to *extract* (his term) new material. He comments: "In the course of this difficult work I began to attach a deeper significance to the resistance offered by the patient in the reproduction of her memories and to make a careful collection of the occasions on which it was particularly marked" (1895, *S.E.* 2:154).

Elisabeth von R was quite blunt about her resistance. When asked why she had not provided a piece of information, she replied simply that she withheld it because she thought she could avoid telling him about it. Freud became curious rather than angry or disappointed, and tried to learn what it was that had deterred her, a model of the technique for dealing with resistance. In contrast, however, some of his writings betray that he did have difficulties with his countertransference. It has been said of Freud's writings that when he was clear he had arrived at a definitive idea, and when he was hazy or contradictory he was working out his ideas while writing them. In his "Lecture on Resistance and Repression" (1916) he is quite inconsistent about resistance. He calls a patient "to account for having broken the sacred rule" (288); he views resistance with "pained astonishment" (288); he uses a metaphor about criminals finding sanctuary; he decries the fact that the resistance "is successfully defying us" (289); he laments the fact that when "we succeed in extorting a certain amount of obedience to the fundamental technical rule from the resistance— [it] thereupon jumps over to another sphere" (289). Yet he also states that resistances provide the best support for treatment if the therapist gives them the right turn. He maintains that resistances should not be one-sidedly condemned and that the therapist should be dissatisfied if the resistances have not been worked through. Of all the difficulties in developing as a therapist, respecting the patient's resistances as necessary for defense is probably one of the most vexing because it is likely to evoke undesirable countertransference reactions powered by therapeutic zeal.

When the defensive function of the ego was clearly described (A. Freud), no doubt remained that resistance is a sign of ego competence. In structural terms, a competent ego is one that has developed to the point where it can recognize anxiety as a signal and employ competent defense. The understructured patient has to be regarded differently because the ego is not usually as capable of elaborating high-level defense. But there are both structured as well as understructured persons who come for treatment lacking motivation. This begins to suggest that resistance and lack of motivation are not precisely the same. We shall discuss that shortly.

Resistance vexes some of the most outstanding theorists of technique. Fenichel (1941), Menninger (1958), and Greenson (1967) write about the defending ego as the enemy, and as disruptive of the analysis. One still hears phrases like "breaking through the resistance," which suggest an embattled analyst in arms against the foe because the patient is not behaving as the analyst would like. Glover (1955) writes about resistance as crass. He says: "Crass resistances as a whole can scarcely be overlooked. They resemble the rashes and tumours of clinical medicine, which are recognised by simple inspection or palpation. The most crass of resistances is of course where the patient decides to abandon analysis" (1955:52).

Obviously, when the defense takes the form of abandoning treatment, the resistance is untreatable unless the patient returns. But what about the patient who remains in analysis but appears to be going against the analytic purpose? The structured patient is behaving exactly as he or she should, using defenses to protect against anxiety. Perhaps those writers fell into error, not simply because therapeutic zeal brooks no opposition in the direct march toward "uncovering" but also because they were dealing with intersystemic conflict only. By "resisting," the ego was accused of failing in its function of revealing unconscious fantasy and wish, while succeeding all too well in its defensive function. When intrasystemic conflict is taken into account along with intersystemic, the concept of resistance acquires a new dimension.

The very word *resistance* tends to mislead because one learned it first in the ordinary English vocabulary, where it usually connotes undesirable opposition. Even in science, physicists seek conductors with minimal resistance to electrical current. Patients sometimes say, "I'm resisting." They are hardly correct. Since, in the vocabulary of psychoanalysis, resistance is the *unconscious* use of defense, it cannot be something the patient does deliberately and consciously. Sometimes patients say this because, although they are not aware of its content, they "feel" that a resistance is in progress. "I feel stuck," is the way the patient usually expresses it. Often patients use the term *resistance* to forestall anticipated criticism for being unable to come forth with associations. There the ego is using the defense mechanism of identification with the aggressor, especially where the resistance is based on anal withholding of associations. If the patient is understructured and thereby less able to employ a defense mechanism, the self-criticism might be a reflection of experience in being criticized—for example, for not functioning at the level of object relations where giving is reciprocal. That, too, appears like identification with the aggressor, but the ego is using identification there, not to separate, but to retain the criticizing object representation as part of the self representation. The patient anticipates that the therapist will agree with objects from the past who have accused him or her of being ungiving, uncooperative, oppositional.

When resistance is viewed as "a part of a patient's wishing, part of his hope, part of his identity, as well as part of his handicap" (Friedman 1969:150), then technical means must be found to affirm that part of the resistance that expresses the patient's wish, hope, and identity.

It is not a truism that the better the motivation the less the resistance. Lack of resistance is not desirable where that means lack of an ego capable of defense. The patient with such an ego can be highly motivated, yet high states of resistance will appear repeatedly in the analysis. Resistance fluctuates and, even within the same session, as Greenacre (1972) has pointed out, the patient will work at a lowered level of resistance at one point and become embroiled in resistance at another.

A major shift in the theory of technique evolved out of the structural theory and the later work of the ego psychologists. With knowledge of the component elements involved in identity formation, analysts became able to work with resistance more effectively. Use of drive theory alone demanded that resistance be attributed to destructive aggression or libidinal fixation. Now that we understand that the aggressive drive serves separation-individuation and that the libidinal drive serves integration at a higher level, an entirely different light is shed on resistance.

We see a wider range of defensive behaviors now that we bring the understructured patient into our purview—from various degrees of reluctance, through being unable to do more than come to the session, sometimes not even that. Probably the largest group of unmotivated patients consists of those who do not come when treatment is indicated.

In addition to elaborating considerably on our understanding of transference, the therapeutic alliance, and the much deplored negative therapeutic reaction, our newly expanded object relations theory helps us understand resistance and absence of motivation in a new light. Added is information about how object relations patterns become fixed and how they determine the manner in which one individual will deal with another. Where the self and object representations are preponderantly negatively cathected, there may not be enough trust to motivate some people to come for therapy; since both the self representation and the object representations are negatively cathected, there would be little reason even to want help for oneself, or to believe that help is possible. In other instances, such a person might come with negative object expectations that are difficult and, in some instances, impossible to overcome.

As a function of the ego, the nature of the resistance reflects the relative success or failure in structuralization. The therapist's first task is to find his or her diagnostic bearings, to determine the developmental level at which the patient is functioning and to note whether this represents an arrest or a regression. If it is an arrest, structure building becomes the main therapeutic task. If it is a regression, it is important to ascertain the highest developmental level that had been attained and what anxiety caused the regression. Regression to a lower level of functioning means, by definition, that a higher level had been reached. Those situations call for therapeutic measures different from structure building; structure is already there even though it has been lost regressively. Like a pathway through a jungle that has become overgrown, the basic pathway is still there and can be retraced, once the therapist understands why the regressive route was chosen.

The therapist may find it baffling that manifestations of resistance take the same superficial forms in both structured and understructured personalities. This refers to those ordinary behaviors, such as arriving late, forgetting a session, having nothing to say. It is only the form that is the same in both kinds of structure; the underlying meanings are quite different and dictate different interventions.

The kinds of defenses available to the ego are products of the level of structuralization. The well-structured patient has mechanisms that are not fully available to the less competent ego. Defense, and especially defense mechanisms, are sometimes thought to be on a hierarchy. In that line of thinking, projection and denial are regarded as more primitive, while such mechanisms as reaction-formation, isolation, and regression are believed to be middle-range, and repression is regarded to be the most efficient defense mechanism. Thinking about the so-called hierarchy of defenses has shifted somewhat, especially about those that used to be regarded as primitive. We still think of repression as the most efficient. But the view of the so-called primitive defense mechanisms has altered with developmental theory.

Jacobson regards projection as the consequence of absence of boundaries. In her view, it is not that a thought or wish is projected from one mind into another, but rather that, in the unseparated state, the individual assumes that the two minds are one with no boundary between them.

Denial has also been regarded as "primitive," the simple turning away from that which is unpleasant. But denial may be used across the diagnostic spectrum and is not necessarily analogous to the ostrich's head in the sand. It can be used, for example, by a competent ego in order to buy time for mastery of a trauma. It may be used adaptively to screen out some of the more unpleasant realities of the world in order that everyday life be bearable. To think every moment about death, nuclear accidents, war, earthquakes, and other disasters is maladaptive; it prevents life from being lived because one is preoccupied with worries that one cannot prevent. To involve oneself actively in political movements against preventable disasters, however, is adaptive.

Some mechanisms that used to be regarded as defensive are part of the normal developmental process. Identification is a good example. At first Freud thought of it as defensive only. Now we have come to understand that, although it may sometimes be used as a defense, its main purpose is developmental. The self representation evolves in part by means of *selective identification* (Jacobson). And in its combined form—identification with the aggressor—it is essential to the attainment of the third organizer of the psyche (Spitz). We have even come to believe that the Oedipus Complex is attenuated by means of identification with the parent of the same sex (Jacobson 1964; G. Blanck 1984). Toward termination of psychoanalysis selective identifications with the analyst are believed to take place, making termination possible as the patient takes away with him or her the object representations that make continuing self-analysis possible (Loewald 1980; Blanck and Blanck 1988). Then analysis may be continued for life; what terminates is contact with the analyst.

Repression and some of the so-called middle-range defense mechanisms do not rove over the entire diagnostic spectrum because they are not available to the less competent ego. But the attitude toward repression is different now from the days when analysts were so intent on uncovering id content that they were hard at work "lifting" repression. We now realize that some repression is essential to organization. If it were possible to render the unconscious conscious all the time, the individual would exist in chaos. Even in psychoanalysis proper, we no longer have as our objective the lifting of *all* repression. And in the treatment of the less structured personalities, often the objective is the opposite of lifting repression; it is building structure so that the ability to repress is acquired.

Developmental theory posits that all defense is in some way adaptive, especially at the time when it was first adopted. This adds a new perspective to the way therapists view defense and resistance; it reinforces the position that they are necessary to the maintenance of equilibrium. Also to be considered is Hartmann's postulate that there are inborn apparatuses in the conflict-free sphere (chapter 3), later validated by Mahler and Emde, who show that adaptive-defensive potential exists in the innate endowment. To that Spitz adds that ineradicable permanent impressions are acquired in the period of coenesthetic reception.

Are resistance and absence of motivation synonymous? Not always. Motivation is a phenomenon of the beginning of treatment. Its absence in the structured personality is usually indicative of an ego syntonic neurosis. Yet if the person comes for therapy there may be a chink in the armor. The task here is to seek ways of rendering the problem dystonic. Consider the following dialogue between patient and therapist:

Patient: My wife says I am too logical. There is no such thing as too much logic, especially in my profession (law).

Therapist: Is their no validity to her complaint, then?

Patient: Well, she says that I value logic over her feelings, but I think that when I am right I have to establish that fact.

Therapist: Even if it makes her feel bad?

Patient: Maybe I do choose the wrong time.

A slight dent has been made in his righteousness and self-justification—not much, but enough to inform the therapist that matters are hopeful because the patient has been led to think that he can be ever so slightly mistaken in his priorities.

This clinical illustration is a form of preanalytic therapy to enable the person to "own" the problem and become a patient. That is likely to be more successful than plunging a person into psychoanalysis or psychotherapy against his or her will.

Excessively narcissistic patients also feel no need for treatment. The impervious narcissistic arrangement does not usually bring the person to the therapist's office unless someone else has complained about it, or it is not working efficiently enough (Blanck and Blanck 1979). Those patients do not want the therapist to change the arrangement; they want the therapist to make it work better because the arrangement, whether ego syntonicity or narcissism, is getting the person into trouble with the real world. The patient has to be enabled to look inward. In chapter 13 we presented a clinical illustration of a man who wanted the therapist to "fix" his wife.

The understructured patient is likely to be unmotivated for reasons that appear, superficially, to be similar to those of the ego syntonic or narcissistic patient. They all locate the problem in the external world. But the structured patient who was so devoted to logic and reason had reached the level where he could appreciate that his wife is a separate, other person. He was in the throes of an obsessional neurosis that uses intellectualization. The demands of the defense against the anxiety of being disorderly were so great that, even though he had attained object constancy, he was forced to override it lest the anxiety become too great.

The narcissistic patient is different in that, for him or her, other persons are not cathected with value. The understructured patient, on the other hand, cathects the other person, but only as part of the self representation. There the problem is projected onto an incompletely differentiated object representation. "She doesn't care about what I want" is to be read by the therapist as "She is part of me; why does she fail to understand without words?"

That defenses have an adaptive purpose, at least when initially established, is a theoretical shift that also changes the task of the patient. What is the patient's job? As we have stated earlier (chapter 14), in the older days of psychoanalysis it was neatly circumscribed. The patient was the provider of material. Matters are not so simple now, even in the psychoanalysis of the structured patient. The patient's task does not end with providing material; the patient is required to organize the material and even, as Kris describes, to interpret it sometimes. This is not difficult for the structured patient if we insist on it. A common form of resistance in well-structured patients is to answer our question, "What do you make of what you have been saying?" with "I was free associating, what more do you want?" The working alliance is temporarily askew when this happens. Of course, one does not get into a struggle over this well-known abuse of free association. It is often sufficient to overlook the hostility in the challenge and respond encouragingly, "Try to add it up." That will usually help restore the alliance and put the structured ego to work again.

Within the therapeutic situation, where it is no longer so much a matter of motivation, the resistances can appear superficially to take the same forms in these different structures. Two patients with different structures forget to come to their regularly scheduled sessions. The better-structured patient has repressed the appointment because he was defending against an unconscious fantasy that was beginning to emerge in the analysis. The less-structured patient was unconsciously afraid of wished-for merger with the therapist, a longing for symbiosis. This patient fails to come because fulfillment of that wish would mean engulfment and loss of identity. Both are using defenses in the service of resistance—the one uses repression; the other lacks ability to repress and therefore must use absence to maintain a safe distance.

A variation of forgetting altogether is the case of a well-structured patient in analysis who comes late because he has trouble parking. He had been driving around for ten or fifteen minutes looking for a metered parking spot. There is a parking garage in the building where the analyst has his office. Granted it costs more than a parking meter. But if the patient is already late, missing so much of the session is also costly. The analyst has to proceed on the assumption that the patient has an unconscious need to curtail the session lest material come through that will bring on more anxiety. We follow Sharpe's advice not to pounce. Most desirably, the patient himself will begin to think aloud about why this is happening. That will be a sign that the resistance is diminishing. Then analyst and patient may work together to bring the matter into consciousness.

It does not happen so easily and did not in this case. Instead, the resistance increased. This told the analyst something else. In the previous session this patient was approaching his repressed competitiveness with his father. It appeared in transferential form as he was talking about his knowledge that the analyst is a writer. Free association led him to venture to say that he is a better writer than the analyst. He needed the lateness because his boldness brought on signal anxiety; repression increased in strength.

Persons with poor motivation constitute a large segment of the patient population of many psychotherapists. Probably most children whose parents brought them into treatment fit this category. Marital partners who are having trouble tend to project blame onto the partner (Blanck and Blanck 1968). They arrive at the consultation room seeking self-justification rather than insight into their own defenses and object relations patterns that affect the marriage. Those schools of psychotherapy that see the problems in the transactions and interactions between persons as interpersonal rather than intrapsychic tend to affirm the defensive projections and displacements. Our approach would promote use of these defensive arrangements as a doorway that leads to understanding the deeper layers of the intrapsychic conflicts.

Often the language, the manifest content, is misperceived by the therapist as indicative of better or poorer motivation. The patient who says "I have a problem" is not necessarily better motivated than the patient who tells the therapist that he is there because his wife threatened to leave him if he did not seek therapy. All patients come with varying levels of ambivalence; the negative side of the ambivalence tends to take over once they enter the consultation room. According to Glover: "The patient has been unconsciously repenting his temerity ever since he rang the bell" (1955:19). It is not necessarily a lack of motivation that prompts a patient to say "I only want a little help." If the therapist listens closely, he or she may hear that the patient is announcing ambivalence. Attending to the negative side of the ambivalence, one hears "only a little." Listening to the positive side, one hears "I want help." It is more useful for the therapist to connect with the positive side. To join the negative side would propel the patient out the door.

The unmotivated patient sometimes pays a severe price for his or her overtly expressed reluctance. Challenges to the motivations of prospective patients will convince many that they were right in avoiding treatment. "If you think your wife is the problem, why are *you* here?" will cause many a man to decide that he does not belong there. "You say you don't believe much in therapy, so why have you come?" discourages that small fraction on the positive side of the ambivalence that brought the patient to our door. Challenges such as those are the result of listening to the manifest content only. Even in cases of "sent" patients, a latent wish for help brings the patient to the consultation room.

"Unmotivated" does not mean that the wish to feel better is absent. It has far more to do with negative (hostile) internalizations that originated in inadequacies of early experiences or distortions; these prevent optimistic anticipation and comprehension of the therapeutic experience as holding out favorable possibilities. For the most part, such patients view therapy with foreboding, with fears of damage to self and therapist because of the hostile cathexis.

We do not imply that the therapist always wins. Some resistances cannot be interpreted, especially in an initial consultation where the transference potential is dormant. Theoretically, however, it is inconceivable that there are more and less preferable kinds of resistance. Since the unconscious is always present and may never be overlooked, the therapist may almost always feel secure that the patient's approach behavior will contain both the wish to get help no matter how well it is concealed, as well as defenses against the anxiety that must inevitably militate against that attempt.

Where there is failure to come, the best we can do is try to help the referring person deal with the lack of motivation. Often this can be quite effective. If it is a spouse, for example, who thinks her husband needs treatment, we can help her deal with him in a way that makes the matter appear less threatening to him. One is not likely to approach a therapist because another person points out one's flaws. We can invite a referring spouse to come for one or a few sessions in order to help her approach her husband with a suggestion that will feel supportive and loving instead of critical. And such sessions, more often than not, open the opportunity for the wife to come to an understanding of her part in the problem as well.

Untrained referring persons and those in related helping professions usually welcome suggestions that provide a useful approach to the person they wish to refer. We can suggest, for example, that the emphasis be shifted. Instead of focusing on the symptom or the anxiety or the behavior, we might propose empathizing with the discomfort.

Legally mandated treatment for offenders and for the addict population, and divorce laws that demand predivorce counseling, all contribute to the ranks of the unmotivated or poorly motivated patient population. Those kinds of referrals are useful attempts to bring into treatment the person who would not seek it voluntarily. Precisely because we agree with these attempts, we wish to contribute techniques for the baffling problem of engaging the unwilling person to the point where he or she becomes a willing participant in the treatment process.

The convicted felon whose prison term was abbreviated on condition that he enter therapy uses the sessions to protest his innocence of the crime for which he was convicted. The therapist's role is not to review the trial, and it must be made especially clear that a therapist cannot overturn a conviction, but that the patient is entitled to a therapeutic hearing. One responds to his need to go over the matter, without holding out hope that one can alter the decision, but in order to encourage a therapeutic alliance out of which one can lead him to a psychological understanding of how he got himself into trouble.

We are stressing that one can only create and maintain a therapeutic alliance by not opposing. But that with which we agree is of critical importance. We agree with the affect and purpose but not necessarily the behavior. Always to act on one's feelings fails to interpose the ego functions of judgment, delay, and thought as trial action.

It is inaccurate to refer to persons with lowered motivation as *patients* until we have sought out and encouraged a reasonable amount of volition. The unmotivated "patient" is not a patient, is not treatable before the lack of motivation is overcome to the extent necessary to tap the interest in getting help. It is much easier to have the patient announce firmly that he wishes to be treated and then delve into the more familiar unconsciously determined resistances that psychoanalysts and psychotherapists have long known how to treat. When lack of motivation is viewed as a challenge, the therapist may become interested in meeting it.

That a person arrives at a therapist's office lacking motivation is not as paradoxical as it appears. There are reasons why persons come without wishing to be there. It is not unusual for someone to "bring the body" compliantly because he or she was sent by a spouse, by the court, by the physician, or others who are better motivated than the person they send. It is an error to begin "treatment" before the person has decided to participate. A patient is forced to come for therapy because his wife was "accidentally" hurt in the heat of an argument. He stresses to the therapist that he has already apologized profusely to his wife. Why can she not forgive and forget? As he presents his life history, it is fraught with injustices that continue in the present without a boundary line between present and past. He works hard at his job, but feels unappreciated. Possibly, out of this, we may speculate about why his anger erupted outside his control; his self representation is that of a permanently unappreciated person. He feels that his wife is nurturing her grievances instead of attending to his. He does not think he needs therapy but has come because he feels so contrite. The therapist meets him at that point of entry. Nothing is lost by agreeing, in order to get started, that it is better to resolve a dispute than nurse a grievance forever. But the fact that he feels so bad about the incident gives the therapist a handle. A better understanding of what went wrong might be arrived at by exploring it further, especially in relation to his feeling of being unappreciated. This calls for a stance on the part of the therapist that accepts the patient's feelings, but not necessarily his behavior. We do not support action in lieu of verbalization in any event; never is it supported where another person, or even the patient himself or herself, is physically hurt. It is the therapist's task to summon the skills necessary to enlist the patient's interest, discover why his feelings have caused him to act in a way that troubles him. This illustrates a way of engaging a patient in a therapeutic alliance. His hostility and lack of control will be dealt with after that alliance is solidly established.

Where the unwilling spouse arrives for his initial consultation sweating so profusely that he must take off his misted eyeglasses and is unable to control the jerking of his knees, one may assume that anxiety is not used as signal; he has become so anxious that it falls just short of overwhelming him. This patient requires the kind of supportive welcome that affirms that he has done a great deal for himself by keeping the appointment, painful as it is for him. The therapist's task is to do nothing that will make him more anxious, since such persons are likely to walk away from their anxiety because more competent defenses are not available to the ego.

Some unmotivated persons come willingly enough but are unable to take on the task of being participants in the treatment because they have meager capacity to extract from the environment. We do the best we can to promote extraction in those cases, but the prognosis is extremely guarded when dealing with an insufficiency in the innate endowment. Most patients who do not participate well, however, are not necessarily lacking in that capacity, but rather are unaccustomed to exercising it. Those patients wait for the therapist to do the work. This used to be designated globally as "passivity," which is dangerously close to being pejorative. We have to "teach" the patient how to perform his or her part of the mutual endeavor. This does not advocate offering didactic instruction in how to become a patient. The task is learned as we refrain from taking it over. Eagerness to get the treatment under way sometimes tempts the therapist to do the work for the patient. This exercises the therapist's ego functions and could well leave him or her exhausted at the end of the day, while the patient leaves unaffected.

Sometimes the therapist has to endure the patient's impatience and even anger that the therapist is not doing the work for him or her. Understructured patients may be helped to work by suggestions similar to those used with the structured patient, but with a slightly different objective: "Why don't you give it a try?" The difference is that the structured patient's ego is competent but sluggish; it *can* function. Because understructured patients are at such varying levels, some have egos that can function almost as well as those of the structured patients but others do not. In the latter instance, the less-structured patient has to be challenged gently to function at a higher level than exists. This is analogous to erecting hurdles when teaching the horseback rider to jump. We do not make them too high all at once. A little at a time raises the level of structuralization a notch by expecting a bit more than the patient thinks he or she can do.

This requires that the therapist assess how much the patient can do. We try not to assign tasks that are beyond the patient's ability because that tends to discourage. The word *try* is always encouraging and lacks the connotation of blame if the patient cannot go that far. A good guideline for the therapist is never to ask an unanswerable question or impose an impossible task. It is also desirable to refrain from expecting more than the level of object relations permits. For example, it harries a patient to expect object constancy where that is the very problem, before therapy has had the opportunity to help the patient attain that developmental position.

Getting the patient to do his or her part of the work will not be easy. The patient will engage in maneuvers that resemble ball games. He or she places the ball in the therapist's court. The therapist tosses it back to the patient *when it belongs there*. In that way the patient learns when the ball belongs in which court.

A structured patient comes to an apparent impasse in the analysis. Material does not flow; the analyst thinks the resistance links to fixation in a psychosexual phase. Desirably, one attends first to the adaptive function of the ego, which here involves protection of autonomy by refusing to comply (chapter 21). That may at the same time be a manifestation of the anal phase, but we postpone that interpretation, giving precedence to adaptation. This is consistent with Jacobson's description of the totality of the experience at any given psychosexual phase. The psychosexual factor exists in the context of the object relationship. Here we look at the drive manifestations from a new perspective, a part of a larger whole. It does not destroy an analysis to postpone dealing with this factor. This is one of the places in the technique of psychoanalysis that has been vastly enhanced by ego psychological and object relations considerations.

One school of thought would describe failure to comply as *passive-aggressive*. That is one of the more pejorative terms in the therapeutic vocabulary. It implies that the patient is intent on having his or her way in a devious fashion. But if we respect the thrust toward autonomy, it matters little whether opposition is overt or covert. We are pleased to find that it is operative.

Both factors, psychosexuality and object relations, exist also in the understructured patient. In such cases it would destroy the treatment to overlook the object relations factor. It is vital to defer interpretation of psychosexual elements while treatment attends to the striving toward autonomy. Contrasted with the psychoanalysis of the structured patient, dealing with psychosexuality only in the understructured patient would fail to build structure.

The strivings for autonomy in these patients represent the developmental thrust, the psychic pulling away that was thwarted in the first round of development. These can take forms that, when looked at from the behavioral aspect only, appear resistant and hostile. The patient refuses to speak or comes late or misses sessions entirely. Structured patients engage in the same forms of behavior. But there, those actions are true resistances and may be interpreted as such at the proper times. It is a grave error to interpret that same behavior as resistance in the understructured patient. To interpret based on behavioral manifestations not only destroys the therapeutic alliance but it repeats the developmental impediment, the unattuned responses of the primary objects or object representations. The alliance is retained by siding with the healthy employment of the aggressive drive in the service of separation-individuation.

Problems in object relations that impede beginning treatment can now be restated in terms of lines of development. For example, fixation in an early level of need gratification will be reflected in inability to accept the frustrations of therapeutic abstinence. For such patients, proper balance of gratification and frustration, missed in initial development, may be fruitfully employed as a motivating factor. Especially where avoidance attitudes have become embedded in character structure, technical means must be sought to overcome the serious misunderstandings of such patients about the intentions of the object. The person who arrives with magical expectations of the therapist is already a step ahead of the one with negative expectations. The optimistic person perceives from a position of infantile omnipotence, but such perception is at least favorable. The more serious developmental failure is reflected in incapacity even to expect that the therapist might be a need-gratifying object. We do not imply that the therapist's role is to gratify. We refer here only to the patient's object expectations.

The silent patient presents a special problem. Some therapists find silence to be most uncomfortable for them and tend to rush in with words to fill in where it might be far better to the allow the patient some space. In earlier psychoanalytic thought, silence was almost invariably interpreted as a resistance against verbalizing negative feelings in the transference. Now we are required to think of a variety of meanings, such as the understructured patient's need to be together without words in replication of the symbiotic experience, and hostility as an affect that accompanies the separating thrust. Here, too, the therapist would want to encourage separation and so would overlook the affective charge with which the patient tries to exercise this important developmental thrust, knowing it is being risked within the benign therapeutic climate that encourages venture.

With an understructured patient who is having difficulty discussing a given matter, we do not take it as a resistance or a violation of the rule of free association. It is more likely an attempt to maintain the modicum of boundary formation that does exist or even to create a boundary that begins to appear possible to the patient within the more benign climate than existed for him or her ever before. The therapist might say: " Obviously, the more I know about you the better I will be able to be of help. However, it is still in your best interest for us to wait until you feel ready to tell me about this matter rather than surrender the information to me." That guards autonomy at the level at which it exists. This is likely to be the first time the patient enjoys affirmation rather than disapproval. Affirmation encourages the use of the aggressive drive to advance to yet higher levels.

This technical measure used to be described as "supporting the ego." That was a most baffling, albeit correct, precept. We have described the precise measures the therapist employs in greater detail to lend precision to the theoretical reason behind ego support. That opens the opportunity for each therapist to create his or her own style of "supporting the ego."

Another term, *developmental level*, is also too global, given the more precise knowledge we have today. To learn more specifically what the level of functioning is, the therapist needs to seek out the forms of interaction between the self representation and the object representations, the degree to which they are cathected, and the balance of positive and negative affect. All this may be determined from the content of the transference manifestations and by the patient's behavior in other relationships in his or her life.

It favors an objective therapeutic stance to bear in mind that the therapeutic alliance, at its best, is not reciprocal. From this it follows that the therapist remains an ally with even affect while the patient, if he or she finds it necessary, expresses a wide range of affect and oppositionalism that may or may not be resistance.

Always, the therapist avoids gratifying inappropriately. Needs that may appear legitimate to the patient may be growth retarding. Considerable skill is required for the therapist to distinguish between gratification that will build structure and gratification that will infantilize. We can state a kind of truism: the patient's *demands* are not always right, but his or her *affect* is always right. The therapist can understand why a patient wants to be gratified, can empathize with the feelings that motivate the demand and with the frustration of not having the demand met. But a therapist only lends himself or herself to that which will promote growth and structure building.

We have used examples of dealing with the resistances of the well-structured patient for purposes of comparison, but we have not explicated the technique of psychoanalysis in depth. Our emphasis is on the resistances of the understructured personalities. We stress that serious technical errors can be made in both directions: resistances of the structured personalities may be treated with overgratification; resistantlike behavior of the understructured personality may be dealt with as though the ego is capable of better-structured defense. It is difficult indeed to make this distinction because, more often than not, the behavioral manifestations are the same.

19

▼

Reconstruction of Preverbal Experience

Preverbal experience is both unrememberable and unforgettable: unrememberable because, as it is not registered in the verbal realm, it is therefore not subject to verbal recall; unforgettable because of the intense cathexis and registration of affectively tinged images of self and other.

We have referred to Spitz's finding that life, in the early days and weeks, is perceived by means of coenesthetic reception, a global intaking process; registry of those very early experiences is lasting and may not always alter with later experience. When diacritic reception begins, registry is also of affectively tinged *inter*action, albeit capacity to recognize that there is another person is far from clearly established. Repetition of those experiences, with alterations dictated by increasing capacity for reality testing, begins to shape the pattern or template of object relations that will remain for life.

We have described the interaction between innate endowment and maternal response as the building blocks for structuralization by means of internalization of self and object representations as these become established over time. We remind ourselves here that object relations is the *resul-*

tant of interaction, at first between self and object and later between the self representation and the object representations.

If it is unrememberable, how do we reconstruct preverbal experience? Adult behavior is influenced because the enduring nature of the object relations pattern guides the individual in his or her attitudes and behavior throughout life. Although considerably altered by the time adulthood is reached, the template remains. In the therapeutic encounter, because the therapist does not interact in the established object relations pattern, he or she can view the patient's behavior in pure form—that is, without the contamination of interaction that takes place in ordinary social encounters.

That is of great moment to therapy. Obviously, it is not in accord with those forms of therapy that would have the therapist interact with the patient for the purpose of providing a new experience. We think it desirable to refrain from interaction initially to be able to detect how the "old" experiences have influenced behavior before providing new ones. Even then, we do not advocate *provision* of experience in an artificial manner. Rather, we rely on the treatment to lead to better capacity for reality testing that enables the patient to distinguish between past experience and present reality, as we have described in chapter 17.

When we first advocated the desirability and feasibility of reconstruction of preverbal experience, the matter was still controversial. Twenty years ago the value of preverbal experience in treatment of the adult patient was hotly debated. Today one hears more of the danger of misinterpreting the data rather than challenging its usefulness. The newer neonatal studies are so rich in heretofore unknown aspects of infantile life that that controversy is resolved in the minds of most analysts. It follows that the significance of infant observational research for clinical work is no longer in question. Inevitably, both theory construction and elaboration of techniques for treatment will continue to be influenced not only by the wealth of information about early life that we now have available, but also by that which is yet to come. We have predicted that, with the invention of more sophisticated instrumentation, not only postnatal but also prenatal life will be explored to provide data not yet foreseeable.

Detailed information about the developmental processes of very early life provides the therapist with guidelines in discerning the pattern of the patient's attitudes and behavior as it is revealed in the therapeutic relationship. It enables the therapist to make assumptions about what might have been experienced by a given patient and how that individual has processed that experience. It also provides us with more solid theoretical underpinning for elaboration of techniques for reconstruction.

Acting out is thought to be a way of repeating instead of remembering in words. Used cautiously, it may constitute a guide to reconstruction of preverbal experience if we can bring it into the verbal realm. A patient rings the doorbell and, not getting an instantaneous response, elects to leave rather than try again. A surge of affect triggers the "memory" of no response, resulting in action based on past experience. At the next session this may be brought into the verbal realm.

Moore and Fine (1990) would confine use of the term *acting out* to the behavior of patients who are capable of verbalizing remembered experience and who, in the service of resistance, repeat in action rather than remember. Their definition is "the expression through action, rather than in words, of a memory, an attitude, or a conflict by a person in psychoanalysis or another form of treatment that is based on verbalization (2–3).

In general practice, the term *acting out* is often used more broadly to apply to all behavior that is not verbal. We believe that the restricted definition is more useful. It distinguishes between the behavior of the well-structured patient who is capable of semantic communication but who uses action as a resistance, on the one hand, and the patient who *acts* because he or she is understructured and therefore has not cathected experience in verbal form, on the other hand. This keeps matters clearer because it serves the therapist in making a decision with regard to treatment techniques; it reserves the concept *acting out* for the more highly structured patient who can be invited to put the action into words. For the understructured patient *acting* more clearly suggests that the behavior is a form of communication for experience that has never entered the verbal realm. Freud implied much of this as early as 1912 in his paper "The Dynamics of Transference," in which he states that not all impulses of infantile life go through a process of development in accord with reality; some remain as they were originally established, having been kept away from the conscious personality and from reality testing.

Impulses that are *acted upon* are not the same as repressed material that is *acted out*. Acting does not demonstrate to the analyst that there are repressed wishes and fantasies from verbal life. Repression is the defense mechanism *par excellence* of the better-structured patient. One searches in vain for repressed memories and unconscious fantasies of the understructured patient because most have not developed to the point where repression can be employed and where fantasy life exists to an appreciable degree. There are exceptions. Those borderline patients who are close to the neurotic border may have unconscious fantasy and ability to endure conflict, to use repression, and may show other characteristics of neurosis while retaining some borderline features as well.

Anna Freud was not optimistic about retrieval of preoedipal life:

> There is, further, the question whether the transference really has the power to transport the person back as far as the beginning of life. Many are convinced that this is the case. Others, myself among them, raise the point that it is one thing for preformed, object-related fantasies to return from repression and be directed from the inner to the outer world (i.e., to the person of the analyst); but it is an entirely different, almost magical expectation to have the patient in analysis change back into the prepsychological, undifferentiated, and unstructured state in which no divisions exist between body and mind, or self and object.
>
> (1969:40–41)

And she adds: "I myself cannot help feeling doubtful about trying to advance into the area of primary repression, i.e., to deal with processes which by nature are totally different from the results of the ego's defensive maneuvering" (1969:39).

Anna Freud bases her argument on the conviction that only the repressed can be retrieved in psychoanalysis. That disputes the findings of the infant observationalists who provide data that unlock the secrets of "primary repression." They proceeded in the direction that Freud indicated when he said: "The direct observation of children has the disadvantage of working upon data which are easily misunderstandable: psycho-analysis is made difficult by the fact that it can only reach its data, as well as its conclusions, after long detours. But by co-operation the two methods can attain a satisfactory degree of certainty in their findings" (1905:201).

Mahler takes direct issue with Anna Freud. She says:

> Psychoanalytic observational research of the first years of life touches on the essence of reconstruction and on the problem of coenesthetic empathy, both so essential for the clinical efficiency of psychoanalysis.
>
> At one end are Melanie Klein and her followers whose *a priori* opinions cannot be refuted by behavioral data.
>
> At the other end of the spectrum stand those among us Freudian ana-

lysts who look with favor on stringent verbal and reconstructive evidence. We organize these on the basis of Freud's metapsychological constructs; yet some of us seem to accord preverbal material no right to serve as the basis for even the most cautious and tentative extension of our main body of hypotheses, unless these, too, be supported by reconstruction, that is to say by clinical and, of course, predominantly verbal material.

Yet Freud's hope was that his fundamental body of theory—that truly monumental basis of clinical and theoretical work—would remain a *living heritage*. Even his genius could not work out every detail in one lifetime; these, added bit by bit, should eventually coalesce to form a general psychology. (1971:404)

To accept that some drive impulses escape the course of development of reality testing presents the therapist with the task of attempting to identify these processes as they are reflected in the affect and behavior of the patient. While relatively impervious to traditional psychoanalytic interpretive (verbal) efforts, this does not mean that they remain impervious to other therapeutic devices. The therapist's task of seeking to understand in a stance of flexible attunement to the patient's productions—verbal, postural, behavioral—reverberates with the earliest moment in life when, for fortunate babies, someone tried to understand before they could communicate in words.

A patient who is a talented musician suffers unbearable anxiety at every performance. Because of this, performances are limited, sometimes canceled; at other times the performance goes on with memory lapses that leave the patient with profound feelings of unworthiness and humiliation. Her mother suffered from lifelong depression. The patient remembers her mother's lack of interest and her inability to approve or affirm childhood performances, not only in music but on almost any level. These memories are of some limited value; largely, they are intellectual, isolated from affect.

There is much reliving in the transference. The therapist is usually successful in eluding being trapped into repeating the negative maternal role, but this does not relieve the anxiety, depression, and expectation of disapproval and failure. The patient can articulate the problem: "I really believe by now that it is not you who are cold and uninterested. Certainly I do not feel angry with you as I did at the beginning of treatment. Yet all this does is make me more upset and miserable each time I find myself in the same state."

Here is an example of how a therapist's attempt to be a better parent would be ineffective. The patient is already a "filled vessel" with no room for new experiences until late in treatment. The therapist, by maintaining the benign climate, even mood, and receptive attitude, and by not reacting countertransferentially, presents an attitude that contains potential for new selective identifications to be made.

In the case we are discussing, this happened. In more positive moments the patient began to express recognition that there has been a fair degree of success in treatment. The anxiety was no longer totally pervasive, and no longer impaired work, play, relationships with family, to the disabling degree that it had. But improved autonomous functioning always took place away from the therapist, suggesting that the patient felt that separating thrusts are dangerous to the relationship. We have referred to this rather common phenomenon as reflecting a "disapproved-of self image," which comes about when the natural developmental thrust is thwarted by the disapproving object who cannot tolerate the child's need to separate and individuate. One sees this frequently in the mother-toddler action in the practicing subphase, for example, where the intrusive mother does not allow the child to explore the world at his or her own initiative. We have seen mothers who intrude upon the crawling baby's movements, turning the child in the direction of the mother's choosing even when there is no potential physical danger.

Because the individuation track is less prone to conflict with the object, fairly often it will proceed autonomously despite disapproval. Many such persons function well but do not feel good abut it. Some abandon autonomy and functioning in favor of object retention. Those persons may feel better because they have averted object loss; the price is failure to develop their potential.

It is important to note that the patient we are now describing can employ isolation, a mechanism of defense that is available to the ego where there is a fair amount of structuralization. She can remember having had temper tantrums and shouting at her mother, but she cannot recall having felt angry or resentful. Affect is isolated and repressed while memory of the event is retained.

The recovery process was slow. It cannot be otherwise because the patient was confronted with an enormous task. The separating, individuating steps that are so difficult for the child at the age-appropriate time become infinitely more difficult in middle-age. Continuing organization had proceeded for so many years, embodying the developmental deficit in ways that enabled structuralization to go forward, and relatively strong defenses to be installed. But, at the core, fear of object loss remained, a fear so deeply buried that any attempt at verbal interpretation feels incomprehensible to an intelligent adult. Yet the patient reached a point where she became able to perceive the therapeutic differential; reorganization is at least possible, a giant step away from where the patient had begun.

Most vexing for therapists are the silent patient and the so-called acting-out patient. As we have said, silence, all too often, is regarded at least peevishly and at worst judgmentally as a blatant violation of free association, inconsistent with the concept of the "talking cure." Traditionally it is thought of as a resistance, usually the withholding of negative thoughts in the transference (chapter 18). In 1961 the American Psychoanalytic Association held an all-day symposium on this irksome problem, and it began to be suggested that there could be more to it—that perhaps silence could represent the wish to be together with the mother. There ensued a rash of interpretations of silence as "I am your babysitter." This was a half-truth because theory and technique had not yet developed sufficiently to enable therapists to understand such silence thoroughly enough. In 1971, at the meetings of the American Psychoanalytic Association, Nathaniel Ross suggested that silence could represent not necessarily resistance in the sense of repression of negative feelings in the transference but enactment of the symbiotic wish. Thus it took ten years longer for theory to illuminate an aspect of silence that resonates with preverbal life. By definition, this kind of silence cannot be verbalized. It is the therapist's task to help the patient apply words retroactively to a wish to be together in perfect understanding without words, to be one with the therapist. This is a far cry from the interpretation to a structured patient who is withholding negative thoughts. Some patients are silent for that reason. Even in such cases, it is not helpful to expect that silence will yield to an accusation disguised as an interpretation. "You are withholding" is not conducive to maintaining a good therapeutic alliance.

In 1974 we said that reconstruction of preverbal experience is a pioneering endeavor, with successful reconstruction rare. Added knowledge emboldens us to go forward. As the object relations patterning becomes clear in the relationship between patient and therapist, it lends itself to gradual questioning that alerts the patient to the fact that behavior that had once seemed natural and logical is no longer as logical as it had appeared. Since that introduces a new element into an already established curriculum—the patterned behavior of the patient—it must go through the equivalent of a developmental experience.

A man reenters therapy after a long hiatus because of difficulties in his marital relationship that cause him to react to his wife more violently than suits his self-image. Exploration discloses that, while he can function brilliantly in his profession, at home he is passive, demanding, and becomes passionately angry. The frustration tolerance that he can maintain for his daily work disappears entirely in his wife's presence. That his wife, who also works, could be suffering her own frustrations is not in his field of object perception. Pointing this out to him would be antitherapeutic since the problem is not interpretable; such confrontation is not conducive to growth in a developmental medium. The therapist remembers that in his previous period of treatment, when his wife went back to work, this patient cried happily, "Now *my* income will double." That this reflects a symbiotic wish is not mentioned to the patient now. But the therapist is able to introduce the enormous contrast between his behavior with his wife and his behavior with his daughter, with whom he is fondly overprotective. The patient's attention is called to this contrast, which introduces a jarring note to his simplistic explanation that his wife is not attuned to his needs. While that is certainly true at times, the therapist can now press the point that this cannot be the complete explanation for his rages. This introduces a demand on his ego to try to understand his own behavior better, without the criticism implicit in confrontation. It is a first step toward possibly finding the unrememberable pattern that influences his present behavior.

Understanding a patient's behavior in the light of repetition of preverbal experience is valuable even when it is not used directly in the form of a reconstructive interpretation. Such understanding can be used diagnostically to broaden the therapist's grasp of the case. Kris (chapter 5) illuminates the importance of creating a climate conducive to remembering. While he agrees that anamnestic data might not be recoverable because of the telescoping of events, of condensation, distortion, and defensive arrangements, he finds value in uncovering patterns that could lead to the lifting of defensive countercathexes. At the time he could only allude to defense against the anxiety of the conflictual state in the structured patient. An understanding of the behavior and defenses of the less-structured patient had not yet entered the theoretical scene.

The question may well be raised as to why verbalization is of such central importance in psychoanalytically oriented psychotherapy, in contrast with so many nonanalytic therapies that promote the more primitive forms of expression, such as acting-out, ventilation, experiencing, encountering, touching, confronting, and so on. We have described verbalization as a complex process. Speech and verbalization are not synonymous. Hartmann (chapter 3) shows how the schizophrenic who has learned to speak uses words as things. Without the bridge of distinct self and object representations and acceptance of the reality principle, the psychotic has not acquired secondary process thought (or has lost it regressively). The major ego functions that enter the complex function of verbalization are, more or less in order of their development: object comprehension, intentionality, object relations, symbolization, speech, and semantic communication.

In a seminar on developmental theory, Frank (personal communication, 1979) anticipated that we would find object relations to be the context within which development takes place. This preceded Emde who proved it observationally. Normally proceeding development leads the wordless infant into the world of semantic communication as a step in the continuing process of structuralization.

Speech begins with global words. Spitz traces in fine detail the complex ego development that paves the way for speech. Yet the thought or affect behind the first spoken words remains relatively unexpressed. One word, best understood by the attuned mother in symbiotic union, contains myriad meanings. Piaget (1955) believes that the word "Mama" is formed by jaw and mouth movements that are only one step beyond sucking. The child who utters this global word may be saying "I am hungry"; "I am afraid"; "I am content"; "Where are you?"; "I see you and remember that it is you who usually brings me comfort"; and so on. But that child may not even be communicating to that degree; he or she may be moving lips and jaw in coordination with the vocal apparatus. That would be an exercise in coordination. Combined in this way are recognition of the object; symbolization—by applying a word (symbol) to the object representation; using the physical apparatus to form the word.

As the child proceeds in the conquest of language, he or she begins to speak in words joined together but not yet as grammatically constructed sentences. These tend to be concrete and simplistic. "Teddy Bear," means "I want my Teddy bear." Subject, verb, and predicate enter later. Even then the sentence does not convey the entire thought, which could be: "I feel lonely and the texture, odor, and closeness of Teddy Bear comfort me by reminding me of the closeness of Self and Mother that has felt so good in the past." Or the sentence: "I won't"—a sentence, to be sure, but it does not necessarily mean " I refuse to do as you say." It may mean "I am beginning to feel like a person in my own right and, having noticed that when I refuse it creates a stir, I am trying out my newly discovered power to disconcert the adults." Or "You have said no to me so many times, which frustrated me and made me angry and anxious because I have felt so separate from you at those moments. You made me realize that we are no longer one. So now I can retaliate. When I imitate your no I find I have the same power that you have. And it will show you how it feels to be on the receiving end of a no."

Psychoanalysis is known as the "talking cure." Psychoanalysis and psychoanalytically oriented psychotherapy remain verbal forms of treatment, in disagreement with those therapies that promote regressive modes of discharge. Fromm (1951) discusses with nostalgia *The Forgotten Language* of the primary process as though its retrieval would have therapeutic value. Her idea is close to that of primal scream "therapy," now superseded by newer fads. The thinking was that expression (ventilation) of preverbal affect eliminates the pain. To be able to communicate and to understand the communications of others in the primary process is questionable therapy, except for psychotics who need to begin by being understood at the only place where they can be reached. That is done, however, only for the purpose of helping them advance. For all others, to understand without words would make inroads on identity and autonomy and would impair many ego functions—the integrative and synthetic functions, symbolization, defense, intentionality, frustration tolerance, reality testing, including the ability to distinguish inside from outside and self representation from object representations. To put it another way, the ego would be permitted to remain inoperative, impeding the therapeutic purpose of building structure.

Not every experience is a therapeutic one. We have heard sincere reports of exhilarating experience in encounter groups, for example. Breaking down inhibition, encouraging closeness, attacking defenses, ventilating affects both loving and hostile are not structure building. In fact, for the nonneurotic patient, a necessary therapeutic goal is to help him or her acquire distance from the other person as part of the process of acquiring identity. The aloof patient may have meager object representations, or may be defending against the wish to merge because that threatens to erase the modicum of identity that has been attained. It is not desirable to assail defenses; the therapeutic task is to understand them. It is especially harmful to force closeness in working with the understructured patient who needs distance as a defense. And to force ventilation of primitive affect exposes the ego to more than it can tolerate, incurring the danger of decompensation.

Learning to convey one's feelings in words protects identity by guarding privacy. The fact that one has to communicate one's thoughts to another person "across a chasm" (Spitz 1972) implies differentiation of self representation from object representations. Many borderline and psychotic patients come to their therapists with the conviction that their minds can be read. They hold such notions because, relating in the symbiotic mode, they assume there are no boundaries between themselves and others. Some are quite terrified of this threat to an already shaky identity and are relieved to know that their therapists cannot know anything not told them. Others, less defended against symbiotic longing, are disappointed when their minds cannot be read. Some patients say openly that they would like it if their therapists could know all without needing to be told. Others fear that their therapists will know too much. Some resort to interesting defensive devices. For example, they try not to have thoughts during their sessions so there will be nothing to read. The best technical procedure for those with the wish for merger is to understand it without gratifying, for gratifying it would continue to infantilize. Withholding gratification is both disappointing and growth promoting. We repeat that not all growth results from gratification; sometimes frustration, if tolerably dosed, serves growth.

Aloofness in defense against the wish to merge is the most common form of borderline resistance. Those patients should be allowed to maintain distance until they feel assured that the therapist does not have the need to engulf. That diminishes the danger. In direct contravention of the basic rule of free association, regarded as a must in the psychoanalytic treatment of neurosis, understructured patients have to be assured that they need not say everything. This supports the ego functions of decision making and volition. When it feels safe, when the patient owns his or her thoughts, they will be voiced voluntarily. Awaiting that time keeps the patient in alliance with the therapeutic purpose, instead of in compliance with or in rebellion against the demands of the object. Consider the following case:

A patient was so afraid of losing her identity because of her unconscious wish for merger that she sat in the far corner of the treatment room for a long time before she could risk moving closer. She said as little as possible, thereby carefully guarding the minimal autonomy that had been attained. She considered all the therapeutic arrangements—hours, fee, frequency—to be because of the therapists's need. The paranoid tinge was particularly evident in the little that she did verbalize. The therapist had to turn the initiative over to the patient by saying "If it's for me, don't do it." This was designed to bring to the attention of the ego that she was not required to obey, that she had the opportunity to choose, and especially that she and the therapist were more differentiated than she believed.

It is not difficult to force patients to comply with rules, but that impairs autonomy. In these sophisticated times, patients have to be assured that their desire for privacy is not necessarily resistance, and not necessarily in opposition to the therapy. The therapist will know, but not convey to the patient in theoretical terms, that opposition and desire for privacy may represent an unconscious insistence on retention of a dearly won separate identity that is still fragile.

The development of the ego and its functions is the decisive factor in determining whether the form of communication in therapy is growth promoting. Therefore we do not necessarily abide by the psychoanalytic rule of abstinence that is appropriate for the well-structured patient, especially in the early phases of treatment. Preverbal modes of establishing object connection and of conveying affect may prompt the patient to write notes, bring gifts, keep diaries, display photographs or art work, and the like. To forgo these, as one would in psychoanalysis proper, is to reject the only way the patient may have of making a connection. It would constitute asking the patient to function beyond his or her communicative capacity. One of the principal purposes of therapy with such patients is to enable them to communicate on higher levels of object relations, that is, verbally. The therapy will proceed to higher levels if we begin by connecting at the level that exists at the outset. We have already said that about treatment of psychosis. It applies at higher levels as well, although it takes different forms in borderline structures. More aware of the separateness of the therapist, borderline patients may bring gifts. We have said that to reject the gifts and similar forms of seeking connection would repeat early injury to the patient's narcissism and would retard the therapy. The means the patient uses to make a connection by communicating nonverbally provide important clues to preverbal experience. As one comes to understand the nonverbal attempts to connect, one can begin to try to help the patient put the matter into words. In psychotherapy the "rules" change with developmental advances that the therapy brings about. With the growing ability to verbalize, we may expect the patient to cease communicating in action.

Reconstruction of preverbal experience is made possible by using developmental object relations theory to observe the patterning of object relations as they appear in the therapeutic situation. This is facilitated by the fact that the therapist does not engage in the prepatterned formulas, thereby providing a clear field for the patterns to unfold. Sometimes dreams also provide clues to preverbal experience. Always, affect is a guide to that "unrememberable" time of life.

20

▼

The Use of Dreams in Psychotherapy

There is a fairly large literature on the meaning and use of dreams in psychoanalysis which we shall not repeat here. Less is written about the use of the dream in psychotherapy although, with increasing interest in the borderline conditions, that subject has begun to enter the literature.

Freud's (1900) landmark work on dreams was not concerned with psychotherapy. He regarded dreams as the royal road to the unconscious at a time in the history of theory construction when uncovering the unconscious appeared to him to be the therapeutic goal. Now there is more to psychoanalysis than making the unconscious conscious and, in many psychotherapy cases, we may want to postpone uncovering until the ego is competent to deal with conflict. Because the so-called borderline personalities have such wide variation in their degrees of structuralization, the therapist may decide to use dreams differently in different cases. This does not offer a secure guideline. Again, as we have pointed out about the technique of psychotherapy in general, we cannot have solidly established rules for the use of dreams because degrees of structuralization vary from one psychotherapy patient to another.

In the treatment of many understructured patients, one would not want to use dreams at all. That refers especially to those cases that fall into the category of close-to-psychotic where the main task is to build structure, to make defenses operate more effectively. So there are two opposite considerations, again depending on the level of structuralization. With the structured patient, one would use whatever means are presented to deal with the defenses in order to uncover unconscious conflict; with the understructured patient, the therapeutic purpose is to improve the defensive capacity as a large part of building structure. With a middle-range borderline patient one might want to use a dream now and then to further the treatment, but not necessarily to uncover the unconscious. With close-to-neurotic structures, one would probably work with dreams in a way that approaches the use of dreams in the psychoanalysis of neurosis.

Before we illustrate the uses of dreams in these different situations, we discuss a matter hardly mentioned elsewhere. Different therapists and analysts feel differently about dreams and that, of course, determines the way they use them. Unanalyzed psychotherapists, we find, are not familiar with their own unconscious and therefore usually are not comfortable with dreams. Their tendency is to ignore them or to make sweeping interpretations of the manifest content. The ideal form of dream interpretation, not often attained, is described by Kris (chapter 5). The patient is the best interpreter of his or her dreams if resistance does not bar the way. The analyst's task is only to interpret resistance. We remind ourselves that Kris referred not to a single resistance but to the crumbling of a resistant structure that is accomplished as an analysis approaches termination .

We cannot say that after studying the *Interpretation of Dreams* and the additional literature, and after attending dream seminars and using dreams in supervised cases, all therapists and analysts are uniformly equipped to work with dreams. Basically, there are varying degrees of talent for understanding dreams which remains relatively unalterable. And there are other variables. In particular, there is the matter of whether and how dreams were dealt with in one's own analysis. Since an analysis is for therapeutic purposes first and only secondarily didactic, dreams in a training analysis have to be dealt with in relation to the therapeutic needs of the analysand. Therefore when we say that much depends on how the analyst *feels* about dreams, we infer that his or her own analysis has been the training ground for those feelings. If dreams have occupied a major place in the analysis, such a person is likely to place more emphasis on dreams in his or her work with patients. We do not imply that copious use of dreams makes for a better training analysis; there can be a good analysis with few dreams. We imply only that a person who has not worked much on his or her own dreams is not as likely to value dream work with patients and is less likely to develop a "feel" for dreams.

Let us begin with the use of dreams in psychoanalysis, not as a comprehensive treatise on that subject but to illustrate how dreams are used there differently from their use in the less-structured personalities. It has long been known that Freud's demonstration of how he analyzed his own dreams in *The Interpretation of Dreams* is not a manual for dream interpretation. He intended to present a theory of how dreams come about, what their function is, and samples of his analysis of his own dreams. From it we learn a great deal about the dream work (how dreams are formed), about differences between the primary and secondary processes, and about metapsychology in general. We do not learn specifically how to analyze a patient's dreams. That is left to the therapist's judgment of what in the analysis is being worked on at the time the dream is presented. In other words, in an orderly analysis priorities play a large role.

Freud believed that a patient's first dream should never be analyzed. He reasoned that the first dream in psychoanalysis contains the entire neurosis in its latent content and should be left to unfold at the appropriate times. This means that one approaches the issues where they can have more than intellectual meaning, that is, in the context of a transference. He was not concerned about losing the material, nor should the analyst be. It remains in the unconscious, to emerge again perhaps in another dream in a different manifest guise or by free association with or without a dream. Freud's dictum about first dreams has been modified somewhat now that we are comfortable about not analyzing the entirety of a dream in the orderly manner of seeking associations to each element as he did in his dream book. One can select a piece of a dream that fits in with the purpose at hand, leaving the rest for another time. It is sometimes better to do something about a first dream than to follow Freud blindly in this matter. It is not contraindicated to communicate to a patient beginning an analysis that something in his or her dream is of importance at the moment. We illustrate:

A patient who has made all of the preliminary arrangements for an analysis began without stressing what analyst and patient both knew—that this analyst was not the patient's first choice. He had seen the analyst he would have preferred, who was fully booked and who referred him to a colleague. The patient began with a long dream about his displeasure because his wife had bought him a tie he did not like; he was in a dilemma because he was loathe to tell her that he didn't want it. The dream had other elements, but the analyst selects this one only because it contains the patient's thinly disguised reluctance to begin with an analyst he does not want. If left uninterpreted this will become an obstacle to their working together, whereas if it is brought into the open the patient will learn not only that the analyst can tolerate a negative attitude but something about his own character— that he finds it hard to say what he feels openly. This fosters a therapeutic alliance without analyzing what would be too much for the time being.

The rationale for this manner of selection also holds for the understructured patient, so we cite it as a generality about the use of dreams—one selects that element of the dream that serves to propel the treatment at the moment. This implies not only that one may use part of a dream without concern for whether a complete dream analysis has been done, but also that one may choose to use a dream in its entirety or even overlook a dream altogether in favor of other material more pressing at the moment. For example, an understructured patient who was in treatment three times a week for more than a year kept bringing long, chaotic dreams. The therapist chose to work with the chaos in the patient's psychic life without direct reference to the dreams.

This follows a dictum we adhere to with little or no variation: Every dream is to be dealt with *in some way*. That does not necessarily mean that it is to be analyzed. To be "dealt with" can mean that one interprets a part of a dream, as we have illustrated, or the entire dream, or that one may decide to deal with the dream by making silent note of its content and style. By making a considered decision, the analyst or therapist is "dealing" with it.

Some understructured patients do not bring dreams. We do not press them to do so. The dream studies (Fisher 1965) reveal that we dream approximately four times in the course of the night. But that does not mean that all dreams are, or should be, remembered. There is also the opposite situation—some understructured patients remember too well. Even those who attend only once a week can occupy almost the entire session with the telling of a dream. There we do have to intervene. Usually it means that the patient believes we want rapid access to the unconscious and that we can know all of his or her psychic life through the dream. We do not interpret this, but use it to round out our own diagnostic impression about the patient's degree of structuralization. The patient usually does not know consciously that he or she believes that minds can be read. Often the disguise in the dream is transparent because the defensive function is weak. In neither instance do we want to uncover. Fairly often an understructured patient will ask the therapist what his or her dream means. It may be a tour de force for the therapist to "read" a dream, but that would go against the therapeutic objective by exercising the therapist's capacities at the expense of the patient. It must always be borne in mind that the manifest content of a dream, which can sometimes be understood by a skilled therapist, contains a latent meaning that is not so patent. It is even possible to understand the latent content if one knows the patient well. Again, that is an exercise of the therapist's skill that does not serve the patient.

Patients learn how to work on their dreams as they learn in general how to work in therapy, not by instruction but out of the structure-building experiences in the therapy. Telling the patient that we cannot read the dream may, for example, interfere prematurely with the patient's need for the therapist to be omniscient; it is more desirable to titrate disillusionment than to impose an aspect of reality for which the patient is not yet ready. One might, for example, interrupt the telling of a long dream to ask the patient whether he or she wants to use the entire session in that way. This avoids forbidding it, a function of the therapist's superego, and puts the ego of the patient to work on thinking it through. Sometimes it is appropriate to deal with style rather than content.

Chaotic dreams are often diagnostic signs. We do not usually advocate making a firm diagnosis via a dream, but here we are still speaking of style. One might well think that, since dreams employ the primary process, every dream would be chaotic. But where there is a structured ego, secondary revision reorganizes the disorder so that dreams are told as though they are coherent stories. That is so even when the dream contains some bizarre elements. The intact ego will note and usually comment on that which is strange. The less competent ego tends to be confused whether in dreams or in waking life. That is a cogent reason for dealing with the dreams of the understructured personality with great caution. Some understructured patients are altogether unable to distinguish between dream life and waking life. In those instances we do not work with the dreams, but use the knowledge to help that patient distinguish between fantasy and reality, between conscious and unconscious, between sleep and waking; in other words, we strengthen the ego—that is, build structure—by helping the patient establish more sharply delineated boundaries.

Dreams of both structured and understructured patients can sometimes provide a royal road to preverbal life. This is because the dream work includes elements from the past as well as from the day or days before the dream, the so-called *day residue*. Sometimes the past that is "unrememberable" is nevertheless remembered in a dream, in disguised form to be sure. We have discussed that preverbal life is both unrememberable and unforgettable. Thus dreams are not necessarily the royal road only to the unconscious.

A patient dreams that he wants to get somewhere in a hurry. He feels unsteady on his feet; he falls, crawls, stands upright again. He tries hard, but cannot reach his destination as quickly as others who pass him by. If this is a structured patient, the dream might connote that the patient is dealing with oedipal conflict; he cannot overtake his rivals. The manner of approach to this oedipal conflict, however, has a template in the subphases—practicing in particular (G. Blanck 1984). Therefore, even though this patient is structured, we see the affect of feeling defeated in preoedipal as well as in oedipal life. Whether one is treating a structured or understructured patient, affect from earlier life is "remembered" in such a dream.

If the patient is understructured, the theme might be frustration and lowered self-esteem represented in the dream by the toddler who feels inadequate and incompetent compared to the other children and even adults around him. We can visualize the patient as a practicing subphase toddler, standing, trying to walk, reverting to crawling, while others walk easily. All practicing subphase toddlers have similar experiences. We have to go on to explore with this patient why this "memory" is so highly charged with affect that he has retained it. Therefore we seek out the affect, noting that that is what is omitted from the manifest dream. Always to be borne in mind is that the dream of an adult is not simply a "memory" of the past. Even if the manifest dream appears to recapitulate preverbal life, the action is a metaphor for latent content, and especially latent affect.

We present examples of the use of dreams for structure building. These techniques, by and large, do not apply in the psychoanalysis of the structured personality. There, traditional dream analysis is appropriate. We have said it is not our purpose to describe the use of dreams in the psychoanalysis of neurosis, but rather to show how dreams are used where structuralization is the therapeutic objective.

A patient dreams that his shoes are too big for him. This dream is not at all chaotic. Yet we need to be clear about the diagnosis. If this were a structured patient, once again, this is very likely an oedipal dream; the patient feels like a boy who cannot fill a man's shoes. But if he is understructured the dream would have a different meaning, connoting perhaps that he is struggling to live beyond what his structure can comfortably bear. Especially in cases of superior intelligence, patients note the behavior that is expected of them and may try to live up to it. But if the structural level is not consonant with the behavior, it is carried out with discomfort and becomes too difficult to live up to at all times.

This explains, in part, why some persons function so well in the world and yet are at a more primitive level of structuralization than meets the eye. A professor of mathematics who held a high-level position was esteemed by his colleagues—no small feat in the rivalrous world of academia. Yet his personal life was chaotic. A well-built man, over six feet tall, his first stance on entering the treatment room was to curl up in the chair in the fetal position and become mute. Before rushing him into functioning at a higher level in the therapy session by demanding that he speak, or asking him to sit up, it is wise to try to understand why his regression is so deep. To hazard a guess, it may well be that the rivalry he deals with daily in his work takes its toll. If it were oedipal rivalry, however, we doubt the regressive floor would be so low.

An understructured patient close to psychosis dreams about a group of people sitting on a beach. Suddenly they turn into seagulls and fly away. To be noted is that there are objects in his psychic life, but not an identifiable object. A first hypothesis might be that the dream connotes that the *libidinal object proper* (Spitz) had not been attained securely enough in the first round of development. As the second organizer of the psyche, this developmental level is reached normally within the first year of life. We note also that the patient has a shaky species identity, which is far more primitive than a shaky gender identity. These observations are speculative and designed only to provide a framework around which to enlist the patient's interest in working on the dream with the therapist. One might begin by asking "How do you feel about this dream?" Such a question is appropriate because the dream was told without affect and we want to know whether the patient was frightened by it. The patient answers, "I was scared. I was left all alone on the beach." This adds considerably to our knowledge about the absence of objects. Not only do they "fly" away, but an affect—fear—was in his picture at one time, has been defended against even in the dream, and is now somewhat recaptured in response to the therapist's question. We add to our speculation that as a young child the patient was probably alone too much at a time when a young child needs the object as part of the self. Each step in our speculation has to be validated by the patient's responses. Validation is not so reliable with the structured patient who is more capable of using the defensive function of the ego and may therefore offer a resistant response. But the understructured patient has to be "tracked" (Blanck and Blanck 1979). We define *tracking* as staying with the patient, following his or her responses, especially those with affective charge, and responding in accordance with the cues these responses provide. This is analogous, but not the same as, the mutual cuing that goes on between mother and child. It cannot be the same with an adult who, no matter how understructured, has proceeded with organization, skewed as it might be.

It may be noted that "tracking" is the opposite of the considered silence in the psychoanalysis of neurosis that is designed to allow for free association without deflection by the analyst. Such an analytic stance with a patient on a low level of structuralization would add to the aloneness. Many therapists recognize this and try to fill the void with words. Talk that merely fills up the silences is not useful. The talk has to "track"—that is, to follow the cues. This describes *attunement* as well as *tracking*.

The therapist asks this patient: "Do you feel alone now?" This brings the matter into the here and now for the purpose of eventually eliciting the affect to bring it to life in the present. One does not expect it to arrive miraculously at this moment; one is merely setting the stage. The patient answers: "Yes, all the time. I know that I am here with you, but I feel alone all the time." The patient is not psychotic and knows intellectually that he is with the therapist, but it has no affective meaning because being with someone is not part of his pattern of self and object relations. To put that another way, there is paucity of a self representation in interaction with object representations.

We speculate silently that there were objects in this persons's early life. They flew away. This resembles what the baby feels when the mother has left the room at a time of life when the child does not yet have a mental representation of her to bridge the aloneness when she is out of sight. That is a speculation, not to be used as an interpretation, but again only as a frame of reference. The therapist goes on: "You feel alone all the time.

Although you know I am here with you, that knowledge does not connect with your feelings. Do you mind the aloneness a lot?" The patient responds: "No. I'm so used to it I don't feel it most of the time." He has established whatever defense he can muster against the pain of aloneness to protect himself from feeling perpetually frightened. Therefore he can have a dream without affect. The therapist does not want to attack his defense, so stops here for now.

The next step will be to help the patient begin to establish a mental representation of an object who is with him. Again, this would build structure. The therapist will have to await material that will come to hand. Perhaps it will become desirable to have him telephone when he feels lonely. That would have to be arranged in a way that must not feel to him as though the therapist needs it, as many such patients assume if they are asked to call. One hopes that the patient will begin to complain about the loneliness. The ideal time to plunge into things is when they trouble the patient.

Other devices may be used when the patient has given a cue. If it can be arranged, frequent contact can revive need that has remained latent because it is defended against. This is one of the several reasons why one session a week is not optimal in most cases. In this case we think there was a modicum of need gratification in early life because, if the patient had not had objects at all, he would not see them in his dream. So another way of using a dream is to note whether there are objects in the patient's psychic life. Dreams are especially useful in this regard with patients with defenses similar to those of this patient. They behave as though they need no one. The dream tells us that it is because the object "flew away" before internalization made it possible for this patient as a baby to acquire a mental representation of her.

Our speculation is that he had been left alone too much too soon. A child can tolerate longer and longer periods of the mother's absence as mental representations of her are built. Much later in the treatment the therapist learned that his mother had tethered him on a leash in the backyard as soon as he could walk. Thus she could keep him safe while she went about her household tasks. But it deprived him of the interaction so essential for building and storing up (internalizing) self and object representations. And it deprived him of a free, approved of, and thereby elated practicing subphase.

Because of the defense, the therapist does not move in too quickly, but move in he or she must if structuralization is to be furthered. Another opportunity might arise around the therapist's vacation. This replicates the early abandonment and must be seized upon in order to make therapeutic mileage. We do not like patients to suffer, and never arrange it deliberately; life provides it. Over several summers this patient felt nothing about the therapist's vacations, yet he always returned at the appointed time. When the patient begins to feel bad about the therapist's anticipated absence, it will be a mark of progress. Vacations, whether the patient's or the therapist's, have to be dealt with long in advance to quicken the ego functions of anticipation and to master the loss.

After several years this patient began to ask whether there was a phone number where he could reach the therapist. We do not advocate offering substitute therapists while on vacation. The request for a phone number is for *the* therapist's phone number. To offer a substitute at such a time is a medical model that, in psychotherapy, misses a dramatic opportunity; the patient needs the specific object! It resonates with his original developmental thrust toward the second organizer—the acquisition of the *libidinal object proper*. That repetition in the transference offers a therapeutic opportunity. We avoid repeating the original disappointment. Such patients cannot verbalize the need because it was preverbal. More usually the observable consequence of repeated disappointment is that the case comes to an impasse; it may take a very long time for another opportunity to reappear in a new guise. On the reassuring side, if such patients stay in treatment long enough it connotes that they are still searching for the object and so will give the therapist another chance. Although repetition of disappointment is undesirable, the best of therapists can miss subtle cues.

We present the dream of a middle-range understructured patient:

I was sitting in a chair. A little girl, maybe two or three years old, was holding me. My mother was standing in the middle of the room with her back to me. The little girl suddenly turned away from me and walked over to my mother. She pulled at her dress to get her attention, but my mother just looked at her indifferently. After a while the little girl turned away from my mother, came back to me, and put her head in my lap. Then I found myself in a bathroom flushing the toilet and was afraid that I'd be flushed down too.

Associations established that the patient identifies both little girls as herself. The dream appears to recapitulate a rapprochement disappointment and the defensive adaptation to it, which has a narcissistic quality; she has become her own comforter. As an adult in therapy, she reported that she was described as an unresponsive child. But the dream depicts that it was the other way round; there can be no response to an indifferent mother because she provides nothing to which to respond. Becoming her own comforter is very different from the more normal developmental phenomenon of transfer of the soothing function to the self representation. In normal development acquisition of the function of self-soothing is desirable, but can only come about if, first, soothing has been provided. Because this patient's mother was indifferent, the child acquires what the mother has provided—indifferent affect. She becomes her own soother, not as a developmental gain but as an adaptive-defensive arrangement that results in a form of pathological narcissism.

The dream also shows the patient's attempt to extract from the environment: the little girl tugs at the mother's dress trying to get her attention. This is promising for the therapy. Because that capacity is depicted in a dream, it can be used by the therapist, after overcoming the narcissistic defense, to encourage the patient to try again. It is impossible to predict when and how an attempt will be made. The dream may be used in this instance, not for analysis, but to alert the therapist to recognize the attempt when it comes. Again, it is important not to disappoint the patient.

How may the therapist enter the narcissistic arrangement? In this case it appears to be less impervious than in many. Here, entry is gained by sharp attunement to apparent trifles. For example, the patient may linger when the time is up. Almost imperceptibly, a patient may signal that it is hard to leave. Often, it takes the form of slowness in standing up and in picking up one's purse or other belongings, taking a long time to leave the room, leaving something behind that then has to be retrieved.

As this sort of lingering is repeated many times, the therapist verbalizes that it is hard for the patient to leave. As these observations accumulate they inform the patient that the therapist cares how she feels. Repeated experience of the therapist's attunement to the affect may encourage the patient to venture to reach out once again. She might, for example, ask for another session because it is so long between sessions. That would be an enormous victory. It is important to respond to that, even if it is difficult to find time for that extra session.

Fear of being flushed down the toilet is a common fear of childhood that normally passes as the child gains a sense of her own size in relation to space. This patient is presumed to have that sense in the present, but the dream harks back to the time when that was one of her fears. That it is retained over the years and finds its way into a dream is a message that she still feels unprotected. It also provides a condensed memory of the time in life when toilet training was experienced affectively—as uncaring at best and wishing to flush her away at worst. Bergmann (1966) suggests that all dreams have a communicative aspect. Because the understructured patient is less verbal than the structured, especially in the affective realm, the therapist can use these communications to search out affect. We place recovery of affect on a higher order of therapeutic priority than recovery of memory. It is the affective aspect of the experience that is retained in the structure. Recovery of affect in the therapeutic relationship provides an opportunity for dramatic change in the self and object relations pattern. Alteration of that pattern can make for a more benign self representation, as well as a new and more benign view of the object world.

With the better-structured borderline patient who is close to neurosis and even has some neurotic (conflictual) features, the therapeutic objective is different. There, because structuralization is more nearly complete, the patient possesses some of the attributes of the well-structured person, such as a greater degree of self and object constancy, capacity to tolerate frustration and anxiety, a defensive structure, and many other features that weigh on the structured side of the Fulcrum. In most such cases, the skilled analyst can apply the techniques for the psychoanalysis of neurosis with modifications where understructured features appear.

There are pitfalls. Logically, it would appear that all one has to do is attend to the understructured features in order to enable the patient to move up to a neurosis proper. Very precise and delicate diagnosis is called for. Is this case to be diagnosed as borderline with neurotic features or neurotic with borderline features? That is more than simply a matter of emphasis. The diagnostic challenge is to distinguish between the true high-level borderline patient and those neurotic patients who seek regressive refuge in preoedipal object relations as a defense against the oedipal conflict. In the one instance development has not proceeded far enough; in the other the individual has reached the oedipal position and has regressed.

Whether there can be a "pure" neurosis without developmental flaws is arguable. Mahler believes that developmental affronts before rapprochement are corrected by an adequate rapprochement experience. Certainly an inadequate symbiosis is irreparable, and it is unlikely that all differentiation and practicing subphase failures can be corrected. At issue is whether experience in those subphases has been good enough not to impair progression to formation of neurotic structure. Rarely would an analysis not benefit from attention to preoedipal factors. The diagnostic issue is delicate because it is essential to be clear as to whether the flaws are truly structural or whether they have become comfortable points for regression in defense against oedipal anxiety. A misdiagnosis can result in treating the structured patient on the regressed level as though structure is faulty. That is an error and a disservice. The patient will have succeeded in enlisting the analyst in perpetuating the defense by casting the analyst in the role of the protecting preoedipal mother, a collusion to protect against oedipal anxiety.

A patient began her treatment in a disorganized state, bringing numerous, long dreams with obvious oedipal content. The analyst's first task is not dream analysis, but to aid organization by barring the pathway to primary process productions. This is accomplished not by forbidding dreams but by not becoming involved in them. Patients will abandon a trend as they find that the analyst does not respond to it. If it should turn out that the patient cannot organize her thoughts, the treatment plan will have to be altered because the patient would not be analyzable. This patient, with the analyst's help, moved more and more into secondary process productions. The procedure followed here would appear to be the opposite of the classical analytic objective of fostering regression in the well-structured patient in order to arrive at more primitive productions. But where borderline features predominate, these require our first attention.

In this case organization was well-enough accomplished in the course of the treatment, and the patient again began to present oedipal-appearing dreams. As we have said the latent content of the dream, if not analyzed at once, remains and reappears later. In this second round of oedipal dreams, however, the maternal figure was noticeably absent. How could they be oedipal where there is no triad? The therapist has to look closely to be sure that they do not represent a dyadic relationship with the paternal representations or that those representations are not used to disguise the maternal ones. The patient's history was the fairly common one of paternal overseduction, not in overt sexual behavior, but in words and attitude. The father found the daughter more interesting than his depressed wife. Marked maternal affective neglect because of the mother's severe depression dominated the preoedipal and oedipal pictures. Because the oedipal position is one of triadic object relations, the conflict cannot be resolved by excluding the parent of the same sex. A benign representation of her is essential. It may be argued that maternal representations were meager because of matricidal wishes, and that is often the case. Even so, the patient would have to bring them to life again because the wish to kill the parent of the same sex is an infantile solution that does not presage resolution.

A large portion of the analysis had to be devoted to the mother's inability to be affectively available. This patient was saved from more severe pathology by good endowment, especially the capacity to extract from the environment. More favorable maternal representations were built as the patient experienced being "touched" by the analyst. This is not literal; we believe firmly that physical contact is contraindicated in all cases. Here it refers to the patient's acute sense of the analyst's affect, which at crucial moments resonated with hers. We are describing a reparative experience that cannot be provided artificially. Analysts cannot force themselves to feel with the patient. It comes about at random moments. Those who would regard such affect as empathic are only partly correct. It is so but cannot be arranged and used as a technique out of our therapeutic tool box. It must come about naturally.

In this case it improved the therapeutic alliance, became an experience in the therapy, and combined with the few favorable experiences there had been with the preoedipal mother, resulting in an alteration in the self and object relations pattern, specifically in the expectation that there is no one to appreciate how she feels. With innumerable testing out of whether this newly acquired object representation would remain steadfast, oedipal dreams that were truly triadic began to appear in the transference; the analyst's husband, whom the patient did not know, began to appear in dreams. That describes an understructured patient whose neurotic features could be analyzed after attention to structuralization.

Another patient began treatment in a moderately regressed state, needy and tearful. He was an only child who insisted, defensively, that his mother had been ideal. The analyst was cautious about yielding to his demands for more time, for response to numerous distressed telephone calls, for sympathy with the various plights in which he found himself. The diagnostic impression was that there was enough structure so that the patient could tolerate frustration of these apparently pressing demands.

In a dream in the early part of treatment he depicted himself sitting on the floor in despair because he could not get his socks on. Two teddy bears were nearby, but they did nothing to help him. His first associations were to the affect. With some surprise he said that the affect in the dream was the same as he feels these days when he is so desperate for comfort. The teddy bears puzzled him. Could the dream refer to a time when he had a teddy bear? The analyst asked why there were two. Associations to numbers led to the speculation that this dream contained a memory of something that occurred when he was two years old. But what? There were no people in the dream, only inanimate teddy bears. Could his mother have been absent?

We rarely ask a patient to check with the family, but this patient was curious enough to do so on his own. We do not suggest it because the answers are usually distorted and defensive. Also, it is preferable to deal with the patient's memory and affect, not with those of the parents or siblings. On the other hand, if a distinct event has occurred, the therapist sometimes finds it useful to know that. The patient learned that his mother had been seriously ill and was in the hospital for more than two months when he was approximately two years old. The number in the dream, then, had a dual meaning: It doubled the comforting teddy bears in compensation for his mother's absence and also provided the age at which that absence occurred. Does this doubling mean that someone provided compensatory comfort, or that he provided it for himself via the teddy bears?

The preoedipal trauma was severe. But he also had exceptionally good endowment, combined with having had a good enough mother when she was with him and a father who was attuned to the boy during the mother's absence, augmented by an aunt who took over lovingly. Most important, the mother returned. All these factors served to pull him through the trauma with minimal damage. Nevertheless, the impact of the experience remained and was retrieved in the dream. This illustrates how a person might become well structured despite object loss. With less supportive surrogates and with permanent absence of the object, failure in structuralization would have occurred. In this case object loss resulted in retention of the affective memory. At the outset of the analysis, that was acted out to announce the intense need that remained with him. It was a regressive position that fortunately was not reinforced by the analyst. It might be interpreted as a defense when the oedipal conflict becomes the issue in the analysis. Then the therapist might say, "You felt that you needed me to comfort you just as you needed your mother when she was away, but now we are dealing with another matter with which your mother could not have helped." This affirms that the two-year-old's need was real, but the mother cannot protect the four-year-old from oedipal anxiety. By then he must rely on his own defenses.

We have described a variety of dreams at different levels of structuralization, not to show how dreams are analyzed but to illustrate how they may be used for other purposes as well. This does not detract, however, from the value of dream analysis.

21

▼

Interpretation

Interpretation is the prime technical tool in the psychoanalysis of the structured personality. Although it has undergone many changes, as we shall show in this chapter, it has a long and honorable history. Its honor lies in the flexibility of psychoanalysts who have been able to regard it differently over the last hundred years—beginning with Freud's willingness to abandon hypnosis and his step after hypnosis, pressure on the forehead to encourage the patient to produce memories. Finally, he discovered that free association is the most productive way to elicit interpretable material because it loosens cathexis to the secondary process, allowing primary process thinking to seep through without compromising autonomy. That applies to the structured patient who is already firmly rooted in the secondary process and can therefore regress in the service of the ego. For most understructured patients free association is not desirable, but Freud had no advice about dealing with those "narcissistic neuroses."

It is a long leap in the history of psychoanalytic theory from the discovery of free association to the present. Today, understanding the developmental vicissitudes of the patient's early life has changed much in the technique for the psychoanalysis of the structured patient and has provided the theoretical backing for elaborating techniques for the psychotherapy of the understructured patient. In this chapter we deal with interpretation in both modalities but with emphasis on interpretation in psychotherapy.

Early psychoanalytic purpose was to seek out what was then thought to be the truth that lay buried in the unconscious. For a long time, therefore, the therapeutic objective was to uncover forgotten (repressed) memories. Interpretation and constructions were used to make those memories conscious; the ego would do the rest—that is, the adult ego would process the childhood experience and put it into perspective by integrating it with adult wisdom. It was an important lesson when analysts discovered that the truth that lies buried in the unconscious does not always set the patient free.

The first major alteration in the theory of technique became inevitable upon the introduction of the structural theory in 1923. Psychoanalysis was no longer a simple theory of force versus counterforce but became a theory of conflict, defense, and compromise formation. That has an important bearing on our subject because it marks the first change in the objective of interpretation; now interpretation is no longer restricted to repressed memories that come into the preconscious by means of the clues provided by free association. Defense (resistance) and the two sides of the conflict are also interpreted. Analysts still welcome the lifting of repression but they realize that that mechanism of defense is not available in all structures, and so lifting repression is no longer the ultimate answer to the psychoanalytic endeavor.

Freud says of the analyzable person: "We all know that the person who is being analyzed has to be induced to remember something that has been experienced by him and repressed; . . . The analyst has neither experienced nor repressed any of the material under consideration; . . . his task is to make out what has been forgotten from the traces which it has left behind or more correctly to *construct* it" (1937, *S.E.* 23:258–59).

As reflected in the slogan "where id was there shall ego be," there is enduring confusion between the id and the repressed, on the one hand, and between the ego and consciousness, on the other. This stems from 1900 when Freud thought of these two agencies as force (id) and counterforce (ego). Apparently Freud's masterpiece, *The Interpretation of Dreams*, has left so powerful an impression that it is difficult for many to alter their views of id and ego to accord with later theoretical correction. Freud's dual drive theory (1920) redefined the id as the repository of the two drives. His structural theory (1923) redefined the ego and made it clear that ego is not synonymous with consciousness, that part of the ego is unconscious.

Those are structural concepts. The topographic theory also has to be considered. A major alteration in the theory of interpretation was imposed by emendation of the topographic theory to include the *preconscious* as well as conscious and unconscious. It meant that interpretation could no longer be thought to enjoy direct access to the unconscious; the material from the unconscious first has to be brought into the preconscious for it to become interpretable, requiring that the analyst devise techniques to facilitate movement of material from the unconscious to the preconscious. But that did not alter the therapeutic objective that dominated the analytic endeavor; it merely added an extra step. The major task remained to convince the patient to give up repressions, to "find the picture of the patient's forgotten years that shall be alike trustworthy and in all essential respects, complete" (1937, *S.E.* 23:258). Freud makes a distinction between *interpretation* and *construction*. He says:" 'Interpretation' applies to something that one does to some single element of the material, such as an association or a parapraxis. But it is a 'construction' when one lays before the subject of the analysis a piece of his early history that he has forgotten" (1937, *S.E.* 23:261).

Contemporary theory would add that the material may also be a piece of the patient's history that he or she is only now beginning to know, first affectively and later by applying language retroactively. Freud (1937) and Sharpe (1950) were perhaps dimly aware of this even though the theory was not yet clear. They were quite comfortable in reformulating interpretations flexibly. Sharpe expressed it as simply saying to the patient something such as, "Today we know a bit more than we knew yesterday when I said that, and so we have to change it" (53).

At issue is whether the interpreter is attempting to locate or construct a complete truth. That presupposes that such a truth exists, that it is possible to find it, and that the analyst is equipped to succeed in such a venture. Understanding the understructured patient is usually less a process of learning something new about the unconscious and more about being able to tune in to developmental factors that were experienced in early life. But we must not overlook that the structured patient, too, has had a preoedipal life, more favorable to be sure but exerting its influence in some way that requires therapeutic attention nevertheless. In all but the lowest levels of understructuralization some intersystemic conflict exists; in the structured personality some intrasystemic conflict persists. We have shown on the Fulcrum of Development that weights may fall on both sides of the scale. That the preponderance of weights falls on one side or the other suffices for tentative diagnosis. For treatment purposes, the smaller number of weights have to be taken into account along with those that make up the weightier side of the balance scale.

Now with the enlargement of our theoretical underpinnings, we have to revise our thoughts about what material is being sought for interpretation and whether, indeed, that which is sought is interpretable. Unraveling elements of structure formed during the very early months and years of life does not rest simply on lifting repression. The distinction between repression and normal childhood amnesia would not bear much discussion were it not that early experience, although unrememberable, is not forgotten. That is a paradox only if we think of memory as literal recall. We speak here, of course, of the importance of the earliest *affective* processing, beginning with coenesthetically received experience during the first few weeks of life.

The "giants" of theory after Freud were less sanguine about their ability to find a "complete picture." Interestingly, in the light of contemporary theory, they relied more than is realized on the interaction within the therapeutic relationship. Fenichel says: "We show *connections* which are calculated to make the patient curious. Moreover, we try to bribe him by showing him, whenever an opportunity presents itself, how analysis can be *beneficial* to him" (1941:35). That statement expresses less confidence about discovery of objective truths to be interpreted; it also relies less on the analyst's knowledge and more on the analyst's effort to engage the patient and stimulate his or her curiosity.

Sharpe (1950) and Glover (1955) advocate a flexible approach to interpretation. As Sharpe puts it: "We cannot command the unconscious; we cannot browbeat resistance. We get a picture of the psychical disturbances in odd and isolated fragments which we have to put together as we go along and small wonder if at times we put a piece that we rescue into a too prominent place, or find that what we passed over as insignificant must be put in a high light" (1950:53).

We see in these early writings the germ of a theory of technique that Kris was to make explicit—that the task of the patient is far greater than to provide material and that of the analyst is more discreet than simply to interpret. Yet Kris's influence has not permeated all contemporary thought. Brenner refers to interpretation as "what the analyst tells his patient about his psychic conflicts" (1976:36). Moore and Fine define interpretation as "a process whereby *the analyst* expresses in words what he or she comes to understand about the patient's mental life" (1990:103).

The manner of arriving at interpretation is appreciably altered by the manner in which we enlist the patient's participation in the process. Although interpretation remains the prime tool in psychoanalysis, there are auxiliary techniques, mostly designed to lead up to and augment interpretation. Greenson (1967) refers to *confrontation, clarification,* and *working through,* in addition to *interpretation,* all designed to further insight. The analyst also asks questions. Boesky believes that these accomplish more than simply eliciting an answer; they alter the established psychic equilibrium. He says: "Questions the analyst asks of the patient are a powerful but neglected aspect of psychoanalytic technique. Their importance lies in the dynamic impact on the psychic equilibrium of the patient because of their ability to destabilize existing compromise formations" (1989:579).

Some therapists tend loosely to designate everything they say as *interpretation.* To serve precision we suggest the generic term *intervention,* which subsumes interpretation as well as the other technical moves of the therapist. By maintaining a sharp distinction between interpretation and the other measures, interpretation is preserved from the dilution that blurs its meaning. We have sometimes found it necessary to inform supervisees who report having made an "interpretation" that what they have engaged in is merely *conversation,* which is not a therapeutic technique.

That repression is altogether undesirable is an older attitude that has been modified over the years. Not only has it less bearing in the treatment of the understructured personality, but it is now seen as a normal phenomenon as well as one that is sometimes used pathologically. Many an error has been made in education as well as in psychoanalysis because repression was regarded as undesirable. The child, for example, has to repress the oedipal wish in order to enter latency. We have seen cases where the oedipal wish was interpreted to a child with the idea that that would aid resolution; it had the opposite result.

A male college student, understructured, was in treatment with a male analyst. The patient was preoccupied with sexual fantasies, which the analyst mistakenly tried to bring into the transference. Showing that he wished to maintain the modicum of repression that his structure could allow, the patient asked, "Do you really want to know?" It takes considerable sophistication about the weakness of repression in the understructured personality to be able to recognize, in that question, that the proper technical intervention would have been to aid repression. Instead, the analyst followed the basic rule by answering, "Of course."

The patient plunged into a detailed exposition of his sexual wishes toward the analyst. His material covered all perversions known to the analyst, and a few new ones. It would have been far better had the analyst heeded the patient's question, "Do you really want to know?" by asking himself "Why is the patient so hesitant?" Taking the degree of structuralization into account, the therapist would know now that polymorphous perverse fantasies emanate from very early childhood and, especially where structure is inadequate, the defensive function of the ego is to be strengthened by supporting repression, not removing it.

This patient's father died when the patient was four years old. He was immediately taken to sleep with his mother and remained in her bed until he was fifteen. This was a severe trauma at the oedipal period, not only because of loss of the paternal object but because the father's death and the boy taking his place in the mother's bed was too real a fulfillment of the oedipal wish. That combination of events promoted rapid regression to the polymorphous perverse position psychosexually and to a borderline state structurally. A more orderly therapeutic procedure would have tended to strengthen defenses so that the perverse fantasies would give way to oedipal ones as the ego becomes able to tolerate them in the benign climate provided by therapy.

The interpretation of conflict involves three basic assumptions—that one is dealing with a structured personality, that therefore the conflict is intersystemic, and that the principal mechanism of defense is repression. None of these applies to the understructured personality.

What of psychotherapy, then? It may be said that therapists use interpretation in psychotherapy only if the definition is broader than making the unconscious conscious and of interpreting intersystemic conflict. Lifting repression is certainly not an objective because repression is not usually a mechanism available to the seriously understructured ego. In fact, the very goal of psychotherapy is to strengthen the ego to the point where repression can be used in place of the less efficient defenses of the under-structured personality. With lower-level understructured personalities, we hardly use interpretation at all. There the prime technical objective is search for affect, and the technical tool is tracking. As the affect is captured within the context of the uninterpretable transference, the therapist "tunes in" to give the self and object relations pattern a better turn. We do this by using Loewald's concept of the therapeutic differential. With time and patience it becomes evident that the therapist is not responding as had the primary object, forcing an alteration in the pattern.

A middle-aged married man would fly into rages with his wife when she did something that touched off his separation anxiety. This did not always mean that she went somewhere without him. She could be at home in another room or reading a book. To him these ordinary activities felt as though she was not with him. The therapist thought that alteration of his object relations pattern could be more effective than couple therapy because so much of the difficulty arose from his early life. He was born to an unmarried mother who had to go to work. She left him to be brought up by an aunt and saw him weekends only. The aunt provided good phys-ical care but little warmth.

He preserved the pattern of abandonment by provoking his wife with small taunts, about the way she dressed or wore her hair, so that she did not feel like being with him. That behavior came into the transference as he tried to irritate the therapist with trivial taunts and by threatening to leave treatment—that is, to use the defense mechanism of reversal, "I will do to you what has been done to me." This is not always hostile in principal intent, although of course it is secondarily hostile. The chief purpose is to convey affect in action because it was first experienced preverbally. If the patient terminates therapy, the therapist will know what it feels like to be abandoned. As happens more often than not, the patient did not carry out his threat to leave; the intensity of object need kept him in therapy.

The therapist noted that the same thing that happens with his wife seemed to be happening in the transference and realized that he, the ther-apist, must not "play the game." He overlooked the taunts for a long time. The patient began to get a bit edgy. After many sessions, the therapist asked, "I notice that you seem a bit anxious. Do you think you are trying to get me to give up on you?" The patient had not been aware of that, but now began to think about it. Then he said, "You mean you intend to stick it out with me no matter what?" The object relations pattern began to alter gradually as he became aware that the therapist was going to stay with him as long as he needed him.

What happened there? The relationship between the self representation and the object representations were such that abandonment had to be repeated. We have termed that *replication of early object experience*. It appears paradoxical that the only way the patient could keep his abandoning mother with him was to maintain her representation as an abandoner. A second objective of the repetition was to gain mastery over the trauma of abandonment by bringing it about in his own time. Since the therapist did not follow the "script," it was a matter of time before the patient would notice that and become a bit anxious. The benign climate created a therapeutic differential that would require a change in the representations of the object. When one set of representations alters, the self representation alters as well because both are in tandem. The patient no longer needed to feel he was not worth being with, and no longer needed to master what he was convinced would be the end result of any relationship—abandonment. As this alteration took place intrapsychically, the marital quarreling diminished.

Where interpretation is used in psychotherapy, it is more likely to be of *intrapsychic* conflict within the context of a transference that emphasizes the object relations aspect of the conflict. In the forgoing clinical illustration, interpretation in the sense of telling the patient what was in his unconscious was not used. What we have shown is that in an uninterpretable transference, reorganization of the quality of the cathexis of the self and object representations from negative to more positive, and redistribution of the quantity of those more positive cathexes, is a form of "interpretation" of the uninterpretable.

Kris alters simplistic ideas about revival of childhood memory. Interpretation is no longer a single statement of a single traumatic memory. It is a series of statements that, in the main, interpret the defensive structure. Kris also promotes a theory of technique that requires more of the patient than simply to provide material for interpretation. The patient becomes a participant in an active, dyadic endeavor. It does not duplicate the mother-child interaction but perpetuates the uniquely human form of communication that begins in the mother-child dyad and becomes the template for our lifelong interaction with others.

Cavell regards interpretation as a special form of semantic communication because it is carried out in a dialogue involving language. She says:

> Interpretation . . . unlike introspection and soliloquy presumes a multiplicity of mind sharing and common language. It takes interpersonal understanding as a model of self knowledge . . . And it views the clinical setting less as an occasion for private catharsis than as providing space for a kind of dialogue in which transferential and countertransferential relationship between patient and analyst are crucial.   (1988:860)

We showed in chapter 19 that experience that precedes semantic communication does not become cathected to language and that early life exerts powerful, albeit subtle, influence on the character nevertheless. The effect of the "mute, invisible tides" (Spitz) that persist from the period of coenesthetic reception render the problem of "memory" far more complex than was thought to be the case when theory was simpler. By the time of acquisition of the third organizer of the psyche, at approximately eighteen months of age, much experience has accumulated, providing the child with his or her unique impressions of life. To be sure they become altered and modified by later experience, but they are never obliterated. And as we have stressed, impressions from early life cannot be interpreted directly. Noting object relations attitudes, and especially affect, within the therapeutic relationship is our only avenue toward capturing some of those impressions as they have influenced the self and object relations patterning. These are patterns that emerge very slowly in the therapeutic relationship out of an interactive process in which the benign climate, neutrality, evenly suspended attention, and like attitudes on the part of the therapist enable the patient to bring forth material. But the material may turn out to derive from a very early period of life when repression played no role. That which at first appears to be a complete picture may turn out to be nothing more than a hazy sketch with missing details.

It is valuable to review the precise meaning of semantic communication, that uniquely human form of communication. That it includes speech is only a small part of the matter. Of prime importance is the object relations factor. We have to assume that semantic communication is not attained at a given moment. By designating it as an indicator, Spitz implies that considerable organization has preceded its appearance. That means that it has taken a span of time for the child to grasp that one needs to communicate in words across the chasm of separation between self and other. That has a profound impact on the nature of the relationship between the self representation and the object representations. Although it is a major move forward in the separation-individuation process, the child, at the time of that third organizer, is only midway in the journey toward establishment of a separate identity. Therefore the object representations, insofar as they have been formed, are still experienced as part of the self representation in some degree. Because of that relative incompletion of the separation-individuation process, the wish to be understood without words lingers on. It probably never leaves us altogether; the well-structured person, at moments of normal regression, also wishes to be understood without words.

Some understructured persons who conform to the demands of everyday life communicate well, but often reluctantly. They perform a task that the intellect understands as a requirement, but it is not accepted affectively. In the therapeutic situation, patient and therapist may become affectively disconnected by carrying on verbalizations that have little or no affective meaning to the patient. The therapist needs to be aware of this in interchanges with the understructured patient. We have to consider the developmental level of the person to whom we are speaking in words. Is the patient merely complying without having attained true semantic communication in the sense of having accepted that degree of separation? This gives us reason to wonder whether our interpretations and other verbalizations are having an impact. Although a similar problem may occur in the psychoanalysis of a regressed structured patient, it can only be temporary because regression, by definition, is via a pathway from a higher level of development and is therefore reversible. The greater concern is about how we communicate to patients who yield intellectually and compliantly to the necessity to use words in order to get along in the world. Are we doing them a service if we go through the motions of making "excellent" interpretations that do not get across affectively? And is it not ironic, now that we see that talking does not always cure, that laypersons refer to psychotherapy as the "talking cure"?

We have described a patient who functions at a high level of professional performance but, in the treatment situation, curls up into the fetal position and does not speak (chapter 20). In some of our earlier writings we advocated informing the patient that we cannot understand without words. We have to revise this now, because it serves only to tell the patient how far apart we are. It does not meet the patient where he or she is affectively. How to bridge the gap? The therapist might say: "When you curl up that way it suggests to me that you are not in the mood to talk, or even to hear me talk. I feel that you want us to be together without imposing the chore of speaking." It joins the patient. Yet great caution has to be exercised because, although we want to join the patient, we have to be clear that it is merely to establish a point of departure. Therapist and patient meet in order to be together to begin a journey, but remaining together at the railroad station or airport terminal does not constitute travel. The patient will want to linger in preverbal union. Our objective must be to move on together, so we may have to devise gentle nudges. This involves doing two things at once—being with the patient and yet being one step ahead. That gives the patient the task of joining the therapist. It will succeed because once the patient's interest in being together has been captured, the patient's tendency will be to continue the union, even if that precludes lingering at the meeting place. The therapist goes ahead so that the patient will want to keep pace.

How is this done? Many understructured patients begin the session in a silence about which they feel awkward. As early as 1912 Freud advised that the patient is to begin the session. That, of course, was for the structured patient in analysis. What about the understructured patient who cannot begin? The very silence may be a message that semantic communication is not the desired form. It relieves the awkwardness of the situation to tell the patient that silence has its value. And it joins that patient at the preverbal level where he or she is. But we do not conduct the entire session in silence. One might say, "May I help you begin?" or one might refer to the last session, something that is hardly ever appropriate in psychoanalysis proper. This joins the patient and moves ahead at almost the same time.

These clinical illustrations describe the technique for dealing with what we have designated *uninterpretable transference*.

Some will think of this as being in keeping with the current vogue of using an empathic approach. Surely it is empathic. But we use the term *empathy* hesitantly because it has been so overused and misused that it has acquired different meanings to different therapists, thereby losing its communicative value. It has even gone so far that some believe it to be a technique in and of itself. Cavell captures its meaning when she says: "Empathy . . . cannot be a matter of my seeing things from your point of view, getting somehow outside my own mind and skin and into yours, but discovering and widening the base we share, exercising my imagination as to the beliefs and desires you may have in respect to which your behavior seems more or less reasonable to you" (1988:874).

Let us turn now to interpretation proper. Timing is critical. Many theorists of technique have said that an interpretation must be correct in timing as well as in content. Freud referred to timing as *tact*. He thought it could not be taught and was probably correct. But it may be reassuring to those who have not learned it out of talent and experience that the potential for harming the case is diminished if the therapist allows room for the patient's participation. Then, if we are mistaken, the patient will offer the correction. Sharpe believes that the only error in interpretation that may steer a case off course is a mistake in interpretation of transference. Even there, the patient is more likely to become angry rather than damaged. If the analyst can endure the anger, he or she will learn how to correct the course. Glover (1955) is not altogether in accord with Sharpe. He distinguishes between inexact and incomplete interpretation. Inexact interpretation, he believes, can be harmful because the patient seizes upon it precisely because it leads away from the source of anxiety. He means, by incomplete interpretation, that the entire unconscious fantasy is interpreted, not all at once but in fractions.

Glover's thoughts about incomplete interpretation match our own suggestion about the style of interpretation. We do not favor lengthy interpretations that appear like supreme court decisions. They tend to overwhelm the patient and run the risk of forcing compliance rather than insight. The therapist remains an authority about the treatment but is not authoritarian. We suggest piecemeal interpretations in the form of a pyramid. The "complete" interpretation is the base of the pyramid. The interpretation begins at the top and is the shortest. In interaction with the patient, the cues that are provided constitute the basis for the next somewhat larger statement. It may take many sessions, delayed by resistance, before the interpretation approaches completeness.

Not to be overlooked is that the patient does not always welcome our interpretations with loud applause. An interpretation disturbs an existing equilibrium and intrudes upon a defensive arrangement. More often than not, a signal that an interpretation is correct is that it is *not* "accepted." The experienced therapist knows that the apparent rejection of an interpretation is no measure of its correctness. In fact, it may signal that the interpretation has hit the mark. Resistance heightens with correct interpretation because the equilibrium has been disturbed and, before the patient can relinquish all resistance, a new defensive arrangement has to be organized. Therefore rejection of an interpretation may be the patient's way of buying time to formulate a new resistance. The beginning therapist is likely to be put out by the patient's "No, you are wrong." We are dealing with the unconscious and so are guided not by the *negation* but by the *effect*. That may not be felt until the next session or even later. After the new resistance presents itself and is interpreted, new material will be the signal that the interpretation has fulfilled its purpose; the analysis marches forward.

What we have added to already existing theory of interpretation is emphasis on affect and object relations patterns. The literature on interpretation for the psychoanalytic treatment of the structured personality implies, but does not make explicit, that affect is important. It does so by advising that interpretation, whenever possible, be made in the context of the transference. That emphasizes the importance of capturing the affect as it comes "alive" in the here and now, with the therapist or analyst as surrogate for the object representations that were internalized in early life. For the structured, analyzable patient, interpretation of these transference phenomena is effective in enabling the patient to distinguish past from present. For the understructured patient in psychotherapy, interpretation of uninterpretable transference is usually in the therapeutic interaction until the patient can truly engage in semantic communication.

22

▼

Depression

What makes us into human beings is, indeed, the
organization not only of our thought processes, but
also of a wide range of feelings, of complex emotional attitudes and affective states unknown to the
animal.   E. Jacobson, *Depression*, 1971:53

Being human means that we are able to enjoy the pleasurable
affects—happiness, serenity, love, joy, sometimes even ecstasy. But
the wide range of feelings that Jacobson speaks of renders us subject to the unpleasurable affects as well—sadness, grief, disappointment,
anxiety and, perhaps worst of all, depression.

More than anxiety, depression is the affect that is of concern to the
therapist because of his or her empathy for the patient who is experiencing such anguish and because of the danger of suicide in certain forms of
depression. The normal affects usually reflect response to an external
event. Although depression may be precipitated by external factors, its etiology is to be found in the structure of the personality. The external event,
if there is one, falls on the fertile ground of an already existing predisposition.

What makes the human being depression prone is the uniquely human
mode of adaptation. We are born in almost total helplessness, to develop
in the medium of the dyad. Factors may go awry on either side of that complex object relationship. Inborn capacities enable the child to extract from

the environment in varying degrees of efficiency. On the side of the environment (mothering person), attuned partnering is essential.

At an earlier time in the continuing evolution of theory construction, Jacobson (1964) said something similar to what Mahler et al. were to say in 1975. Jacobson's thoughts, because they came earlier, were less specific. She emphasized Freud's 1917 observation that object loss is a major predisposing factor in depression. Object loss is not necessarily literal loss of the object. It can connote paucity of object representations because of insufficient internalization of self with object experience. Again, the failure may be precipitated by factors on either side of the dyad.

Now that so much is being discovered about the biochemistry of the brain, we cannot omit reference to the neurotransmitters that are found to influence mood and behavior. Biochemistry can be altered by chemical means, that is, by drugs. This applies to anxiety, psychosis, and obsessional behavior as well as to depression, although the role of medication in depression is of outstanding importance. We do not oppose the use of such medication where it may serve to make the person feel better, and especially where suicide is a danger. However, in the enthusiasm for new discoveries, the old tends to be discarded as superseded by the new. The discoveries of biochemical elements in psychosis and depression have created passionate proponents who contend that those discoveries prove that psychological factors do not exist. We think that both play an interlocking role.

Long before the biochemical investigations, Spitz found that very young infants who were taken from their mothers became depressed. He termed this *anaclitic depression*. That type of depression is not the same as depression as an affective state because, at that early time of life, there is not yet cathexis of self and object representations. The infant in an anaclitic depression has also not yet reached the level where affects are differentiated. While a depressed individual *feels* helpless and hopeless, the anaclitically depressed infant *is* in a hopeless, helpless state. In current pediatric terminology, "failure to thrive" is a diagnosis. The debate about whether these infants suffer from abnormal brain chemistry or from insufficient object connection polarizes the issue. Our answer, until future research clarifies matters further, is that neurotransmitters can be stimulated by the human "touch" as well as by medication. Animals "know" this instinctively, so the mother cat licks her newborn kittens to "start them up," that is, to promote production of neurotransmitters.

Billy, age nine months, was in a life-threatening condition because of failure to thrive. When he was hospitalized he improved rapidly because he experienced hands-on nursing care—the human touch. Discharged to his home, he again failed to thrive and had to be rehospitalized. A social worker who visited the home after one of the several hospital discharges noted that the mother showed no interest in him. He lay in his crib listlessly, ignored by her. Antidepressant medication had not yet been developed, and only recently has it been recommended for infants and young children. Would Billy have been better off with such medication, or should the mother have been referred for treatment of her indifference to her child? And are these measure mutually exclusive?

Whether medication is administered for depression or for other forms of behavior, it alters *the behavior or the affect only*. Ideally, it should be administered in conjunction with structure-building psychotherapy if the individual is to be rendered more human, cathected to self and object representations, rather than simply better behaved or in a less troubled affective state.

Antidepressive medications are of value, with the obvious limitation that a drug does not deal with the self and object relations factor. Nevertheless, suffering need not be perpetuated if it can be relieved. We think of medication as analogous to anesthesia in surgery. One can treat the patient without being cruel where relief from pain is possible.

The question arises: what difference does it make whether the brain is stimulated by a drug or by mothering? The difference is huge; medication cannot build structure via self and object experience. Especially in infancy and childhood, when structure is being built, drugs do not provide object relations experiences that build an inner world. Therefore the child so treated would not acquire adequate self and object representations; that would make for a most significant deficit in structure.

That it does not cure the object relations problems has become a social problem because so many psychiatrists, to the delight of the insurance carriers and the drug manufacturers, insist that the cure for depression is medication. There is even a return to electric shock therapy in intractable cases, which had been briefly discarded in the past in favor of medication but resumed because medication is not effective for all patients. We regard these as adjunctive to psychotherapy, important because they may make the patient feel better and thereby become more available to psychotherapy, and vital where there is suicidal risk.

By now we have iterated and reiterated that the transactions between neonate and mothering person establish enduring patterns of self and object relations that become internalized. Those transactions are between two unequal partners, one of whom is totally dependent on the other. The mothering person cannot always be available, nor would it be desirable if that were possible. Therefore there is always a modicum of object loss that is tolerable and growth promoting if the dosage is neither too much nor too little. Both closeness and distancing on the part of the mother are necessary and should be in tune with the changing needs of the developing child.

Since the neonate is not yet capable of cognizing that he or she exists in a situation in which there are two individuals, neither can that neonate cognize that it is another person who is absent; the neonate experiences the mother's absence as though part of the self is missing. In the first weeks of life the mother's appearances and absences constitute part of the chaos that requires, and probably even propels, organization.

As development proceeds and the infant becomes capable of cognizing the human face sufficiently to experience a surge of positive affect (the smile and its accompanying physical activity), attention becomes focused on the external world; the percept of the human face is cathected. Although organization has begun, it has not yet proceeded to the point where the infant can distinguish between self and object. This is why the absence of the object is still experienced as loss of part of the self. Here is the first precursor of depression.

Repair is accomplished quickly enough to avert an abnormal predisposition to depression where the good enough mother returns within a reasonable period of time. For the infant, reasonable time is brief. The good enough mother plays the peek-a-boo game intuitively to give her baby the opportunity to master object loss followed by quick restoration. The child learns the game, covering his or her face (often with the transitional object) for as long as that self-inflicted object loss is tolerable. In this way the infant achieves complete ego mastery over the loss and restoration. As one observes this game, the squeals of delight as the object is restored after having been lost informs us that this is far more than an interesting game. It is a vehicle that carries the child on a developmental leap. The object is lost and regained over and over again *at the child's behest* until the object representations are internalized, which insures resumption of object connection on a next higher level of integration. With gradual internalization, the child gradually loses interest in the game because the object representations are secured.

When upright locomotion is attained, gratifying experiences that had hitherto been provided by the symbiotic partner now come about by the toddler's own efforts. A sense of mastery and intense narcissistic gratification, a sense of liberation from passivity and from the totality of dependence on the symbiotic object, account for the noticeable elation of the practicing subphase.

Elation leaves lasting memory traces in the affective realm. But at the time of the waning of the practicing subphase, elation is temporarily lost. Reality testing informs the toddler not only that he or she is a small person in a large world but that the symbiotic partner that one expected to be there always is not omnipresent at the child's behest and, even more disillusioning, is not omnipotent. Massive disappointment results; paradise is lost forever. This is why Mahler regards the rapprochement crisis as so critical to whether the elation of the practicing subphase remains as a memory trace or is erased by rapprochement disappointment.

The rapprochement movement is an attempt to return to the comfortable past. Even at best—that is, where the mother accepts the child's return to "home base"—paradise cannot be regained. Child and mother no longer fit together as before. The child must move on to become part of the imperfect world. But if the mother meets the rapprochement adequately, predisposition to depression is attenuated. We have said that we do not believe that all subphase inadequacies are made up for if rapprochement is adequate, but where object retrieval is concerned, adequate rapprochement is, of course, essential.

Even at best, a low-keyedness accompanies the rapprochement subphase out of the realization that there is no going back. We believe this brings with it the capacity to mourn. The individual mourns for, and often tries to regain, symbiotic union. This is not a totally negative aspect of the human condition. Normally, symbiosis can be regained momentarily at times of regression in the service of the ego, for pleasure and creativity (Kris). In some forms of depressive pathology, however, suicide is attempted where the object has been lost and the wish to reunite with the object takes this unrealistic form.

Rapprochement leads to an internal process that is less concerned with the behavior of the external object and more with resolution of the split in the affective relationship between self and object representations. The "all good" gratifying object and the "all bad" disappointing object must be fused into a single set of object representations of a person who sometimes gratifies and sometimes frustrates. Polytheism is thought to have been a more primitive form of object relations because it created a number of deities, each with a specific function. Monotheism is regarded as a progressive step in human object relations because all functions are fused into a single set of representations (Freud 1939). Without a cathected object, one may be spared the pain of object loss. The price is to live in the objectless world of psychosis. With object cathexis, we are compensated by the capacity to love. Where there is true object loss, such as death, normal mourning must be endured.

Freud (1917) distinguishes mourning from melancholia (depression) by the fact that the person in mourning is engaged in the process of withdrawing cathexis from the lost object in order to recover and become able to invest in a new object. Melancholia, on the other hand, is not a process; it has no end. This is because negative cathexis of the object representations pervades the self representation as well. Because he did not have the language of contemporary theory, Freud put this idea more simply but also more poetically. In mourning, he says, the world feels cold and empty; in melancholia, the ego (we would now say self representation) feels cold and empty. Thus he knew, even though he could only use the terminology of his time, that depression is a pathology of self and object relations.

Little has been written about the oedipal disappointment as yet another potential for depression. Freud, of course, believes that the Oedipus Complex is resolved in childhood by means of the castration threat. We, along with other developmentalists, maintain that the Oedipus Complex is not "resolved," but goes through repeated rounds at different phases of the life cycle, leading to more and more attenuation at each round. Loewald (1979) prefers the term *waning* rather than *resolution* or *dissolution*, which terms were used in the various translations of Freud's word *untergang*. Loewald's term stresses that the Oedipus Complex does not have a distinct terminal point. Calef and Weinshel (1983) believe that all persons, even those who complete an analysis, suffer oedipal disappointment because the oedipal wish is not consummated. That disappointment demands the utmost of the adaptive function, necessary because consummation would ensure enduring pathology (chapter 12). The success or failure in dealing with oedipal disappointment exerts a powerful influence on the success or failure in forming a satisfactory spousal relationship with a contemporary. A form of depression that contributes to some marital problems is the result of realization that the spouse is not the oedipal object.

So we have to think about oedipal disappointment as the next step in the series of disillusionments and disappointments that begin with the realization that the object is not part of the self, proceed to the bitter reality of the imperfect world that confronts the rapprochement toddler, and culminates in the realization, at the oedipal level, that the parent is not available as a sex partner. All of these developmental vicissitudes tax the individual's capacity to master disappointment and render the human being depression prone. That does not mean that everyone is subject to true clinical depression. In good developmental circumstances, lowered moods and transient depressions are facts of life. They occur in all persons from time to time.

We allude to depression, not as a diagnostic entity, but as an affective state. That posits that its status is a symptom, not a diagnosis. Depression, as Jacobson indicates, has its roots in object loss at varying levels of development. It has different meanings and different prognoses at different levels. Therefore it is inaccurate to describe a person as "depressed." That refers to the affective state, but not to the structure in which the symptom is embedded (Eissler 1953).

Psychotic depression is based in the objectless state caused by failure of adaptation—that is, failure to find a partner with whom to fit together. Now that we know that object relations is the very medium of development, it becomes ever clearer that life without an object to be internalized as an enduring representation is unbearable. It may occur because no partner is available or because the partner is an inadequate one or because deficiency in the innate endowment impairs ability to connect with a partner. Hallucinations create a psychotic object world in lieu of a real one.

In the borderline conditions there is an object representation but it is not yet fully separated. Potential for depression is created where the experience of separateness is too great for the individual to tolerate, stemming from the time when there was a failure in the dyad while the toddler still needed to experience the object as part of the self. Again, this may be because the object is insufficiently attuned or because there is a flaw in the innate endowment.

In one form of narcissistic pathology the object representations are overvalued at the expense of the self representation, resulting in poor self-esteem and possibly depression.

Neurotic depression can also result from overidealization of the object representations at the expense of the self representation, but there are differentiated self and object representations in neurotic structure that render the depression less serious although not less painful. More often than narcissistic imbalance, neurotic depression is precipitated by guilt. The superego punishes the ego. Thus it is an intersystemic matter. Since Freud's essay, "Mourning and Melancholia" (1917), the role of the superego in depression remains prominent in psychoanalytic thought.

A dilemma is posed by the fact that, with the advent of developmental theory, we no longer believe that the superego plays a role in all structures because, at the lesser levels of structuralization, it has not yet come into being. In neurotic structure and in some of the higher-level borderline structures, the superego as the third and final aspect of structuralization is functional. Only where it exists can it impose guilt and depression punitively on the ego (the self representation, in more modern terminology).

Even before developmental theory, it was known that the superego in the borderline conditions is more severe than in ordinary neurosis. It was referred to as an *archaic* superego, meaning a less merciful one, untempered by identification with some benign object representations. This is understood today as stemming from identification with the still insufficiently separated but negatively cathected object representations. Lacking are sufficient "good" internalized object representations who make the self representation feel good.

A common type of depression consists of identification with the affective state of the object—most usually a depressed mother. How this will affect the life of the child once again depends on the continuing process of structuralization and whether sufficient differentiation enables the child to develop an identity separate from the object. Because it is difficult for any child to separate from the maternal affect, that affect always plays a role in identification and structuralization. Fortunately, depression is not the predominant maternal affect in every instance.

A young man in a painful, but not suicidal, depression came for treatment because he could never feel good. His father had died two months before he was born. Even though his conscious wish was to feel better, he had transference difficulties. He complained that the therapist appeared too cheerful. Actually, the therapist was neither cheerful nor glum, merely in an even mood, ready for work. The patient wanted the therapist's mood to match his; in that way they would be joined together. It was speculated that this patient, in infancy, had had to use his capacity to extract from the environment by entering symbiosis with a mother who was in mourning. That affect remained with him for life and, as was found in the transference, became his manner of uniting. It was an adaptive measure that saved him from an objectless state. The prognosis, however, had to be quite guarded because the basis of the depression lay in very early life and was therefore difficult to treat. The therapist had to be exceedingly careful not to deprive him of the object connection with his mother as the sole parent, even though that connection was maintained by the affect, depression. That does not mean that the therapist joins the patient in his affect. It means only that one interprets with great caution because connection must be maintained regardless of its quality until the treatment can enable the patient to tolerate greater separation.

There are erroneous techniques for treating depression based on misunderstanding Freud's essay. Out of his formulations about melancholia as representing hostility toward the object turned against the self, some therapists have evolved a technique we have termed the *reversible raincoat theory*. They believe that if the turned-against-the-self hostility can be turned outward, against the object world, the patient will feel better. There is a modicum of truth in that. The error lies in trying to elicit rage toward the therapist by provoking it. Then it is no longer in the transference but is a real response to a real provocation. To provide a real cause obscures the basic cause.

A second objection is that hostility (and any other affect) must always be under the control of the ego. "Ventilation" is nothing more than uncontrolled discharge of affect. That cannot enable the ego to attain control over behavior—to delay, to exercise judgment, to employ thought as trial action. In addition, ventilating hostility can be dangerous because it risks severing object connection, which can exacerbate object loss. For all these reasons, provoking an outburst of anger at the therapist, under the misperception that this will discharge the patient's hostile affect, is an error in logic and in practice, even where at times it has been said to "work." We think, with Jacobson, that what happens to the already overly hostile cathexis of the self and object representations is that cathexis is reinforced.

It is theoretically incorrect to speak of *treatment* of depression, since affects are not treatable. We do not treat anxiety, joy, grief, or any other affect as such. It is the person experiencing the affect who is treated through the ego. Because suicide remains a danger in depression, emergency measures are sometimes necessary to deal with crises. Lifesaving devices always take precedence over rigid adherence to technical "rules."

All depressions are to be taken seriously. It is an error to deal with depression, and especially suicidal depression, as simple hostility or attention-seeking arranged for the benefit or anguish of the therapist. That fails to recognize the existence of the unconscious and of the internal world. Never is depression a problem of interpersonal relations between patient and therapist, although it can easily become the therapist's problem if he or she takes it that way.

Whether interpretable or uninterpretable, the patient's relationship is transferential. A patient may formulate his or her thoughts in interpersonal form; it is not useful for the therapist to accept that at face value. Every suicidal threat is to be taken seriously, not as casual or idle. Instead of minimizing these threats, we must consider: what is the nature of the therapeutic relationship where the patient makes such threats? Does he or she wish to alarm the therapist, to punish? Even the wish for attention carries a message. Especially troublesome is the suicidal "gesture." How many suicides that were intended only as gestures succeeded?

Some therapists ask a patient whether there is suicidal ideation, and even what form of suicide the patient is contemplating. This is contraindicated. Often the patient's plans have not gone that far. We are interested in the method the patient contemplates using only because we want to know how far along the plans have been carried. To ask how the patient plans to do it joins in with the formulation of a suicidal plan that the patient might not have developed too far. The therapist must avoid becoming an ally in the self-destructive plan.

If the patient does speak of suicidal thoughts, one might say something like, "Let us try to find out what makes you feel so desperate." This has the advantage not only of attending to the affect but even suggests that the feeling might pass. A person in physical as well as psychic pain endures it better when he or she knows that it will not go on forever. One might add, "While you feel so desperate let us make some arrangements for your protection, because you will change your mind when you feel a little better."

That may mean hospitalization, but other solutions may be possible. The best of these is a loving parent, friend, companion, or spouse who will cooperate with the treatment. The therapist must also maintain availability. The patient should be encouraged to use the telephone before acting.

Even if the patient is not contemplating action, the therapist must welcome these calls whenever they come.

Many depressed patients come to a low point at specific times of the day. Some find it hard to get out of bed, others get depressed at dusk. Interest in these specific times is comforting to the patient, and one might suggest that the telephone be used then. Patients who are reluctant to call feel easier if a telephone appointment has been made so that they know the therapist will be available.

We are not implying that much therapy is accomplished on the telephone in the middle of the night. Usually, merely raising a question gives the patient something to think about, which buys time. Suicide may be delayed while the ego has the unfinished task of finding the answer. If necessary, the therapist should offer to see the patient but he or she must be able to carry out that offer with full libidinal availability. Compliance will not suffice as the patient will probably feel like a burden, which will exacerbate the situation. Most nonpsychotic patients will want to preserve the "good" object, and so night calls will usually diminish when the crisis is past. These are emergency measures for the duration of the crisis, not for the duration of treatment.

It is important to be interested in the patient's appetite and nutrition. Severely depressed patients tend to lose their appetites, some to the point of becoming anorexic. That can reach life-threatening proportions, so it is necessary to be sure they are not slowly starving to death and to take strenuous measures if one finds this to be so. Even short of starvation, interest in the patient's food habits might stimulate the appetite. In that way, the therapist allies himself or herself with whatever modicum of cathexis of the "good" object representations exist. Even if the patient is well-enough nourished, interest in what the patient eats meets him or her at the primitive oral level.

When the patient feels better, such expressions of interest are usually met with defensive rebuttals but the therapist need not be dismayed. The "bad" object representations are prominent in depression, and the patient may attempt to provoke the therapist in that direction. One patient jeered repeatedly at the therapist's persistent interest in what she ate. Nevertheless, she looked forward to the sessions with concealed pleasure. After feeling assured that the therapist would still be interested in spite of frequent rebuffs, she began her sessions with, "I suppose you are going to ask me what I ate." The therapist's matter-of-fact response was "Yes, of course," a way of welcoming the assertiveness (and the mild hostility).

The therapist's libidinal availability to the patient's need, loneliness, and distress presents an attitude different from his or her primary object experiences. While we do not believe that the benign attitude is intrinsically curative, because distorted self and object representations remain, we do propose that a consistent, benign atmosphere may become one that the patient can trust when his or her distortions are corrected. Then the hope is that the patient will be able to use the therapist's libidinal cathexes to build more positive self and object representations.

At the very least, expressing interest in the patient's verbalizations conveys that we understand that the patient wishes to communicate something. This will alert the ego to that fact and induce an effort to express the feelings and wishes in words rather than in an irreversible action. Although we have discussed that before in relation to action in general, it applies specifically in relation to depression because action can lead to self-destruction.

One becomes a reliable "good" object slowly at best. When this has been achieved, however, it can turn the tide in times of stress. Where such favorable balance is attained, the telephone contact becomes simpler; the therapist can then say, "We will be able to talk about that in your session tomorrow," affirming continuity in this way and beginning, with appropriate timing, to encourage diminution of use of the telephone just as, when it was needed, one encouraged its use.

Hospitalization is a last resort, not because we are averse to it but because of the discontinuity in treatment. Very few hospitals allow the treating therapist to continue treatment in the hospital unless he or she is on the staff. It is confusing to the patient to have different therapists in and out of the hospital; it impairs whatever object connection had been made before hospitalization and makes it difficult to resume on discharge. Nevertheless, if life is in danger hospitalization is necessary. This despite the unfortunate arbitrariness of insurance carriers. They usually limit hospitalization to twenty-one days. What if the patient needs four weeks or more? Where expedience rather than diagnosis dictates treatment, whether in or out of the hospital, the patient is the loser. If the patient has a supportive environment, it is better that the therapist see the patient every day during the crisis, with appropriate medication, as a substitute for the discontinuity and possible disorientation that curtailed hospitalization imposes.

What constitutes a supportive environment? Each case has to be judged in accordance with the individual circumstances. In many instances, the very familial environment may have perpetuated the desperate situation; there, it is not a useful adjunct to treatment.

Availability is more than physical availability or a good telephone answering service. It is an attitude that pervades the therapist's behavior. At the outset of treatment it is difficult to convey, since words alone cannot carry the entire message. It is done repeatedly in words and by attitude. The patient who cannot use the telephone because she "knows" that the therapist will be annoyed needs to be met with the recognition that it is too difficult for her to take the risk now, but that perhaps she may be able to do it at some future time. This avoids focusing on her failure.

In critical cases it is important to arrange for frequent sessions at the outset. But perhaps even before that, the therapist has to decide whether he or she is willing to treat a case that can be so demanding of time and energy. There is a limit to one's availability, and the therapist must consider carefully before becoming committed to treat seriously depressed or suicidal patients. Certainly one cannot handle too many at one time.

We have discussed frequency of contact in a general way, suggesting that we not see patients too frequently if the prognosis is poor because it implies a promise we cannot keep. While frequent sessions are in order in the critical phase of suicidal depression, when matters stabilize they may be diminished. This guards autonomy and does not encourage regression to an excessive state of dependency.

That there is a tomorrow, a future, needs to be stressed. Not only during the desperate phone call, but throughout treatment, the therapist phrases his or her comments to indicate complete conviction about a future. Statements in the future tense, even the near future, are desirable, such as "When I see you tomorrow we will try to understand more about that." Such statements are reserved for the depressed patient and are used for the special purpose of reminding him of the future. They are contraindicated in all other situations, especially as a means of terminating an ordinary session because, in less critical situations or in the treatment of nondepressed patients, they convey the therapist's anxiety about whether the patient will return the next day.

Some of what is contained in the discussion of emergency measures for dealing with depression apply also to the long pull. In other respects, long-range treatment of the depressed patient depends on the diagnosis—the structure of the ego that is experiencing that affect. In particular, we assume that object loss is involved, whether real or fantasied, and would search the history for its origin as well as for those repetitive experiences that will have confirmed or reinforced the feeling of loss.

In treating depression, as in all therapy, it is important that the therapist remain a reliable object; sometimes this has to be maintained in the face of the patient's efforts to alienate. Gradually, as the therapist understands the life experiences in which self-esteem was damaged and objects lost, the therapist begins to build self-esteem. It is characteristic of depressed patients to blame themselves for their condition. This attitude is designed to protect the object representations from further negative cathexis lest they be lost altogether. The therapist becomes an ally in maintaining whatever modicum of positive cathexis exists. There is always some, which is what enables the patient to function at all. We never gild the object representations to make them appear better than they are or were. But we need whatever exists for the difficult work of helping the patient build self-esteem, that is, a positively cathected self representation, beginning with whatever is already there. The best outcome is one in which we have succeeded in helping the patient feel worthwhile, to understand that he or she is not to blame for not having been treated well in the past. This hews a narrow line because neither do we want to blame the patient's objects. One school of thought holds that if we show the patient that the parents were to blame then a cure is possible. This is fallacious. Our concern is less with how the parents were, more with what the patient was able to extract even from an unfavorable environment, and what his or her capacities for adaptation and reorganization are.

Finally, it must be said that we do not always win. There is serious risk in treating depression. Some very difficult judgments have to be made where suicide is a danger. Even short of that, poorly structured patients are difficult to treat in any event because not all are capable of reorganization. And in depression, some patients are so bent on suicide that no amount of vigilance can stop them.

23

▼

Specific Techniques of Psychotherapy

I n this chapter we discuss the treatment techniques that derive from the theory we have described. It is our hope that the therapist who works with adult patients at all levels of structuralization will have a surer hand as he or she is guided and informed by the theory.

Application of theory to treatment is an art. No two therapists will use theory in precisely the same way. Therefore the case illustrations we present are not intended to show the *right* way to deal with every therapeutic challenge. Used as guides, the illustrations will enable the therapist to devise a unique style; it will certainly vary with the style we present. With sound theoretical backing, the manner in which the therapist approaches the patient's therapeutic needs will inevitably be sound.

Part 1: Clinical Illustrations

The cases will be described in ascending order of structuralization. The first case discusses a near-psychotic understructured personality to illustrate how one helps to build structure and how the patient's innate capacities are "quickened" to become operative in the therapeutic endeavor.

A young man just out of college left his parent's home to come to New York City to work and to pursue graduate study. Finding himself lonely, confused, and at times in a chaotic state, he sought help. Already, this informs the therapist that he does possess a memory, an internalized percept that there might be help to be found in the object world. Had this not been the case he would simply have had a breakdown or committed suicide. So the memory of the helping face (Spitz) provided a beacon of orientation (Mahler 1968) that enabled him to seek help from another person.

Where a patient *functions* chaotically, we may assume that there is a substantial defect in the central steering mechanism (Spitz) or superordinate ego (Blanck and Blanck 1986). This patient is at a lower level of structuralization than others who may *feel* chaotic but who can contain that feeling, bad as it may be. In the latter patient, the defenses are in some working order even though the anxiety level is probably quite high. Where defense is operative, there are mechanisms that enable the person to organize some form of coherence (or seeming coherence) out of the chaotic feeling. This patient was overwhelmed by his anxiety, suggesting to the therapist that basic psychic integrity had not been firmly established and that he could not summon a workable defense. He was easily angered, but usually could confine his rage to verbal expression; his demeanor, however, was explosive.

In psychiatric diagnostic terms, this young man would be described as on the border between borderline and psychotic, with regression into psychotic episodes. For devising treatment techniques, however, it is more useful to view his difficulties in developmental terms. Failure to achieve coherence suggests failure in very early development, in the symbiotic experience that is essential for orientation to self, to reality, and to the object world. Ego deficits are inevitable consequences of such early affront to development. The therapist does not know at the outset whether this is because of failure in the environment (mothering person) or because of innate deficiency. The answer has to be searched out in the life history and in the relationship with the therapist.

The patient spoke often of his father (with very ambivalent affect) but rarely of his mother. Evidently the father contributed much to the patient's development, but he did not repair the damage of a less than adequate symbiosis. Therefore internalization was of fuzzy representations of both self and object, barely differentiated. This, in turn, made for diffuse identity formation, clinically noticeable in that identity appeared to be unclear and unreliable. Separation, insofar as it had taken place, remained fluid, sometimes flowing forward to a more differentiated position, sometimes regressing. This was because he tended to experience in totalities. Whenever he experienced a greater degree of differentiation, he feared it would result in total isolation. To become an individual with a separate identity felt too alone and therefore dangerous. He remained a perpetual graduate student because he was afraid to go out into the world.

He had chaotic and violent dreams which he suffered through all over again in the telling, a sign that he could barely distinguish the dream state from waking life. In one dream, an ambulance siren became louder and louder until it was too loud to tolerate. Even as he described the dream his face became contorted with anguish. One does not analyze such dreams. The first intervention was to comment that the dream took place the previous night, that it is not going on in the present. That was designed to orient him in time and to help him distinguish the dream state from the waking state. It is often desirable for a well-structured patient to relive the past in order to recapture the affect, but that would be contraindicated here. The affect is too much with him, overwhelming the ego. The therapist speculated that the dream represented a painful preverbal experience, unaltered by the passage of time and not reorganized by later experience. It might have been a memory of the sound of his own screaming when, as an infant, he was in distress unrelieved by the appearance of an object. That dates it quite early, when an infant does not yet know that the sound emanates from him.

Speculations are not imposed on the patient. We need the patient's guidance before we can know whether those speculations are correct. The first step in this case is to inform the patient that what had occurred in the dream was not happening to him in the telling of it. Next, a "tool" is offered: "You can wake yourself up when you have a bad dream. You don't have to let it happen to you." The better-structured patients have this tool and therefore do not have to be told this; they wake themselves from a bad dream before allowing the dream to go too far, for there is a self-protective function of the ego even in the sleeping state, acquired by transfer of the function of having been protected. This patient had to be given a way of putting the ego in control instead of becoming overwhelmed by events, even by his own dream, as though it is something that has happened entirely outside his control. The therapist is telling him, in effect, that he no longer has to be like a passive and helpless baby. He now has the resources of an adult.

What help can we offer such a patient? As with every understructured patient, the helping process is contained in the relationship with the therapist who acts as a catalyst of growth. This involves connecting with the patient at the level at which he is functioning at the moment and, at the same time, trying to assess whether he ever functions at a higher level when not overcome by anxiety at the level of fear of annihilation. The therapeutic thrust is always to enable the patient to find ways of doing a little more for himself than he believes possible. One does not expect that the suggestion "It is not happening to you now" will make a substantial difference immediately. It may, however, have a small impact that will exert its influence as similar interventions accumulate. In chapter 21 we said that an intervention is to be worded with a twofold purpose in mind—to advance the treatment in a given session and to constitute a contribution to the larger end goal.

This patient sometimes arrived without an appointment, expecting to be seen. It is important that the therapist try to see him, if only for a few moments, to make him feel welcome. Whenever that happened, the patient was gently informed that if the therapist had known he was coming he might have been able to arrange more time for him. It appears simple; one is merely informing him that there is another person who would welcome him if he could do what is necessary to bring that about. That, too, "stretches" the ego ever so slightly by showing him how he can play his part.

This patient said, in one session, "I want you to make me feel better," to which the therapist responded, "*We* will try to do that, and it would be very useful for you to try to help that along." Again, contained in a simple sounding statement is the steady promotion of growth, once again implying that he can do more than he thinks he can. An important part of that statement is that *we* will do it together. This joins him in a way that he had not sufficiently experienced when, as a baby, he needed another person. It is important to avoid allowing him to feel too alone. These are tiny steps; a large task would appear to him too formidable and too demanding. Yet we also want to avoid infantilizing him by doing too much for him. There are no precise measurements. The interventions depend on the therapist's art and the capacity to tolerate the frustration of trial and error.

The therapist's stability provides a safety feeling, essential if the patient is to relive inadequate early experience not as simple repetition but in order to process it in a new way. It is hoped that new internalizations will be formed. The therapist has to combat the indistinct, fleeting images in which self and object are relatively undifferentiated. By the reliability and stability of the therapeutic situation, the therapist constitutes an environment within which images can become stabilized into representations because they are consistently the same in each session. New internalizations become part of the structure. New object representations alter the self representation as well.

New internalizations are always superimposed on or added to those that already exist. Had this young man not had a modicum of internalized self and object images, he would not be treatable as an ambulatory patient. A therapist cannot replace existing internalizations, nor would it be desirable to try to do so even if it were possible. We do not want to destroy what had been acquired in early development, regardless of how distorted. As we *add* representations of a stable object and a stable self, these newly acquired internalizations may also alter those already in existence as reorganization takes place. This invokes the patient's capacity to reorganize—an essential feature of the innate endowment. Where it is lacking, the patient would remain in a psychotic state regardless of the therapist's efforts. How can we tell whether that innate capacity exists? If, for example, the patient begins to come at the appointed times or telephones in advance if he needs to come at another time, he has accepted the therapist's attempt to help him reorganize. That, of course, is nothing more than the mere beginning, a sign that the capacity is there.

Another such opportunity arose in this case when, at the onset of treatment, the patient would telephone late at night, wanting to chat. The therapist, without allowing himself to be exploited by talking on the telephone all night, responded as best he could rather than confront him too soon with the reality of the late hour. This was in order to avoid discouraging the patient's reaching out to extract from the environment, the feature that led him to seek out treatment in the first place. The therapist accepted the calls at first, realizing that need overwhelmed reality testing—that the level of object relations was such that the other person is not perceived as having separate needs. The patient required a benign, nonjudgmental response, as does the baby who is needy during the night. That the patient is an adult does not alter the fact that his structure rendered it impossible for him to comprehend the inappropriateness of the late night calls.

Another sign that reorganization was operative appeared in one such telephone call at 2:00 A.M. when the patient said, "You sound very sleepy." Awareness that there is another person with separate needs had arrived! From there the therapist can continue to build on the strengths derived from the innate endowment and from the modicum of structure that had brought this man into treatment. It is not possible to predict what effect a new experience in object relations will do for such a patient, but one can follow the signs and cues that inform whether the new experience is becoming meaningful.

The prognosis for such a patient has to remain guarded. As one works along with him, the extent to which the innate endowment and the capacity for reorganization become operative determine whether the prognosis alters in a more favorable direction. A good result in such a case would be a greater degree of separation-individuation and improved functioning. Included here, of course, would be the capacity to be alone and to soothe oneself.

The next case is of a middle-aged man who had developed a bit higher along the developmental continuum. This man had had a troubled but well-intentioned start in life. With a good capacity to extract from the environment and talents he could venture to exercise in working with an encouraging therapist, this patient could move rapidly toward autonomous functioning. The foci of the treatment were object deprivation, object loss, and the difficulties in dealing with objects as separate from himself. This patient *feels* chaotic at times, as distinguished from the first patient who *is* chaotic. Close exploration discloses that there were operative defenses. This is shown by his ability to *verbalize* that he feels totally confused when anxious; he does not *act* in a way that would get him into serious trouble. He found a "shorthand" way of describing his feelings. He used the fact that he had worked in a liquor store many years ago. When he felt confused he would say to the therapist, "I'm dropping bottles again." After many years of treatment he was able to establish a business, which was quite successful despite continuous difficulties with his landlord, with government regulatory agencies, even with customers whom he would give what he thought they wanted rather than what they said they wanted.

He was the youngest of four children. The father was terminally ill with cancer throughout the patient's early life and died when the patient was five. The entire household was dominated by the father's illness, precluding the mother's availability to her baby. His phase-specific developmental needs were either ignored or provided for in an irregular and unpredictable fashion by an overburdened and emotionally beset mother. Feelings of need remain overpowering; capacity to delay discharge is minimal; self-soothing had not been acquired in transfer from the object representation to the self representation because the mother had not been available to soothe him when he needed it. Anxiety was not reduced to a signal. His feeling of confusion represented several affects—anxiety, fear of object loss, need for soothing. Later, the therapist began to think that there was an element of identification in the confusion. This illustrates that the therapist must search for the meaning behind the patient's expression of affective states. Where affect differentiation has not progressed, patients tend to use global words to describe a multiplicity of affects. So the therapist searches out all the different affects that might be contained in the one word *confused*. This is not done all at once, of course, but has to be kept in mind for exploration as opportunities arise.

It also became clear that the patient did not experience himself or the other person as separate and whole. This can be ascertained in the diagnostic evaluation by the patient's behavior with the therapist and his description of behavior with others. He "read" his customer's minds; in trying to please them, he gave them what would please him. With the therapist, he assumed that his wishes could be known without verbalizing them. He was quicker than the first patient to become able to cathect an object in terms other than pure need gratification. Again, the therapeutic moves appear simplistic and even trivial. After many months of helping himself to tissues in the therapist's office, he finally came to wonder why he never carried a handkerchief—a small step toward autonomous functioning. The therapist's response was simply an affirmation, "It would probably be more convenient for you if you could remember to carry one." This also illustrates the value of waiting for the initiative to come from the patient. He is more likely to do something for himself when it is on his own initiative and not in response to a demand or criticism. As a child he had been given many toys and gadgets to compensate for his mother's limited availability, so his object world was "peopled" with material need gratifiers. Other persons were perceived more as suppliers, not as individuals with needs and purposes of their own. Yet he yearned for intimate contact but was unable to express it adequately in words.

He was a skilled extractor in the real world. When his business started to go well, he bought an expensive sports car. As business got even better, he wanted an airplane. His friends and siblings were terrified for him and tried to stop him. When he told the therapist that he intended to take flying lessons, the therapist kept his fears to himself and said, "You will of course make certain that you have learned well before you go up alone." This felt so different to the patient. Rarely had anyone ever expressed confidence in his ability to do things well. He also appreciated the concern for his safety as more genuinely intertwined with his autonomy than his brother's fears that he couldn't or shouldn't try to do it because he would surely kill himself.

Growth proceeded more markedly in this case than in the first because it began on a higher platform. This patient had had more maternal attunement even though his mother was distraught by her husband's illness. Part of this patient's confusion was in identification with an overburdened mother. Having the capacity to extract from the environment, he extracted her confusion in order to acquire the needed closeness with her. We have said that a baby and young child will join the mother's affect in order to arrange for the needed merged state she cannot provide directly. In childhood this is adaptive; in adulthood it becomes maladaptive.

He began one session in the usual way by saying he was confused and dropping bottles. The therapist said, "You know, there was so much confusion all around you when you were little that you caught it like chicken pox." He responded obliquely, by detailing some of the events since the last session. Then he interrupted himself, smiled, looked directly at the therapist and asked, "How are you today?" The level of object relations had taken a leap beyond need gratification. A question such as that calls for immediate acknowledgement, not out of politeness, but something far more profound. The question about the therapist was analogous to the move of the very young child who, without warning, suddenly begins to feed the feeder or in other ways begins to recognize that she is a separate person with her own needs. "I'm very well, thank you for asking," welcomes the effort to address the therapist as a separate person and is sufficient for the moment.

This case proceeded in ever-increasing interaction as the patient connected with the encouragement by internalizing a "good" representation and was able to transfer the "goodness" to the self representation. What he also internalized was the experience with and idea of a growth-promoter. These moves only appear simple. They are backed by sound theory and are effective only when the right moment is seized. It is in a case such as this that being informed by the theory almost "tells" the therapist what to say.

The therapeutic objective was ever greater distinction between self and object representations, in this case promoted by the therapist's unwavering confidence in the patient and attunement to his needs even as they changed. Unusually well endowed, the patient found pleasure in his skills just as the practicing subphase toddler experiences the elation of achievement in the presence of an approving object. The reorganization of this subphase inadequacy in his childhood is reflected in the "second round" in the form of wishing to fly an airplane. In this round the therapist must not repeat the failure of the primary object to accept his venturesomeness.

It is this kind of understructured personality who can proceed in treatment to a more psychoanalytic mode. Then he can be helped through the oedipal conflict, which has greatly contributed to his confusion. We may assume he was beset by the usual erotic feelings toward his mother, accompanied by death wishes toward a father who really was dying. It is far too difficult for a child to separate the reality of his father's illness and death from assumed causal connection with his normal death wishes. In more usual circumstances, the reality of the father's continued existence diminishes the fear of the magical power of the child's wishes. If the father really dies, as in this case, that fear is confirmed and reinforced. That will present the psychoanalyst with a most formidable task. It can be attempted if the patient chooses to go that far in treatment.

Our next illustration is of a person who cathects the object as a separate, whole other person. That means that she has attained a fair degree of separation. But individuation, which is less bound up in conflict, proceeded far ahead of separation. (Mahler considered these to be two separate tracks that do not always proceed in parallel.) Because individuation forged ahead, she could approach living up to her potential. Yet that very fact intensified separation anxiety. She could fulfill herself at the price of retaining a disapproved of self-image.

Her separation anxiety was so intense that it obscured opportunity for the therapist to determine the level of structure at which it originated. The depressive affect was too pervasive and could not be alleviated without long-term treatment. The patient's history revealed that the mother was chronically depressed and relied on help with child care. A significant memory was that when she was about three years old her mother took her to a park after the nanny had been dismissed suddenly. She wandered off, got lost, and was found some hours later about a mile away. This exacerbated the object loss of the nanny and precipitated a disillusionment as well. But children at that age cannot afford to dwell on the realization that the object has failed, so they tend to blame themselves, thereby further reducing self-esteem. Loss of safety feeling also ensued. The idea that the mother did not care enough or was careless enough to permit that to happen brings about enormous rages that must be repressed. To express it openly or even to *think* it would further increase the danger of object loss beyond the endurance of any child. In addition to repression, the hostility is turned against the self representation. The price is lowered self-esteem.

We learned from Kris that there is no single childhood memory, but a condensation and telescoping of many. The therapist took the memory of being lost as descriptive of the patient's picture of failure of the object. In this patient's unconscious, she was at fault for having wandered off in her search of adventure. The mother's representation was retained as blameless. This locates the problem in the conflict between the self representation and the object representations and, interestingly, exemplifies a struggle for individuation.

Because of superior innate endowment, the patient became skilled in a number of areas. She acquired a doctorate and achieved important successes in several fields. But she could not enjoy these accomplishments; she overlooked the plaudits of colleagues and usually found ways of subverting success. The ego could not tolerate the pleasure of achievement because it threatened to separate her from the disapproving object, so she found "safety" by converting achievements into ashes and despair.

The hostile self cathexis preserved a relationship with the primary object; childhood achievements had invariably been responded to with belittling or faint praise. One example will convey the flavor of a relationship studded with similar ones: The patient was chosen to be valedictorian of her graduating class; her mother's only comment on her valedictory address was "You spoke too fast."

That the relationship was preserved enabled the child to grow and develop structure, despite the hostile self cathexis that leaves her vulnerable to depression and even to suicidal thoughts. Those, of course, represent the wish to kill the object, turned against the self. She does not act on suicidal ideation but instead suffers from self-inflicted failures and torture. A less structured patient would feel defeat as emanating from the environment; a near-psychotic patient might act to destroy the merged self and object images. This patient, being more structured, was tormented with guilt; the superego punishes the ego.

She often felt deeply troubled in the intervals between sessions. Some patients do not even think of telephoning the therapist, as contrasted with the first patient who telephoned at random. Here, the therapist said, "Would it help to call me when you feel upset and alone?" The patient replied, "I thought of that but I couldn't do it." Now the therapist has to look into why she finds it too difficult to avail herself of this potentially relieving contact.

The therapist has many questions to ponder. Is there a sustaining object in the patient's representational world? If so, does a negative cathexis preclude reaching out? Was there an adequate practicing subphase; did the negative cathexis form during the rapprochement subphase, or could it be a manifestation of oedipal guilt?

Usually, reflections of many subphase experiences are condensed in a single aspect of adult behavior. The answers to these questions are best found in the transference. Whether the patient can think of telephoning is important to explore. She had already informed the therapist that the thought had crossed her mind, but she could not bring herself to make the call. It is important to know why. The therapist asked her on several occasions and received several answers:

- I did not want to invade your privacy.
- You are entitled to your time off, and I hesitated to disturb you.
- I didn't think that it would do any good.
- I have to learn to handle my problems myself.

These answers reveal the defenses. Protecting the therapist's privacy reflects an attempt to repress primal scene fantasies. Hesitation to disturb is in a similar vein, adding that perhaps she was scolded for doing so. The third response is different, reflecting conviction that the object representation is that of someone who does not help. Finally, the defense is that because no help can be expected from external sources, she has to turn to a narcissistic arrangement (Blanck and Blanck 1979). These thoughts, of course, were not conscious, so she did not know that they were deterring her from picking up the telephone. Yet it is vital that such thoughts be ferreted out in the therapy, to be put to use to alter the self and object relations pattern that precludes help from another person. That is never accomplished by reassurance that the call would be welcome. Reassurance is not a therapeutic technique; it does not alter the structure and the pattern of self and object relations. This patient's reality testing was intact, so she was able to say that she knew the therapist would respond gently even if he were to say that it is not a convenient moment and that he would return her call. The therapist then said, "You know that intellectually. But what is important now is that you *feel* rejection and your feelings are more convincing." The rapprochement crisis comes to mind, with the speculation that perhaps her "return to home base" was met with disapproval. We repeat for emphasis—such speculations are not to be taken as fact and are not material for interpretation. They are to be discarded if further information proves them to be incorrect.

The diagnostic issues in this case are perplexing because diagnostic signs point in opposite directions. On the structured side of the balance scale is that she leads a reasonably successful life professionally as well as socially. That she is highly educated, extremely well thought of in her field, married, with children, friends, and important interests all point to a well-functioning individual. On the other side is the fact that she cannot enjoy her successes, that she feels they are accidental and undeserved. Her self-esteem is alarmingly low; pleasure or success bring immediate thoughts of punishment, so powerful that she considers suicide. The superego is dominated by hostile, disapproving, punitive object representations.

The therapist concluded that the main obstacle to full structuralization lay in rapprochement failure that impaired her ability to tolerate the oedipal conflict when she arrived at that later developmental level. Her functional activity suggested that a high level of structuralization was regressively abandoned in face of the threat of object loss. Rapprochement disappointment resonated with frightening oedipal wishes in the context of a relationship with an object representation who would not tolerate the normal hostile oedipal wishes. Ordinarily, a high degree of structuralization provides a floor below which regression does not proceed; this patient's regressions appeared to go through that floor. Thus the diagnosis became ever more complex as the material appeared to oscillate through a wide range.

As a child the patient sought libidinal connection and found it, in the manner described in the previous case, by identifying with the mother's affect—depression. Separation anxiety predominated. Her greatest fear was that the therapist would tire of her and end treatment. The therapist's vacations left her feeling abandoned and anxious. She would try to allay the anxiety by writing a letter she did not mail, threatening to terminate treatment. She always returned for treatment after the therapist's vacation ended. But the thought of leaving him had two meanings. One was to gain ego mastery by doing the leaving—that is, to be the active "doer" instead of accepting the pain passively. The other was to show the therapist how it feels to be left. This latter reason has a retaliatory flavor, but the principal purpose was to demonstrate the affect. It informs better than words what being left feels like.

As the therapeutic alliance strengthened, outbursts of rage began to come through. These are difficult sessions for both patient and therapist. Yet there can be no therapeutic gain without it. Most important is for the therapist to become the "magnet" for the accumulated rage without becoming personally injured and thereby defensive. For the therapist to become defensive locates the conflict in the interpersonal realm instead of in the intrapsychic. There can be no resolution interpersonally because the conflict is between the self representation and the object representations. When a patient experiences that a lifetime of repressed anger can be expressed without object loss, the uneven cathectic balance between the two sets of representations is altered. Invariably, patients feel better as the hostility toward the self representation diminishes. We have said that the two sets of representations proceed more or less in tandem. Hostile feelings toward the object representations affect the self representation as well.

We do not advocate ventilation for its own sake; the anger has to be reduced to its genetic roots. But first it must be explored in the transference. The therapist looked for what had made her angry and depressed in the last session. That could be done with this patient because she was capable of maintaining continuity from one session to the next. Over a long series of sessions the dialogue continued, with the patient focusing on her perceptions of the therapist's "unfair" behavior and feeling justifiable anger therefore. As this went on without the therapist's defensiveness or retaliation, her focus began to shift. She started looking at her own patterns of functioning. She began to listen more. One time she responded with "I never thought of it that way."

Humor is always a favorable sign that the ego capacity for judgment is taking hold. As patient and therapist considered her improvement, she said, "That's because you have improved as a therapist!" The therapist acknowledged that this was undoubtedly true, but not the whole truth.

This case is cited as an example of long-term treatment of a difficult-to-diagnose patient with considerable structuralization and depressive affect. On a day-to-day level, change is undiscernible; fixed object relations patterns are continually repeated. She had to be "weaned" away from identification with a depressed mother. To begin to identify selectively with the therapist involved the use of the therapeutic differential. It is always difficult, painful, and at the same time liberating for a patient to begin to appreciate that the therapist is a more suitable object for identification. En route, the patient will use every device at her command to create a repetition of the seemingly uncaring object, including interminable accusations, rages, and depressed aftermaths. The end does not come as a dramatic climax. Slowly the patient feels better and termination of psychotherapy looms. This patient, too, could proceed into psychoanalysis if she chooses. There, one would devote more attention to the interesting resonance between rapprochement disappointment and oedipal conflict.

Part 2: Specific Techniques

Because the literature on the technique of psychoanalysis is adequate, our focus has been largely on the technique for the treatment of the understructured patient. Essential to understanding abnormal phenomena is the process of normal development against which pathology is measured. Especially important is knowledge of the critical periods when psychological development and physical maturation must coincide if development is to go forward smoothly. Also necessary is knowledge of the different needs of the four subphases of the separation-individuation process.

The Role of the Patient

We recapitulate what we have described as the role of the patient in the therapeutic process, and we shall then go on to dwell at greater length on the therapist's role and the specific techniques that he or she employs.

Adult patients bring to the treatment situation their unique innate endowment which, in the first round of development, has interacted in the dyadic relationship to build structure. This implies that adult patients come with established patterns of object relations, with particular levels of structuralization, with inter- and intrasystemic conflict, with varying defensive systems, and with varying innate capacities for extracting from the environment and for reorganization.

The patient is expected first to provide diagnostic information, and then to participate in the therapy by using whatever equipment he possesses to work with the therapist, who is there to guide him to ever-higher levels of structuralization. The "equipment" to be used will of course include the resistances.

The Role of the Therapist

The therapist's first task is to make an accurate but flexible diagnosis in order to ascertain where on the Fulcrum of Development the preponderance of weights falls. This enables the therapist to decide on the form of treatment—psychoanalysis for the structured personality, psychotherapy for the understructured. After diagnosis, the practical arrangements are made and therapy begins.

The Techniques of Psychotherapy

The benign climate. This refers to the setting, both physical and attitudinal. The therapist provides a comfortable room, is there and receptive at the appointed time, and presents an aura of reliability. Interruptions are eliminated as far as possible. Telephone calls are not made. If telephone calls are received, they are kept to brief messages only. It is made clear by the therapist's behavior and respect for the patient that the session is for that patient alone. The patient, not the procedure, is the focus. This is in contrast with the medical model of performing procedures. The physician or dentist can work on the body that the patient has to bring. The therapist works with the whole person—soma and psyche. This is taking on ever greater importance as third parties insist that psychoanalysis and psychotherapy follow the medical model of diagnosis "by the numbers," that is, by symptoms, and that each symptom calls for a separate procedure, without consideration of the structure.

The therapist's emotional attitude is of overriding importance. He or she must be in good health, in an evenly positive mood, ready for whatever the patient may bring and able to cope with it. To the patient, this attitude becomes predictable after a few sessions.

In summary, the benign climate is the environment within which therapy takes place. For many patients, to be treated respectfully, to have the session devoted solely to them, even to be seen on time are in themselves new experiences. Rarely is more than this needed for the ambulatory patient.

The therapeutic alliance. Every person who takes the trouble to come for treatment is by that very act using the part of the endowment or structure where the wish to further development and correct distortions is to be found. It is with that part of the personality that the therapist allies himself and expects the patient similarly to join in alliance against the pathology. Against this alliance, defense and resistance are operative. That means the patient is sometimes in alliance with the therapist and sometimes not. When resistance impairs the alliance, it is the task of the therapist to deal with the resistance in order to restore the alliance. Obviously, the therapy goes forward when the therapeutic alliance is operative.

Provision of experience. There is much controversy about whether the therapist provides a new experience. We have said that the benign climate is more often than not a new experience in and of itself. Beyond that, as always, much depends on the patient's structure. The very disturbed patient may need to be told how to manage life in this world. The middle-range borderline patient is best helped to "stretch" the ego, to use his or her own capacities to function better. The well-structured patient already has his or her own resources.

Without deliberately doing anything artificial, however, the therapist provides a great deal. In addition to the benign climate, that the therapist is different from the primary objects provides opportunity for new identifications to add to or alter those already in existence. And, of course, the therapist uses the technical skills summarized here in the patient's behalf.

The therapist as catalyst. A *catalyst of growth* is one who guards autonomy and promotes it to higher levels. He or she stands for optimal functioning. As in chemistry, where the term originates, the therapist is a necessary presence, a promoter, but not an active participant in the patient's functioning.

Reparenting. The therapist does not reparent. We have explained that despite inadequacies in early development, the adult patient has already organized some structure and has acquired object representations, no matter how inadequate. Thus the patient is not an empty vessel into whom new experiences can be poured. The therapist works with the existing internalizations, tries to alter the patterning of self and object relations, and offers opportunity for new identifications.

The therapeutic differential. This felicitous term and concept, proposed by Loewald, explains how established patterns of self and object relations alter in therapy and how new identifications are formed. This usually takes place late in the treatment, after the established patterning is thoroughly understood. The patient experiences that the therapist behaves differently from the internalized object representations and finds it desirable to identify selectively with admired attitudes in the therapist. New identifications alter the self representation as well as the representations of the object.

Transfer of function. In the process of development a separate object does not exist at first. When there is awareness of an external object, the functions of that object may still, for a while, be experienced as functions of the self. With further development, as the representational world is formed, the functions become part of the object representations. Some of these functions undergo transfer intrasystemically, from the object representations to the self representation. We use the example of soothing which at first is the function of the object, later is a function of the object representations, and still later becomes a function of the self representation by means of transfer. We expect that adults, under ordinary circumstances, are able to soothe themselves in such functions as putting themselves to sleep, which was, in childhood, a function of the object representation.

Object relations. We define object relations differently from the other schools of thought, some of which are known as "schools" of object relations. To the developmentalist, object relations consist of the *resultant* of the interaction between child and mothering person in the dyadic experience in early life and, somewhat later, with the father and others in the triadic experience. These experiences have become internalized to form the self and object representations. In this way we differ from those who see object relations as "attachment." In developmental theory, rather than attachment, there is intertwining by means of the action-reaction-action cycle.

Interpretable and uninterpretable transference. Transference interpretation is the backbone of psychoanalytic technique. This remains valid for the structured personality and may apply also to certain higher-level understructured personalities. For the preponderance of understructured patients, however, transference interpretation has no meaning because a true transfer from past to present objects has not been made. In addition to not having developed to the point where the other person is experienced as separated and whole, some of these patients are not yet on the level of true semantic communication. For such patients, interpretation of transference incurs the risk of becoming an empty intellectual exercise.

The understructured patient is more likely to seek replication of early self and object experience, or gratification of need. Rather than interpretation, the interchange between therapist and patient remains on the affective level where the therapist tries to "talk" the patient's affective language.

Tracking. This refers to the process whereby the therapist remains closely attuned to the affective state of the understructured patient. It is analogous to the attunement required of the mothering person by the developing child. In treating an adult patient, however, the therapist's behavior in the present cannot be the same because we are not bringing up a developing child; the patient arrives with a degree of structural organization. As already pointed out, the adult patient is not an empty vessel. We try to stay with the patient affectively. Therefore our interventions and responses must be designed to be with the patient and, at the same time, lead the patient to higher levels of functioning.

Empathy. This has become a much overused term that has acquired different meanings to different therapists. In most instances, the therapist must remain a separate, whole, other person who cannot get into the patient's skin. The few exceptions are when the therapist has to join the lower-level understructured patient in order to bring that patient along to higher levels. We agree with Kernberg (personal communication, 1990) that empathy is not a therapeutic technique. Especially when used to become a more empathic "parent," or to decry the limitations and failures of the real parents in the past, not only is structuralization not advanced but it may even be retarded by destroying the parental representations that are needed to form an object world.

Interpretation. The structured patient who participates in true semantic communication can process interpretation when both content and timing are correct. Much that goes on between therapist and understructured patient is not interpretation proper, but *tracking*. To be avoided is *conversation*, which often occurs because of the therapist's anxiety about silences and because of therapeutic zeal and the urgency to do something.

Guardianship of autonomy. This is not an active technique; it is an attitude. The therapist is not a fount of wisdom about how to conduct one's life and, even when the therapist knows better, it is best to allow patients to find their own way. The therapist does not give advice or make decisions for the patient, but does provide guidance toward decision making. The exception to this, of course, is when the patient proposes to engage in irreversible destructive behavior.

Confrontation. Confrontation is best achieved when the therapist helps the observing ego to confront the behavior. This promotes the use of judgment and of thought as trial action. Rarely is a person helped by being confronted by another person. This keeps the problem where it belongs—within the structure rather than in the interpersonal interaction between therapist and patient.

Ventilation. Ventilation of affect cannot have much value unless it is accompanied by insight. Therefore to encourage a patient to ventilate, especially with the erroneous idea that hostile affect can be discharged like steam, is a fallacy. The process is far more profound. Affect is to be connected with experience and to be traced to its origin if there is to be alteration. It is never desirable to provoke the patient, for if he or she is angry for cause, this has no curative value. Beyond that, it is never desirable to provoke artificially because that would render the therapist untrustworthy.

Evenly suspended attention. This deals with the manner of listening. The therapist listens with the "third ear," which hears the patient's unconscious, the affects, the patterning of self and object relations, the transference manifestations, and the resistances.

Neutrality. Neutrality is related to evenly suspended attention; the therapist maintains a position equidistant from id, ego, and superego. It has nothing to do with failing to take a position that is in the patient's best interest, especially when destructive action can be averted by intervention.

Affect differentiation. This deals with development of an affective repertory beyond "all good" and "all bad." A fully developed range of affect contains shadings of both positive and negative affect. On the negative side the range would be from low-keyedness to sadness to grief to sorrow to depression; interpersonally, the affect would range from dislike to anger to rage to hatred. On the positive side would be happiness, joy, elation, ecstasy; interpersonally, liking, loving, and similar affects would prevail.

Promotion of self-esteem. This is not a simple matter of praise as though self-esteem can be enhanced by the therapist's judgment. It is lastingly promoted by finding the sources of esteem in the relationship between the self representation and the object representations. When a patient has low self-esteem, it is usually because the object representations have been overvalued at the expense of the self representation. This malignant process can have its inception in the first days or weeks of life if the partner in the dyad fails to provide adequate gratification as building blocks for self esteem. It is enhanced in the symbiotic experience of oneness with the object. And it takes a sharp turn in the practicing subphase where elation is the appropriate affect when practicing subphase experience is optimal. Where the object disapproves of the practicing thrust, a disapproved of self-image can result in place of elation.

At higher levels of development, self-esteem is impaired by superego punishment. Thus the technique of self-esteem enhancement rests on an adequate diagnosis to find the origin of the problem. This explains why patients are not helped by simple praise.

Abstinence. This concept is often misunderstood because it is equated with the therapist's silence. It means, in fact, that the therapist does not gratify infantile wishes and fantasies. Because it is the therapist's objective to lead the patient on to higher levels, gratification usually infantilizes rather than promotes growth. The therapist may speak as much as is useful to help the growth process. The only purpose of silence is to allow room for the patient's own thoughts and associations to emerge without clouding or diverting them.

The therapist's role is a difficult one, not because the techniques are difficult to learn but because the therapist is required to function in a disciplined manner beyond what is required in any other profession. As we have said, a person in another profession may befriend a patient or client, may socialize, may discuss personal matters, may use the patient for one's own gratification without necessarily impairing the professional function. Psychoanalysts and psychotherapists may not do anything with patients for their own gratification. That means in the course of a day's work that some sessions may be pleasurable, some may be the opposite. We are obliged to seek pleasure outside the professional relationships.

24

▼

On Ending the Treatment

Freud compares the practice of psychoanalysis with the "noble game of chess" (1912b:123). He contends that only the opening gambit and the endgame admit of systematic presentation; the middle moves, including *tact* (timing), cannot be taught. That is a challenge we have accepted by describing some of the middle moves, including the delicate matter of timing (Blanck and Blanck 1974, 1979, 1986).

In this final chapter we discuss the endgame. It is useful to begin with a historical perspective on ending the treatment because the contemporary points of view are best understood in the context of their evolution from their antecedents. In 1912 psychoanalytic theory and the technique that flowed from it were far simpler than today. Ending the treatment was deemed appropriate when the unconscious had been made conscious. The slogan then was, "where id was there shall ego be." That, of course, was at the infancy of psychoanalytic theory construction when a crude topographic theory delineated two levels of the psyche. Id was regarded as synonymous with unconscious, and ego was equated with consciousness. That early theory is hard to dispel. Its tendency to persist makes for confusion about structural as well as topographic elements. The unconscious was (and in popular thought remains) a Pandora's box that , when opened, spills its contents, presumably making them available for interpretation and attainment of insight. When that was accomplished, which took only a few months, treatment ended.

In present-day theory, the id is still thought to be unconscious, but it is the repository of the drives, not the whole of the unconscious. It is arguable whether repressed material is relegated to the id. Since we are dealing with constructs, it is tidier to think that repressed material "resides" in another sphere of the unconscious, to be retrieved when countercathexis is applied. The drives, on the other hand, are never conscious but are only manifest through their derivatives. (That is why we have argued that the word *aggression* is often used incorrectly when what is meant is an affect, such as *hostility*.) It is also now no longer believed that the ego is altogether conscious. The very motive for Freud's enunciation of the structural theory was his observation in his clinical work that part of the ego is unconscious.

One of the principal results of ego psychological discoveries is a new respect for repression. No longer do we set about diligently to uncover all that is repressed. The structure of the personality as well as the timing determine whether a given patient would benefit from lifting repression in order to resolve conflict. In all cases, repressions that are essential to the orderly organization of secondary process thought are to be left intact. Moreover, in the treatment of the understructured personalities, lifting repression is usually not the goal at all. More often the reverse is true; the goal is to foster repression rather than lift it.

One aspect of the older theory is worth noting and retaining. Achievement of autonomous functioning, although not stated in those terms, was an integral element in the termination process. Although the work of the analysis was considered to have been completed when the unconscious was made conscious, the patient was expected to identify with the analyst and thereby continue with self-analysis. Although that is still believed to be operative, the matter is far more profound, as we shall discuss shortly.

It was at first rather optimistically believed that the work of the analysis produces changes that endure for life. It took Freud from 1912 to 1937 to note that analysis is interminable because one can only deal with the conflict that presents itself at the time of the analysis. A "completed" analysis does not preclude emergence of conflicts later in life as circumstances trigger them.

In addition to making the unconscious conscious, other criteria for ending treatment were enunciated early on. The capacity for love and work was regarded as a measure of completion of an analysis. No one can quarrel with that, although now love can be discussed in more sophisticated terms. We can now explain how the capacity to love develops from absolute need for the object, through primitive love for the object, to object constancy when the object is loved regardless of the state of need. Although Freud did not have the theory to show him how the capacity to love develops, he knew it is necessary—that we must love or perish.

By 1937 Freud thought that analysis could be terminated when the patient was no longer suffering, when much that had hitherto been puzzling had been explained, when resistances had been worked through, and when repressed material had emerged and been interpreted. He alludes to this as a natural termination. He was not optimistic, however, about reaching such ideal results in every instance, especially because he believed that the id is innately endowed with so much power that it can overwhelm the ego. That was especially so, he thought, with regard to the aggressive drive, which he equated with a death instinct.

After Freud's 1937 treatise on termination, psychoanalytic theorists turned their attention to other matters. Not until the 1950s does termination of analysis begin to become a theoretical concern once again. Hoffer (1950) retains the idea of making the unconscious conscious as the end goal of psychoanalysis. Balint (1950) adds attainment of genital primacy as a major criterion for termination (chapter 12). Rickman (1950) joins Balint by stressing orgastic capacity. These are drive-oriented positions.

Ego-oriented points of view, along with object relations considerations, begin to enter the literature as Nunberg (1954) and Glover (1955) write about structural change. Glover stresses structural change over symptom relief. G. Blanck (1966) uses Mahler's early thoughts about separation-individuation to suggest that ending treatment is to be "tailored" to avoid repetition of early separation trauma.

E. Ticho (1972) regards mental illness as a disruption in development. According to him, therefore, termination is appropriate when treatment has brought the patient to the point where impeded development can be resumed. Influenced by the elaboration of ego psychology in which he was an active participant, Kris (chapter 4) shifts the focus of technique in general, including termination. He conceptualizes what Freud knew only intuitively—that the capacity for a greater degree of autonomous functioning is a major criterion in ending the treatment.

Firestein (1978) conducted a follow-up study of cases after termination of psychoanalytic treatment at the New York Psychoanalytic Institute. He found that anxiety at the prospect of termination is related to a traumatic separation early in life. Although by that time Mahler (1963) had worked out the specificity of the subphases of the separation-individuation process and its relevance to capacity for psychic separation, Firestein and his collaborators do not avail themselves of it, thereby depriving themselves of precision about the nature of the original separation trauma that the prospect of termination threatens to repeat.

Later authors focus on specific details about termination. Cavenar and Nash (1976) emphasize the well-known fact that dreams can signal readiness to end the treatment. Calef and Weinshel (1983) note that all analyses end without "true" termination because the oedipal wish must remain unconsummated. Shane and Shane (1984) believe that the transference neurosis is immutable, leaving the question of whether neurotic conflict can be resolved by means of working within the transference neurosis. Goldberg and Marcus (1985), without reference to Freud's thoughts about natural termination, propose a "natural" termination based on a "sense" that ending is appropriate. This leaves the issue dependent on the analyst's intuition, a most unreliable tool in our opinion. De Simone Gaburri (1985) adheres to the concept of the death instinct, abandoned by so many other theorists. She contends that the prospect of termination is equated with death in the mind of the analysand. And she adds that criteria for termination cannot be established.

Many analysts deem termination appropriate when the infantile neurosis, revolving around the Oedipus Complex, has been transformed into a transference neurosis and is resolved as the person of the analyst stands in lieu of the original object or objects. There is question now about whether an infantile neurosis truly exists to be reproduced as an entity in the form of a transference neurosis (see chapter 17). Regardless of the relevance of that question in relation to the structured personality, clearly the patient who has not attained neurotic structure can have neither an infantile neurosis nor a transference neurosis.

It is generally accepted that resolution of the oedipal conflict in its several rounds remains an important goal of psychoanalysis. Looking at the oedipal configuration from the developmental point of view, we find it hardly likely that vicissitudes of preoedipal life do not affect the nature of the Oedipus Complex in some way, often unfavorably, in rare instances favorably. We have said that preoedipal experience determines the "shape" and quality of the Oedipus Complex as well as the capacity to resolve it. Understructured patients suffer from faulty early development that limits their capacities to deal with conflict. The structured personality does possess that capacity. We repeat that the Oedipus Complex in early life is but the first round in a continuing process in attenuating Oedipal wishes. A second round takes place in adolescence (Blos 1962). We (Blanck and Blanck 1968) describe marriage as still another developmental phase and as another round in the continuing reworking of the oedipal conflict. Benedek (1959) suggests that parenthood is yet another developmental phase, and to that we may add that it presents still another dimension to the oedipal configuration because of the dramatic alteration in roles.

Two distinct points of view regarding termination are on the contemporary scene. Bergmann (1988) represents those who apply the concept of transference neurosis, in particular transference love, to termination. By emphasizing transference love, he concludes that treatment may end with displacement of that love to an object in real life. That displacement, however, must be based on an intrapsychic reorganization that has been achieved in the analysis. Bergmann doubts that the transference relationship and the Oedipus Complex can be resolved. He is more certain about the power of the drives than about processes of internalization. He says: "Internalization and identification with the analyst, though important, cannot carry the full burden of termination" (151). Bergmann's approach is largely drive oriented. (See chapter 2 where we discuss the false dichotomy between drive theory and ego psychology.)

Blanck and Blanck (1988) and Loewald (1988) rest their considerations regarding termination on internalization and its power to alter the self representation. Our thrust emphasizes autonomy as a criterion for termination. We suggest that there is an underlying assumption throughout the treatment that the patient will leave in a more autonomous state than at the outset. This stance dictates that the therapist guard autonomy from the beginning, supporting the highest level of functioning that the patient presents, and encouraging growth as we have described. Hartmann (chapter 3) defines autonomy as relative independence of the ego from the drives. We add an object relations dimension that enlarges that definition to include relative independence of the self representation from the object representations. A satisfactory degree of such independence usually already exists in the psychic structure of the neurotic patient. For such patients, therefore, criteria for termination rest on the attainment of relative independence of the ego from the drives and from the superego. For the under-structured patient who is not to go on to analysis proper, the end of treatment is heralded by increased independence of the self representation from the object representations. When the maximum degree of autonomy that can be expected is attained, the continuous physical presence of the analyst or therapist is no longer needed. Freud was correct in considering that identification with the analyst and the analyst's work enables the terminating patient to continue without the analyst. Now we can put it differently—object representations remain "alive" intrasystemically. In this manner, ending contact with the therapist or analyst attenuates intense separation anxiety and object loss because the mental representations of the object continue to exist.

Loewald (1988) describes the dissolution of the relationship with the analyst at termination as involving the process of mourning by means of which identification and internalization replace the lost object. As contrasted with Bergmann's position, Loewald places stress on the power of internalization. It follows, then, that Loewald relies more thoroughly on self-transformation, the resultant of internalization, to enable the patient to leave the analyst autonomously rather than by displacement of transference love. Loewald says: "Transforming these transactions into intrapsychic ones that no longer have the nature of object relations but are becoming elements of the patient's character, of his self (if you prefer that designation), is what I call internalizing" (1988:1).

We find this consistent with our concept of transfer of the functions of the object representations to the self representation. We are also in agreement with Loewald (and he with us) that, as we put it, the end is contained in the beginning. As he puts it: "The end permeates the entire course of treatment" (1988:157). To Loewald, termination is an exercise in coming to terms with individuation, that part of the separation-individuation process that functions autonomously. He adds the important observation that there can be resistance to ending the treatment as well as to beginning it.

Most authors on the subject of ending treatment are concerned with termination of psychoanalysis. That the preponderance of literature on termination does not apply to the understructured personality is a factor of the state of the art. The technique for termination of such cases is in the process of being established hand in hand with understanding the etiology and treatment of those pathologies.

We stress criteria for ending the treatment with the understructured personality because of the paucity of literature on that matter. We have said that the ideal termination of such cases is attainment of greater distinction between the self representation and object representations. That is a long-term goal. Many cases have to terminate before such an ideal ending is possible. Sometimes this is for practical reasons, money being the outstanding one. Others have to do with proximity, change in geographic location, and the like. A large consideration is motivation. Not all people are persistent and wish for the best that life has to offer but are content with small gains. And it must be taken into account that some patients are not capable of achieving optimal success in treatment because of intrinsic factors, such as unfavorable innate endowment.

Psychotherapy patients cannot be as neatly categorized as are medical patients, who ordinarily have well-understood illnesses. They more resemble those esoteric situations that have to be studied case by case. And they do not even share the common features in structuralization of the neurotic patients, as we have mentioned. The endowment, the structure, the life experience, and the interrelatedness among all those factors vary widely from one understructured patient to another. Distinct treatment guidelines are difficult to prescribe, and endings vary widely from one case to another.

Too many cases end because the insurance runs out. We cannot deal with that here beyond having already said that the duration of the case is not to be dictated by the insurance carrier. It should be the other way around, but that is a social and political problem that is beyond our scope.

A person with little ambition for major personality change, or with poor endowment, can be helped to some extent. Some poorly endowed patients wish to carry on treatment beyond a reasonable prognosis. There, it is the responsibility of the therapist to limit the treatment. Patients with low ambition may wish to end when the accomplishment is satisfactory to them. We do not advocate leaving the ending of treatment to the decision of the patient. Ideally, it is a joint decision. Yet the therapist cannot carry motivation and ambition for the patient. Therapeutic zeal is well and good when it does not go beyond the zeal of the patient. The best we can do is try to raise the level of ambition, but we must be cautious about this lest we overestimate the innate potential. Consider the following two cases:

A man who was having an extramarital affair came for therapy because he wanted to end the affair but needed help in doing so. The therapist explored his capacities, as described in chapter 13, and found that the patient was capable of going far beyond his stated goal. The therapist did not force intensive treatment on him. In the process of working out why he engaged in this affair and why he was unable to end it on his own, since that was what he wanted, inevitably a great deal was discovered about his endowment and structure. The therapist found that he had an excessively traumatic early life, which was largely repressed. Despite that, he was functioning extraordinarily well in his business and moderately well in his marriage. He was attracted to other women from time to time for reasons he did not understand. It was important to him that his marriage be preserved, and he realized that it was threatened with continuing affairs. Understanding his excessive need for comfort and mothering wherever it was offered helped him know that almost any woman can seduce him more for mothering than for sex. He was able to end the current affair and was content with that. He feared entering a long treatment that would revive memory of painful trauma. The therapist respected his wishes. He was told that more is possible whenever he should choose to undertake it. That is far from the ideal ending of sorting out self and object representations. Many psychotherapy cases end short of that.

A woman came for treatment because she felt that there was no emotional tie between herself and her husband. She was wealthy and able financially to undertake whatever treatment was prescribed without insurance encumbrance. She described the meager interaction in her marriage. She felt that her husband was not as interested in her as she would like. Yet she did not want to confront this. She realized that she herself was restrained in her affective life. Intensive treatment for her would probably entail treatment for the husband as well and would call for major changes in the personalities of both partners.

She was one of ten children, lost literally and emotionally somewhere in the middle because of her ordinal position. One had the impression that she felt tolerated in the family because she was there but she had no sense of distinction. Neither parents nor older siblings conveyed a sense that she was special to anyone. Again, as in the first case, the prospect of long-term treatment frightened her, not because of the time but because of what might emerge. The major problem was one of self-esteem—that is, paucity of a positively cathected self representation. She feared that the uncertain stability of her marriage would tilt in the direction of abandoning it if she were to become less narcissistically deficient and more assertive. The therapist was not as convinced as she that her husband would leave her if she were to acquire a better self-image but did not insist that she take that risk. She had enough regard for her children to wish to spare them the disruption of a divorce. Treatment ended with her deliberate choice to postpone further therapy, knowing she could return when the prospect of an upheaval would be more tolerable to her and the children.

These two cases illustrate that we do have to end treatment with less than ideal results when the attempt to attain them is not assured of success. To insist in such instances would be more for the satisfaction of the therapist than the patient. Yet we do not always go along with the patient's wish to end where ending would be premature. Some patients leave by acting on their anger or other negative feelings, by wishing to give the therapist a taste of what it feels like to be left, by impulsive decisions that are difficult to reverse. In such instances the therapist has the obligation to try to convey insight into the behavior. Some therapists confuse independence and autonomy with acting and acting out. To act without exercising judgment is not autonomous, and the patient is to be protected against such impulses. Often the therapist's interest in continuing the treatment despite the patient's negative feelings is appreciated, and the patient does continue. That is not always assured, so we terminate in good grace. By that we mean that the therapist ends on good terms with the patient who is leaving prematurely, and always leaves the door open so the patient will feel comfortable about returning.

Often endings feel premature to the therapist because he or she underestimates the gain the patient experiences. To illustrate:

Another patient in an unsatisfactory marriage was able to leave his wife when his separation anxiety attenuated. He divorced and made a more satisfactory marriage after a few years. The therapist thought this man could be analyzed and presented him with that opportunity. But he was content with his new marriage and did not want further treatment. He returned a few years later because of a question about his job—whether to press for a promotion or seek a job elsewhere. That was resolved after a few sessions. Again he did not want to undertake more than that. In the course of that second meeting he told the therapist how pleased he was with the success of the first round of treatment, about how much he had gained through having conquered his separation anxiety. That treatment, although short of what the therapist thought possible, did create greater distinction between the self representation and the object representations, perhaps not maximally but to the patient's satisfaction. Many patients experience great exhilaration with that event because identity and positive self cathexis is enhanced. The wish to end with such achievement is based on feeling better than ever before.

We are reminded here of Mahler's (1968) concept of separation, that it is an intrapsychic process. Two persons can be together physically and yet be separate psychically because there are clearly established boundaries between then. Yet some patients who attain a greater degree of separation through the treatment wish to leave the therapist in order to try themselves out in the real world on their own. Therapists are in a delicate position here. They do not wish to impede the separating thrust. Yet if more work needs to be done, they also do not want the patient to feel foolish for having left too soon because that risks that he or she would find it difficult to return. Each case has to be decided on the basis of allowing maximum autonomy, yet guarding against too hasty a departure.

Some patients wish to remain in treatment "forever." Some even put it that way. This has been frowned on more than treated in the past when analysis was dominated by the philosophy that it should be brief. Of course it is proper to end a case when nothing further can be accomplished. But we recommend that one take a sharp look at why the patient feels that he or she needs the therapist's physical presence endlessly. Loewald is one of the few authors who writes about resistance to ending, although he does not elaborate. We believe that patients who cannot terminate are conveying the message that internalization is incomplete. Then the therapist has the task of ascertaining whether further treatment would complete the process or whether that is as far as that patient can go. A patient whose capacity for internalization is limited would not need to remain in treatment permanently but can be "weaned" with the understanding that return sessions can be held from time to time as needed.

What is implied in this consideration of ending the treatment is that, even more than psychoanalysis, psychotherapy is interminable. In both modalities one cannot predict the new life situations that will arise after what appears to be a suitable ending. But in psychotherapy that has ended with greater independence of the self representation from the object representations, an additional consideration is that conflicts have not been resolved. A good reason for such a patient to return is that he or she may have become capable of enduring the conflict resolution offered by psychoanalytic treatment.

Many presenting requests for help begin with rationalization and especially with displacement. Often the beginning is occupied with dealing with those defenses. It is commonplace, for example, for one spouse to attribute marital problems to the personality of the other spouse. Some patients can work out their own difficulties when they come to understand that the problem lies in their own object relations patterns. Such realization can bring a person to a reasonable ending. They may find that, when displacement no longer impedes them, they alter their interactions.

We have described some of the kinds of psychotherapy cases that end before reaching what the therapist would consider an ideal ending. It was once believed that treatment is a one-time endeavor that either succeeds or fails. Patients may need a lifetime connection with the therapist, which is not to say that a literal connection is to be maintained. Patients can and do return from time to time. Object need brings them back when they need "refueling."

The ideal of maximum autonomy, of distinction between the self and object representations, is most usually reached with long-term treatment. We have described the "opening gambit" and middle moves in such cases. The "endgame" dictates itself as autonomous behavior becomes manifest within and outside the treatment.

References

Alexander, F. and T. M. French. 1946. Psychoanalytic Psychotherapy. New York: Ronald Press.

Arlow, J. A. and C. Brenner. 1964. Psychoanalytic Concepts and the Structural Theory. New York: International Universities Press.

Bak, R. 1953. Fetishism. Journal of the American Psychoanalytic Association 1: 285–98.

———— 1956. Aggression and perversion. In S. Lorand, ed., Perversions: Psychodynamics and Therapy. New York: Random House.

———— 1965. Comments on object relations in schizophrenia and perversions. The Psychoanalytic Quarterly 34: 473–75.

———— 1968. The phallic woman and the ubiquitous fantasy in perversions. The Psychoanalytic Study of the Child 23: 13–36. New York: International Universities Press.

Balint, M. 1950. On the termination of psychoanalysis. International Journal of Psycho-Analysis 31: 196–99.

Benedek, T. 1959. Parenthood as a developmental phase. Journal of the American Psychoanalytic Association 7: 389–417.

———— 1968. A discussion of Mary Jane Sherfey's "The evolution and nature of female sexuality in relation to psychoanalytic theory." Journal of the American Psychoanalytic Association 16: 424–48.

Bergmann, M. S. 1966. The intrapsychic and communicative aspects of the dream. International Journal of Psycho-Analysis 47: 356–63.

——— 1987. The Anatomy of Loving. New York: Columbia University Press.

——— 1988. On the fate of the intrapsychic image of the psychoanalyst after termination of the analysis. The Psychoanalytic Study of the Child 43: 137–54. New Haven: Yale University Press.

——— 1991. Plenary address, Midwinter Meeting, American Psychoanalytic Association, December 1991, New York.

Blanck, G. 1966. Some technical implications of ego psychology. International Journal of Psycho-Analysis 47: 389–417.

——— 1984. The complete Oedipus Complex. International Journal of Psycho-Analysis 65: 331–39.

——— 1987. The Subtle Seductions. New York: Jason Aronson.

Blanck, G. and R. Blanck. 1972. Toward a psychoanalytic developmental psychology. Journal of the American Psychoanalytic Association 20: 668–710.

——— 1974. Ego Psychology: Theory and Practice. New York: Columbia University Press.

——— 1979. Ego Psychology II: Psychoanalytic Developmental Psychology. New York: Columbia University Press.

——— 1980. Separation-individuation: An organizing principle. In R. F. Lax, S. Bach, and J. A. Burland, eds., Rapprochement: The Critical Subphase of Separation-Individuation, pp. 101–16. New York: Jason Aronson.

——— 1988. The contribution of ego psychology to understanding the process of termination in psychoanalysis and psychotherapy. Journal of the American Psychoanalytic Association 36: 961–84.

Blanck, R. 1986. The functions of the object representations. Psychotherapie, Psychosomatics and Mediscine Psychologie 36: 1–7. Stuttgart: Thieme.

Blanck, R. and G. Blanck. 1968. Marriage and Personal Development. New York: Columbia University Press.

——— 1977. The transference object and the real object. International Journal of Psycho-Analysis 58: 33–44.

——— 1986. Beyond Ego Psychology: Developmental Object Relations Theory. New York: Columbia University Press.

Blos, P. 1962. On Adolescence: A Psychoanalytic Interpretation. New York: The Free Press.

Bornstein, B. 1945. Clinical notes on child analysis. The Psychoanalytic Study of the Child 1: 151–66. New York: International Universities Press.

Brazleton, T. B. et al. 1975. Early mother infant reciprocity. CIBA Symposium. Amsterdam.

Brenner, C. 1976. Psychoanalytic Technique and Psychic Conflict. New York: International Universities Press.

Brunswick, R. M. 1940. The preoedipal phase of the libido development. The Psychoanalytic Quarterly 9: 293–319.

Calef, V. and E. M. Weinshel. 1983. A note on consummation and termination. Journal of the American Psychoanalytic Association 31: 619–42.

Cavenar, J. O. and J. L. Nash. 1976. The dream as a signal for termination. Journal of the American Psychoanalytic Association 24: 425–35.

Cavell. M. 1988. Interpretation, psychoanalysis, and the philosophy of mind. Journal of the American Psychoanalytic Association 36: 859–80.

De Simone Gaburri, G. 1985. On termination of the analysis. International Review of Psycho-Analysis 12: 467–68.

Deutsch, H. 1942. Some forms of emotional disturbance and their relationship to schizophrenia. The Psychoanalytic Quarterly 11: 301–21.

———— 1944. The Psychology of Women. Vols. 1 and 2. New York: Grune and Stratton.

DSM-III. 1980. Diagnostic and Statistical Manual of Mental Disorders. 3d ed. Washington, D.C.: American Psychiatric Association.

Dowling, S. and A. Rothstein, eds. 1989. The Significance of Infant Observational Research for Clinical Work with Children, Adolescents, and Adults. Monograph 5, American Psychoanalytic Association. New York: International Universities Press.

Dunn, M. 1992. Personal communication.

Eissler, Kurt R. 1953. The effect of the structure of the ego on psychoanalytic technique. Journal of the American Psychoanalytic Association 1: 104–43.

Emde, R. N. 1988a. Development terminable and interminable, Part 1: Innate and motivational factors from infancy. International Journal of Psycho-Analysis 69: 23–42.

———— 1988b. Development terminable and interminable, Part 2: Recent psychoanalytic theory and therapeutic considerations. International Journal of Psycho-Analysis 69: 283–96.

Erikson, E. 1959. Identity and the life cycle. Psychological Issues. Monograph 1. New York: International Universities Press.

Federn, P. 1952. Ego Psychology and the Psychoses. New York: Basic Books.

Fenichel, O. 1941. Problems of Psychoanalytic Technique. New York: Psychoanalytic Quarterly.

Firestein, S. K. 1978. Termination in Psychoanalysis. New York: International Universities Press.

Fisher, C. 1965. Psychoanalytic implications of recent research on sleep and dreaming. Journal of the American Psychoanalytic Association 13: 197–303.

Fliegel, Z. O. 1973. Feminine psychological development in Freudian theory: A historical reconstruction. The Psychoanalytic Quarterly 42: 385–408.

Frank, M. 1990. Personal communication.

Freud, A. 1936. The Ego and the Mechanisms of Defense. In The Writings of Anna Freud. Vol. 2. New York: International Universities Press, 1966.

————— 1959. The Psychoanalytic Treatment of Children. New York: International Universities Press.

————— 1969. Difficulties in the Path of Psychoanalysis. The Freud Anniversary Lecture Series. New York: International Universities Press.

————— 1971. Remarks made at the Twenty-seventh Congress of the International Psycho-Analytic Association.

Freud, S. 1953–1974. The Standard Edition of the Complete Psychological Works of Sigmund Freud. 24 vols. Translated and edited by James Strachey. London: Hogarth Press.

————— 1895. Studies on hysteria, vol. 2.

————— 1900. The interpretation of dreams, vols. 4 and 5.

————— 1905. Three essays on the theory of sexuality, vol. 7.

————— 1909. Analysis of a phobia in a five-year-old boy, vol. 10

————— 1909. Notes upon a case of obsessional neurosis, vol. 10.

————— 1911. A case of paranoia, vol. 12.

————— 1912a. The dynamics of transference, vol. 12.

————— 1912b. Recommendations to physicians practising psychoanalysis, vol. 12.

————— 1913a. On beginning the treatment (further recommendations on the technique of psychoanalysis), vol. 12.

————— 1913b. Totem and taboo, vol. 13

————— 1914a. Remembering, repeating, and working through (further recommendations on the technique of psychoanalysis), vol. 12.

————— 1914b. Observations on transference love, vol. 12.

————— 1914c. On narcissism, vol. 14.

————— 1915–17. Introductory lectures on psychoanalysis, vol. 16.

————— 1917. Mourning and melancholia, vol. 14.

————— 1918. From the history of an infantile neurosis, vol. 17.

————— 1920. Beyond the pleasure principle, vol. 18.

————— 1921. Group psychology and the analysis of the ego, vol. 18.

————— 1923. The ego and the id, vol. 19.

————— 1925. Some psychical consequences of the anatomical distinction between the sexes, vol. 19.

————— 1926. Inhibitions, symptoms, and anxiety, vol. 20.

————— 1931. Female sexuality, vol. 21.

————— 1933a. Femininity, lecture 23, vol. 22.

————— 1933b. The dissection of the psychical personality, lecture 31, vol. 22.

————— 1937. Constructions in analysis, vol. 23.

————— 1939. Moses and monotheism, vol. 23.

————— 1940. An outline of psycho-analysis, vol. 23.

Friedman, L. 1969. The therapeutic alliance. The International Journal of Psycho-Analysis 50: 139–53.

———— 1984. Pictures of treatment by Gill and Schafer. The Psychoanalytic Quarterly 53: 167–207.

Fromm, E. 1951. The Forgotten Language. New York: Grove Press.

Galenson, E. and H. Roiphe. 1976. Some suggested revisions concerning early female development. Journal of the American Psychoanalytic Association 24: 29–57.

Gill, M. M. 1954. Psychoanalysis and exploratory psychotherapy. Journal of the American Psychoanalytic Association 28: 805–28.

———— 1984. Psychoanalysis and psychotherapy: A revision. International Review of Psycho-Analysis 11: 161–80.

Gillespie, W. R. 1969. Concepts of vaginal orgasm. International Journal of Psycho-Analysis 50: 495–97.

Glover, E. 1955. The Technique of Psychoanalysis. New York: International Universities Press.

———— 1956. On the Early Development of Mind. New York: International Universities Press.

Goldberg, A. and D. Marcus. 1985. "Natural termination": Some comments on ending analysis without setting a date. Psychoanalytic Quarterly 54: 46–65.

Greenacre, P. 1952. Special problems of early female sexual development. The Psychoanalytic Study of the Child 5: 122–38.

———— 1953. Certain relationships between fetishism and faulty development of the body image. The Psychoanalytic Study of the Child 8: 65–78. New York: International Universities Press.

———— 1955. Swift and Carroll: A Psychoanalytic Study of Two Lives. New York: International Universities Press.

———— 1957. The childhood of the artist. The Psychoanalytic Study of the Child 12: 47–72.

———— 1959. Certain technical problems in the transference relationship. Journal of the American Psychoanalytic Association 7: 484–502.

———— 1969. The fetish and the transitional object. The Psychoanalytic Study of the Child 24: 187–94.

———— 1972. Problems of overidealization of the analyst and of analysis: Their manifestations in the transference and countertransference relationship. The Psychoanalytic Study of the Child. New York: International Universities Press.

Greenson, R. R. 1964. On homosexuality and gender identity. International Journal of Psycho-Analysis 45: 217–19.

———— 1965. The working alliance and the transference neurosis. Psychoanalytic Quarterly 34: 155–81.

—— 1967. The Technique and Practice of Psychoanalysis. New York: Hallmark Press.

Greenson, R. R. and M. Wexler. 1969. The non-transference relationships in the psychoanalytic situation. International Journal of Psycho-Analysis 50: 27–39.

Grossman, W. J. and W. H. Stewart. 1976. "Penis envy" from childhood wish to metaphor. Journal of the American Psychoanalytic Association 24: 193–212.

Hartmann, H. [1939] 1958. Ego Psychology and the Problem of Adaptation. New York: International Universities Press.

—— 1953. Contribution to the metapsychology of schizophrenia. The Psychoanalytic Study of the Child 8: 177–98.

—— 1956. The development of the ego concept in Freud's work. The International Journal of Psycho-Analysis 37: 425–39.

—— 1964. Essays in Ego Psychology. New York: International Universities Press.

Hartmann, H. and E. Kris. 1945. The genetic approach in psychoanalysis. The Psychoanalytic Study of the Child 1: 11–30. New York: International Universities Press.

Hartmann, H., E. Kris, and R. M. Loewenstein. 1946. Comments on the formation of psychic structure. The Psychoanalytic Study of the Child 2: 11–38. New York: International Universities Press.

—— 1949. Notes on the theory of aggression. The Psychoanalytic Study of the Child 3/4: 9–36. New York: International Universities Press.

—— 1953. The function of theory in psychoanalysis. In R. M. Loewenstein, ed., Drives, Affects, Behavior. New York: International Universities Press.

Hartmann, H. and R. M. Loewenstein. 1962. Notes on the superego. The Psychoanalytic Study of the Child 17: 42–81. New York: International Universities Press.

Hoffer, W. 1950. Three psychological criteria for the termination of treatment. International Journal of Psycho-Analysis 31: 194–95.

Horney, K. 1939. New Ways in Psychoanalysis. New York: W. W. Norton.

—— 1967. Feminine Psychology. New York: W. W. Norton.

Jacobson, E. 1954. The self and the object world: Vicissitudes of their infantile cathexes and their influence on ideational and affective development. The Psychoanalytic Study of the Child 9: 75–127. New York: International Universities Press.

—— 1959. Depersonalization. Journal of the American Psychoanalytic Association 7: 581–610.

—— 1964. The Self and the Object World. New York: International Universities Press.

—— 1968. On the development of the girl's wish for a child. Psychoanalytic Quarterly 37: 523–38.

———— 1971. Depression. New York: International Universities Press.

Kaplan, L. 1987. Discussion of Daniel Stern's The Interpersonal World of the Infant. In Contemporary Psychoanalysis 23 (1): 27.

———— 1990. Female Perversions: The Temptation of Emma Bovary. New York: Doubleday.

Kernberg, O. 1967. Borderline Personality Organization. Journal of the American Psychoanalytic Association 15: 641–85.

———— 1975. Borderline Conditions and Pathological Narcissism. New York: Jason Aronson.

———— 1984. Severe Personality Disorders: Psychotherapeutic Strategies. New Haven: Yale University Press.

———— 1987. Projection and projective identification: Developmental and clinical aspects. Journal of the American Psychoanalytic Association 35: 795–820.

———— 1980. Internal World and External Reality. New York: Jason Aronson.

Kestenberg, J. 1956. Vicissitudes of female sexuality. Journal of the American Psychoanalytic Association 4: 453–76.

Kinsey, A. C., W. B. Pomeroy, and C. E. Martin. 1948. Sexual Behavior In the Human Male. Philadelphia and London: W. B. Saunders.

———— 1953. Sexual Behavior in the Human Female. Philadelphia: W. B. Saunders.

Klein, M. 1948. Contributions to Psycho-Analysis. London: Hogarth Press.

Knight, R. P. 1954. Borderline states. In R. P. Knight and C. Friedman, eds., Psychoanalytic Psychiatry and Psychology, pp. 52–64. New York: International Universities Press.

Kohut, H. 1971. The Analysis of the Self. New York: International Universities Press.

———— 1977. The Restoration of the Self. New York: International Universities Press.

Kris, E. 1951. Ego psychology and interpretation in psychoanalytic therapy. The Psychoanalytic Quarterly 20: 15–30.

———— 1952. Psychoanalytic Explorations in Art. New York: International Universities Press.

———— 1956a. The personal myth. Journal of the American Psychoanalytic Association 4: 653–81.

———— 1956b. On some vicissitudes of insight in psychoanalysis. International Journal of Psycho-Analysis 37: 445–55.

———— 1956c. The recovery of childhood memories in psychoanalysis. The Psychoanalytic Study of the Child 11: 54–88. New York, International Universities Press.

Lichtenberg, J. D. 1975. The development of the sense of self. Journal of the American Psychoanalytic Association 23: 453–84.

Loewald, H. W. 1960. On the therapeutic action of psychoanalysis. International Journal of Psycho-Analysis 41: 16–35.

——— 1978. Instinct theory, object relations, and psychic structure formation. Journal of the American Psychoanalytic Association 26: 493–506.

——— 1979. The waning of the Oedipus Complex. Journal of the American Psychoanalytic Association 27: 751–76.

——— 1980. Papers on Psychoanalysis. New Haven: Yale University Press.

——— 1988. Termination analyzable and unanalyzable. The Psychoanalytic Study of the Child 43: 155–66. New Haven: Yale University Press.

Loewenstein, R. M. 1957. Some thoughts on interpretation in the theory and practice of psychoanalysis. The Psychoanalytic Study of the Child 12: 127–150. New York: International Universities Press.

Mahler, M. S. 1958. Autism and symbiosis: Two extreme disturbances of identity. International Journal of Psycho-Analysis 39: 77–83.

——— 1965. On the significance of the normal separation-individuation phase. In M. Schur, ed., Drives, Affects, and Behavior, vol. 2, pp. 161–68. New York: International Universities Press.

——— 1968. On Human Symbiosis and the Vicissitudes of Individuation. New York: International Universities Press.

——— 1971. A study of the separation-individuation process and its possible application to borderline phenomena in the psychoanalytic situation. The Psychoanalytic Study of the Child 26: 403–24. New York: Quadrangle Press.

Mahler, M. S. and K. LaPerriere. 1965. Mother-child ineraction during separation-individuation. The Psychoanalytic Quarterly 34: 483–98.

Mahler, M. S., F. Pine, and A. Bergman. 1975. The Psychological Birth of the Human Infant. New York: Basic Books.

Masters, W. H. and V. E. Johnson. 1966. Human Sexual Response. Boston: Little Brown.

Maurer, D. and C. Maurer. 1988. The World of the Newborn. New York: Basic Books.

McDevitt, J. B. 1983. The emergence of hostile aggression and its defensive and adaptive modifications during the separation-individuation process. Journal of the American Psychoanalytic Association 31 (Supplement): 273–300.

Menninger, K. 1958. Theory of Psychoanalytic Technique. New York: Basic Books.

Moore, B. E. 1964. Frigidity: A review of the literature. The Psychoanalytic Quarterly 23: 323–49.

Moore, B. E. and B. D. Fine. 1990. Psychoanalytic Terms and Concepts. New Haven: Yale University Press.

Murphy, W. F. 1965. The Tactics of Psychotherapy. New York: International Universities Press.

Nadelson, C. 1987. Towards the further understanding of homosexual women. Journal of the American Psychoanalytic Association 35: 165–74.

Nunberg, H. 1931. The synthetic function of the ego. International Journal of Psycho-Analysis 12: 123–40.

———— 1954. Evaluation of the results of psychoanalytic treatment. International Journal of Psycho-Analysis 35: 2–7.

Osofsky, J. D., ed. 1979. Handbook of Infant Development. New York: John Wiley.

Panel. American Psychoanalytic Association. 1961. Silent Patient. Journal of the American Psychoanalytic Association 9: 2–123.

Parens, H. 1979. The Development of Aggression in Early Childhood. New York: Jason Aronson.

Piaget, J. 1955. The Language and Thought of the Child. New York: Macmillan.

Rangell, Leo. 1955. On the psychoanalytic theory of anxiety. Journal of the American Psychoanalytic Association 3: 389–414.

———— 1972. Aggression, Oedipus and historical perspective. International Journal of Psycho-Analysis 53: 3–11.

———— 1989. Action theory within the structural view. International Journal of Psycho-Analysis 70: 189–201.

———— 1986. The executive functions of the ego: An extension of the concept of ego autonomy. The Psychoanalytic Study of the Child 41: 1–37.

Rapaport, D. 1951. Organization and Pathology of Thought. New York: Columbia University Press.

———— 1959. The structure of psychoanalytic theory: A systematizing attempt. Psychological Issues 6.

———— 1967. The Collected Papers of David Rapaport. Edited by M. Gill. New York: Basic Books.

Rapaport, D. and M. M. Gill. 1959. The points of view and assumptions of metapsychology. International Journal of Psycho-Analysis 40: 153–62.

Richards, A. 1989. A romance with pain: A telephone perversion. International Journal of Psycho-Analysis 70: 153–64.

Rickman, J. 1950. On the criteria for the termination of an analysis. International Journal of Psycho-Analysis 31: 200–201.

Ross, N. 1960. An examination of nosology according to psychoanalytic concepts. Journal of the American Psychoanalytic Association 8: 535–51.

———— 1967. The 'as if' concept. Journal of the American Psychoanalytic Association 13: 59–82.

———— 1970. The primacy of genitality in the light of ego psychology: Introductory remarks. Journal of the American Psychoanalytic Association 17: 267–84.

———— 1975. Affect as cognition—with observations on the meanings of mystical states. International Review of Psycho-Analysis 2: 79–84.

Sandler, J. 1960. The background of safety. International Journal of Psycho-Analysis 41: 352–56.

Shane, M. and E. Shane. 1984. The end phase of psychoanalysis: Indicators, tasks, and functions of termination. Journal of the American Psychoanalytic Association 32: 739–72.

Sharpe, E. F. 1950. Collected Papers on Psychoanalysis. London: Hogarth Press.

Shaw, R. R. (Reporter) 1991. Concepts and controversies about the transference neurosis. Journal of the American Psychoanalytic Association 39: 227–40.

Spitz, R. A. 1945. Hospitalism: An inquiry into the genesis of psychiatric conditions in early childhood. The Psychoanalytic Study of the Child 1: 52–74. New York: International Universities Press.

——— 1946. Hospitalism: A follow up report. The Psychoanalytic Study of the Child 2: 113–117.

——— 1957. No and Yes. New York: International Universities Press.

——— 1959. A Genetic Field Theory of Ego Formation. New York: International Universities Press.

——— 1965. The First Year of Life. New York: International Universities Press.

——— 1972. Bridges: On anticipation, duration, and meaning. Journal of the American Psychoanalytic Association 20: 721–35.

Stern, D. 1985. The Interpersonal World of the Infant. New York: Basic Books.

Stone, L. 1954. The widening scope of indications for psychoanalysis. Journal of the American Psychoanalytic Association 2: 567–94.

Sullivan, H. S. 1953. The Interpersonal Theory of Psychiatry. Edited by H. S. Perry and M. L. Gawel. New York: W. W. Norton.

Supplement on Female Sexuality. 1976. Journal of the American Psychoanalytic Association 24.

Tarachow, S. 1963. An Introduction to Psychotherapy. New York: International Universities Press.

Ticho, E. 1972. Termination of psychoanalysis: Treatment goals, life goals. Psychoanalytic Quarterly 41: 315–33.

Wallerstein, R. S. 1989. Psychoanalysis and psychotherapy: An historical perspective. International Journal of Psycho-Analysis 70: 563–92.

Weiss, J. (Reporter) 1966. Panel. Clinical and theoretical aspects of 'as if' characters. Journal of the American Psychoanalytic Association 14: 569–90.

Winnicott, D. W. 1953. Transitional objects and transitional phenomena. International Journal of Psycho-Analysis 34: 89–97.

Zetzel, E. R. 1956a. An Approach to the relation between concept and content in psychoanalytic theory. The Psychoanalytic Study of the Child 11: 99–121.

——— 1956b. Current concepts of transference. International Journal of Psychoanalysis 37: 369–75.

Name Index

Subject Index